D1614327

JOHN CHRISTIE
OF GLYNDEBOURNE

JOHN CHRISTIE
of Glyndebourne

by
WILFRID BLUNT

THEATRE ARTS BOOKS
NEW YORK

Published by Theatre Arts Books,
333 Sixth Avenue, New York, 10014.

Printed in Great Britain
by Richard Clay (The Chaucer Press), Ltd.,
Bungay, Suffolk

TO
FRANCIS

Contents

PREFACE   xi
FAMILY TREE   xiv

Part I

1   PRELUDE   1
2   PARENTS AND CHILDHOOD   4
3   ETON BOY   20
4   WOOLWICH, CAMBRIDGE AND CARS   27
5   ETON MASTER   38

Part II

6   ACTIVE SERVICE   59
7   GLYNDEBOURNE MANOR   72
8   AUGUSTUS CHRISTIE   85
9   GLYNDEBOURNE HOST   92
10 ORGANS AND BIG BUSINESS   103

Part III

11 THE GENESIS OF OPERA   113
12 CHRISTIE *v.* OERTON AND NICHOLSON   125
13 MARRIAGE   140
14 THE FIRST SEASON   160
15 THE MID THIRTIES   175
16 INTERLUDE: JOHN CHRISTIE *v.* GIACOMO AGATI   192
17 1939 AND 1940   197
18 THE GLYNDEBOURNE TEAM   203

Part IV

19 THE YEARS OF SEPARATION 211
20 PLANNING A BETTER WORLD 226
21 GLYNDEBOURNE REOPENS ITS DOORS 240
22 EDINBURGH AND AFTER 259
23 THE LAST DECADE 274

INDEX 291

Illustrations

Plate   *Facing page*

1. Daniel Béat Christin (Christie) — xvi
2. The harem of "Surdah Cawn" — 1
3. (*Above*) Three generations at Glyndebourne: William (seated), Augustus and John Christie, *c*. 1895 — 16
   (*Below left*) Lady Rosamond and John Christie, 1888
   (*Below right*) John Christie, 1895
4. Augustus Christie at the Instow Cricket Club — 17
   Augustus Christie as High Sheriff of Devon
5. (*Above*) Tapeley as it was and (*below*) as reconstructed — 32
6. John Christie (*left*) *c*. 1920 and (*below*) in his motor at Ringmer in 1911 — 33
7. Glyndebourne (*above*) as it was and (*below*) as it is today, with the organ room and opera house added — 48
8. The organ room at Glyndebourne — 49
9. John Christie as Beckmesser, 1928 — 144
10. Audrey Mildmay about the time of her marriage — 145
11. Audrey Christie at Glyndebourne in the thirties — 160
    Audrey Mildmay as Zerlina
12. John Christie by Kenneth Green, 1937 — 161
    Childs by Kenneth Green, 1937
13. (*Above*) Audrey, George, Rosamond and John Christie, 1936 — 256
    (*Left*) George, John and Mary Christie (holding Hector) at Hector's christening in 1961

Plate   *Facing page*

14. (*Above*) Fritz Busch, John Christie, Carl Ebert and
     Moran Caplat, 1951   257
     (*Below left*) Jani Strasser and (*right*) Rudi Bing

15. John Christie, 1954   272

16. Family group at Glyndebourne, 1959. John Christie,
     Rosamond, Mary and George   273

Preface

I MUST BEGIN by paying two debts of honour.

Several years ago Mr John Gwynne started to collect material about John Christie's life, and indeed drafted a number of chapters for a biography. When his project was abandoned, he most generously put all his information at my disposal. This included not only his text but also notes of interviews with, and letters from, a large number of people who had known John Christie. I have made the fullest use of all this—I have indeed in places quoted almost *verbatim* what he wrote. Moreover, he added to his other kindnesses by reading my typescript, and made detailed and invaluable suggestions for its improvement. I take this opportunity to express my deep gratitude to him.

Then, just as I was about to start work, there appeared Mr Spike Hughes's full and admirable *Glyndebourne* (Methuen, 1965). From this mine of information I have dug much precious metal. Thus I have had the novel experience of writing a biography for which much of the preliminary spadework had already been done by others. Mr Hughes will not fail to observe how deeply I have put myself in his debt; I tender to him my warmest thanks. All who wish to know the history of opera at Glyndebourne will turn to his book, where the story is told more fully than it is necessary for me to do here.

For the author of a biography such as this, the attitude adopted by the family of his subject is of considerable importance. To Mr George Christie, who encouraged me to write the book, and to Mrs Christie, I cannot adequately express the gratitude I feel for the help they have given me (while allowing me complete freedom), the hospitality they have extended to me, and the understanding they have shown me throughout. George Christie read and re-read rough drafts, final typescripts and proofs; answered endless catechisms, helped me to make useful contacts and in a hundred different ways facilitated my task. His sister Miss Rosamond Christie, and Mrs Christie's brother Mr Brian Nicholson, were also kind enough to read the book and make helpful comments.

To three people who knew John Christie intimately—Miss Rhona Byron, Mr A. S. F. Gow and Mr W. E. Edwards—I am especially indebted for their kindness in reading the book and providing valuable criticisms and suggestions. To Mr F. R. Thompson I am no less grateful, but for a different service. He did not know John Christie and he is not interested in Opera. He read from the standpoint of the "general reader", pointing out where he considered such a reader might be bored or mystified and suggesting passages which could advantageously be abbreviated or deleted.

I must also express my gratitude to the following for kindly giving me permission to quote material of which they hold the copyright: to Shirley, Lady Beecham for a letter from the late Lady Betty Humby Beecham to the late Mrs John Christie; to Lt-Col Arthur Lloyd-Baker for the extracts from his Diary; to Messrs George Harrap for passages from *Ego 3* by the late James Agate; to the Public Trustee and the Society of Authors for a letter from the late Bernard Shaw, and to Major C. J. Wilson for extracts from *The King's Royal Rifle Corps Chronicle* (1916).

My thanks are also due to the following for allowing me to talk with them or quote from their letters (or letters of which they hold the copyright), or for information supplied to me either direct or through Mr John Gwynne:

Mr Nigel Abercrombie, Colonel C. H. Adams, Mr John Allen, Mrs Mildred Archer, Mr Julian Bayly, Mr Donald Beard, Mr Hugh Beaumont, the Lady Elizabeth Beazley, Miss Margaret Belshaw, Sir Rex Benson, Mr Rudolf Bing, Mrs Violet Bridgewater, Mr Benjamin Britten, the late Mrs Mowbray Buller, the Hon Mrs and the late Mr Cyril Butterwick, Mr Moran Caplat, Mr Clive Carey, the late Countess of Chichester, Mr Gerald Coke, Mrs

Daniels, Mr F. W. Dobbs, Sir Everard Duncan, Bt, Professor Carl Ebert, Mr J. J. P. Evans, Mrs Edwin Fisher, Mr G. M. Fitzgerald, Mrs Fleming, Miss Marguerita Fowler, the Viscount Gage, Mr Peter Gellhorn, Mrs Thornely Gibson, Mr Tom Goff, Mr John Gough, Sir William Haley, Sir L. Halsey, Mr F. Harvey, Frau Johanna Hirth, Mr Quintin Hogg, Mr Lawrence Impey, Mr A. Jenkins, Sir Alan Lascelles, the Countess of Limerick, Mr R. G. Longman, the Lord and Lady Redcliffe-Maud, the late Lady Monk Bretton, Dr Patrick Mounsey, Mr E. Scott Norman, Mr Herbert Norman, the Lord Nugent, Mr Peter Pears, Mr John Piper, Col Sir Charles Ponsonby, Bt, Mr John Pritchard, Mr W. N. Roe, Mr Harold Rosenthal, Sir George Schuster, Mrs John Stirling, Mr Jani Strasser, Mrs Rosamond Stutchbury, the late Mr J. Veness, Mrs Oliver Watney, the Duke of Wellington, the late Mr C. M. Wells, Mr and Mrs A. W. Whitworth, Mrs Ella Wilson, Miss Anne Wood, Mr Nigel Wykes and Mr William Yeo.

To any whose names I have inadvertently overlooked I offer my apologies.

Miss Charmian Young kindly retyped my original typescript more than once, and Miss Kathleen Strange checked the page proofs.

W.J.W.B.

The Watts Gallery,
Compton, Guildford.

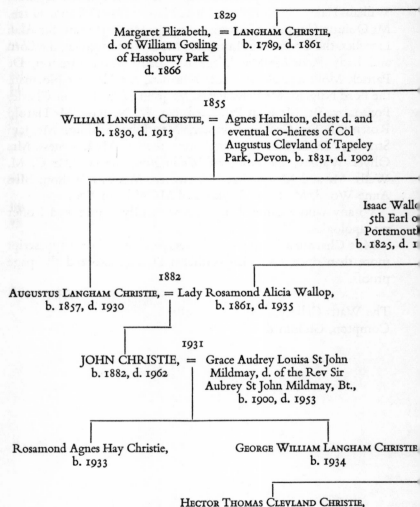

1784

Charlotte, d. of the Rev. = DANIEL BÉAT CHRISTIN
George Bellasis, D.D.,   CHRISTIE
Rector of Yattenden
b. 1761, d. 1784

1829

Margaret Elizabeth, = LANGHAM CHRISTIE,
d. of William Gosling   b. 1789, d. 1861
of Hassobury Park
d. 1866

1855

WILLIAM LANGHAM CHRISTIE, = Agnes Hamilton, eldest d. and
b. 1830, d. 1913   eventual co-heiress of Col
                  Augustus Clevland of Tapeley
                  Park, Devon, b. 1831, d. 1902

Isaac Wallo
5th Earl o
Portsmout
b. 1825, d. 1

1882

AUGUSTUS LANGHAM CHRISTIE, = Lady Rosamond Alicia Wallop,
b. 1857, d. 1930   b. 1861, d. 1935

1931

JOHN CHRISTIE, = Grace Audrey Louisa St John
b. 1882, d. 1962   Mildmay, d. of the Rev Sir
           Aubrey St John Mildmay, Bt.,
           b. 1900, d. 1953

Rosamond Agnes Hay Christie,   GEORGE WILLIAM LANGHAM CHRISTIE
b. 1933   b. 1934

HECTOR THOMAS CLEVLAND CHRISTIE,
b. 1961

5

Elizabeth, eldest d. and co-heiress
of Capt. Purbeck Langham,
b. 1752, d. 1833

Charles William Christie,
b. 1791, d. 1873

1863
Charlotte Christie = The Rev John Henry Brookes   4 other
children

5

Lady Eveline Herbert,   1892
d. of 3rd Earl of   Mary Christie = Major Edward   7 other
Carnarvon   Le Marchant   children

Edward Le
Marchant

1891
Vernon James Watney, = Lady Gwendolen   10 other
b. 1860, d. 1928   Margaret Wallop,   children
b. 1866, d. 1943

Rosalind Watney,   Silvia Watney,   Oliver Watney,
b. 1891, d. 1957,   b. 1896, d. 1966,   b. 1902, d. 1966,
m. Major the Hon   m. Major   m. Christina Nelson
Charles Lyell   Mowbray Buller

ricia Mary, d. of Ivor Nicholson,
b. 1937

gustus Jack Christie,   Patricia Louise Christie,
b. 1963   b. 1966

1   Daniel Béat Christin (Christie)

2   The harem of "Surdah Cawn"

PART I

I

Prelude

IN A LUMBER-ROOM at Glyndebourne—and worthy perhaps of a better fate—is a fragment of what must once have been a very large canvas. It is the work of an Anglo-Indian artist of the latter half of the eighteenth century and portrays a group of Indian ladies in great distress. Two other fragments of the same canvas are also said to have survived: one of these shows the head of Captain Daniel Béat Christie (or Christin) of the Bombay Engineers, John Christie's great-great-grandfather; the other (which cannot at present be found) "the curly head of an angry Hindoo or nigger". The picture in its original state portrayed the gallant Captain Christie rescuing the harem of "Surdah Cawn" from death or at least a fate worse than death. The episode occurred on 8th February 1782 at Tellicherry, on the Malabar coast, during the second Mysore war between the British and Haidar Ali of Mysore; it has been delightfully described by the anonymous author of *The History of the War in Asia, 1780 to 1782*, published in London in 1789:

> When the fortified house in which the unfortunate Surdah Cawn made his last stand was set on fire, many of his family and other adherents, in order to avoid the flames, began to drop down the walls amidst the fire of the Sepoys. Among them were seven of the finest women of the East, who composed the Cawn's seraglio. Captain Christie, who happened to pass by the spot where the women threw themselves down from the battlements of the harem, immediately stopped the firing, and at the

hazard of his life ran up to their assistance and received them one after another into his arms.

In the meantime a party of sailors belonging to the Bombay cruizers that had co-operated with the land forces in the attack came up, and for the sake of plunder began to tear off the women's earrings, while these unfortunate ladies, afraid of even ruder treatment and uncertain of their fate, endeavoured to put an end to their existence. But Captain Christie, partly by his authority as an officer and partly by a seasonable distribution of the jewels, in which the ladies cheerfully seconded him, was enabled, though with difficulty, to save them from further violence by restoring order among the sailors. The poor women, when they found themselves under secure protection, gave vent to their gratitude by embracing the knees and bathing the feet of their protector with tears of joy.

Captain Christie, accompanied by Lieut Hawkes of the Artillery, who had come up to lend his assistance in this generous act of gallantry, immediately led them up to his commanding officer. They were then restored safely to their lord, who had testified the most agonising anxiety concerning their fate. When they came into his presence he looked sternly into their faces, and manifested symptoms of trouble, anguish and despair. But after he had conversed with them for some time his countenance softened into tears of joy, and he expressed the strongest emotions of gratitude for the delicate way in which the women had been treated by the English officers. "You", said he, "enjoy the fortune of the day and you deserve it. Go, therefore, to a room (which he described) in the fortified house and you will find there for your reward two lacks of rupees." Above twenty thousand pounds were accordingly divided among the Army.

Daniel Béat Christin, the hero of this affray and the first of the Christies, was born in 1745 at Payerne, at that time in the Swiss canton of Berne, where his family "had lived for four generations highly respected".* Daniel's father had been "too fond of pleasure and walked to his ruin", leaving his son, a pugnacious youth, to make his own way in the world. Daniel therefore did what a num-

* *Christie of Glyndebourne—being Recollections of her Family narrated by Charlotte Brookes*, privately printed, 1919. Charlotte Brookes was a granddaughter of Daniel Béat Christin.

ber of adventurous young Swiss were doing at that time: he entered the service of the Honourable East India Company's forces, in which he finally rose to the rank of major. On enlisting he changed his name to Christie.

We do not know what cut of the £20,000 came to Daniel, but apparently it was enough to enable him to marry, not long after and in Bombay, Charlotte, the daughter of Dr Bellasis, Rector of Yattenden and Vicar of Basildon and Ashhampstead in the county of Berkshire. But within two months of his marriage Charlotte was dead. Two years later Daniel left India for England where, "in spite of his foreign birth and somewhat humble upbringing"*— and, it might have been added, the fact that he was now over forty —he married in 1786 Elizabeth, eldest daughter and co-heiress of Purbeck Langham, the third son of the fourth baronet.

This judicious alliance was in due course to bring Glyndebourne to the Christie family. After a legal dispute "which lasted for fourteen years and was taken to every Court in the Land",* their son, Langham Christie, inherited the estate in 1833 under the wills of Henrietta and Frances Hay, connections of the Langhams. Though he hunted and shot, and took an interest in his estate and in politics, Langham's tastes were "really more literary and artistic than sporting".* He played the 'cello, and his wife, Margaret, was a competent pianist.

On Langham's death in 1861 Glyndebourne passed to his son William, who married Agnes Clevland, eldest daughter and co-heiress of Colonel Augustus Clevland of Tapeley (or Tapley) in Devon.† For the second time—and it was again through the female line—the Christies were to inherit, on Colonel Clevland's death, large estates and a much renovated Queen Anne house, Tapeley Park. William Christie was Member of Parliament for Lewes and Master of the Southdown Foxhounds; he added to Glyndebourne Manor and increased the estate from the original 1,500 acres to over 10,000.

---

* Charlotte Brookes, *op. cit.*
† Agnes's brother, Archibald Clevland, a Cornet in the 17th Lancers, survived the Charge at Balaclava only to fall by a stray shot at Inkerman. For convenience I have made the spelling of Tapeley uniform throughout this book.

2

Parents and Childhood

WILLIAM AND AGNES CHRISTIE had nine children, but it would appear that husband and wife came in time to realise that they could not live happily under one roof. ("Your mother is I fancy a bit mad," William was later to inform one of his sons, "but not sufficiently so for me to be able to take any definite steps . . ."). He therefore established himself at Glyndebourne, leaving Agnes to make a home for herself and the children at Tapeley.

Augustus Langham Christie, eldest of their six sons and father of the subject of this biography, was born in 1857 and educated at Eton and at Trinity College, Cambridge. In the autumn of 1881, as his time at the University was drawing to its close, he fell in love with the twenty-year-old Lady Rosamond Wallop, third daughter of the fifth Earl of Portsmouth.* In an undated letter Lady Portsmouth wrote to Augustus:

My dear Mr Christy [sic],
    Come & win for yourself my jewel—I believe I may safely trust her to yr tenderness & devotion while you both live.
Yours affectionately
E. Portsmouth

Augustus went—and won her. When, shortly before Christmas, the engagement was announced, it was greeted with warm approval by the members of both families. Indeed on paper it was a most

---

* Lord Portsmouth was the original of Arthur in *Tom Brown's Schooldays*. Many years later John Christie was to tell his wife that, ever since he had learned this fact, he had said his prayers on his knees and not in bed.

suitable alliance: the bridegroom had the prospect of large estates; the bride was the daughter of an earl. Congratulatory letters poured in: brothers and sisters wrote of their happiness in the acquisition of so delightful a brother-in-law or sister-in-law; uncles and aunts welcomed the new nephew or niece; friends were convinced that the bridegroom was "a very lucky man" and the bride "a very lucky woman".

Outwardly Augustus was a typical country squire, fond of farming and hunting and shooting. Physically he was exceptionally powerful—so powerful, indeed, that Sandow,* when he happened to meet him, regretted that he could not take him in hand and make a "strong man" out of him. But his parents can hardly have been unaware that there was a neurotic strain in him —a strain which was to reveal itself within a few months of his marriage and to lead him finally to insanity.

Augustus was by no means tall; but he was thickset, and beside him his bride looked small and frail. Her features were aristocratic, the nose aquiline, the hair reddish; and all who knew her recall how tiny was her voice. She dressed plainly and believed in plain living, considering that money spent on food or clothes was money wasted. She was, however, very conscious of her high birth and ancient lineage;† indeed it may well be that she considered that she had stooped a little in allowing herself to be conquered by Augustus.

But the marriage, which took place in February 1882, was undoubtedly a love match, and for the first seven months everything apparently went well; at all events the letters they exchanged, on the rare occasions when they were obliged to be parted for a day or two, were full of love. Lady Rosamond encouraged her husband's political ambitions—he hoped to enter Parliament as a Liberal—and helped him with a speech he was to make at

---

* Eugene Sandow (1867–1925), professional strong man and exponent of physical culture.

† There were Wallops at Wallop (Hampshire) before the Norman Conquest. Lady Rosamond's nephew, the present Lord Portsmouth, wrote: "Of the known forebears in my English heritage there were a hundred and forty-nine direct (not collateral) ancestors who were Knights of the Garter, eleven who were canonised saints, and sixty-nine who were executed by their rulers, probably rightly." (*A Knot of Roots*, p. 2, published by Geoffrey Bles, 1965.)

Andover; she promised to learn how to run his house economically (which she was disastrously to do); she busied herself with little homely tasks such as adding a hook and eye to his ulster. As for Augustus, when he had to go down to Tapeley for twenty-four hours he carried her photograph about with him all day and at night slept with it under his pillow. "I cannot understand [he wrote to her on 4th August] a husband and wife being separated a day without writing to one another."

At the reception after the wedding a young man, perhaps a little drunk, had knocked the top off the wedding cake before it had been cut by the bride and bridegroom. Superstitious guests had seen an ill omen in this, and their fears proved justified: in October something sinister occurred at Tapeley. Just what this was can be guessed at from various family letters exchanged during the months that followed. On 27th October Lady Portsmouth wrote to Augustus urging him to follow the doctor's instructions in every particular:

The wise course now is to try to occupy yourself with other things and recover that healthier tone of mind which is most likely to bring you ease through a real self control. Everything that gives you strength to *control* your *thoughts* and wishes by bearing cheerfully the present difficulties will, I assure you, help you more than any other thing can do to recover happiness.

The same day Lady Rosamond wrote to her husband:

My darling,
You may not come to me. I know it is hard for you, but only by this conquest over yourself you may hope to win back bright days. Let this trouble bear golden fruits to you, darling. You will try—I ask it of you—to employ your hours and thoughts with plenty of occupations and, my dear Gus, strive to be gentle and loving with your mother. You should not leave Tapeley. You will, my own darling, make the best reparation to God for all the faults and wrong doings by taking the duties and the work he has sent you and fulfilling them manfully. You may write, dear husband, and tell me how you spend your days, the business, the reading, the shooting, the

care for your mother. Take these and refuse to give way to gloomy thoughts . . .

Your loving wife
Rosamond Christie

Next day she writes again that she freely forgives him, and encloses a list of "some specially lovely chapters" of Isaiah, the Psalms and the Epistles to the Romans and Ephesians which might help him; from Lady Portsmouth comes a copy of Lady Anne Blunt's *A Pilgrimage to Nejd* for brighter reading.

But Augustus was unco-operative. He refused to see his father, and only with the greatest reluctance agreed to take specialist advice—and the advice was that he ought not at present to return to live with his wife. Meanwhile Lady Rosamond wrote to him regularly—cheerful letters full of local gossip, of the books she is reading (she was taking "very strong pulls" at Bagehot's *English Constitution*), of her continued affection for him and her firm conviction that these bad days will soon be over. She tells him what he should say at meetings he is about to address, what line he should take about the Army and the Church. She includes little "amusing" stories that he might slip in to lighten his speeches. What she does not mention is that this tragedy has made her ill.

It is alleged (though this is nowhere mentioned in the letters) that one of the causes of Augustus's loss of control in October was his disgust at the sight of his wife's pregnant figure. On 14th December their son, John, was born at Eggesford, her father's house in North Devon. Some seventy years later John said in a broadcast: "The groom went to fetch the doctor (at a gallop, no doubt) but I arrived before the doctor."

★   ★   ★

It was the unanimous verdict of the medical advisers and of the family that Augustus should go abroad for a time, with a suitable companion, and let a change of scene work its cure. There was talk first of America, and Lady Rosamond got quantities of books on the subject from the London Library. She assured her husband that the danger from icebergs was not great, especially since he was thinking of going to the southern States; and she begged him *not* to hurry back, because America is very large, and it would require a visit of several months to study it thoroughly. Augustus, who hated the cold, was suddenly seized with a strange desire to visit the Behring Straits, but this, wrote his wife, "would *never, never* do". Then there is mention of the south of France, or of Egypt . . .

The search for a suitable companion also presented difficulties. Various doctors were approached; an elderly Canon was almost hooked, but he got away. Finally Augustus set out with a Dr Hoggan, and it seems that they went to Egypt and the Levant and certainly they were for a time in Sebastopol. In April Dr Hoggan had to return to his duties in England (or could bear the strain no longer), but reported that Augustus was not yet well enough to come home. "Dear fellow," Lady Rosamond wrote to her husband, "we don't think you are well enough to come back at present to England. I think you would be much happier travelling about . . ." And she warmly recommended that a Dr Howard—"a strong Liberal"—should join him in Venice.

Lord Portsmouth was in full agreement. He felt sure that Augustus's nerves were "still too unstrung" for it to be right for him to return to live with his wife. He begged his son-in-law to continue his travels with the admirable Dr Howard. However, Augustus ignored all advice and came back to England. Lord Portsmouth and one or two other members of his family met and the possibility was discussed of placing Augustus in a private asylum; but Lady Rosamond, though she could not yet bring herself to return to her husband, opposed this. Nor did she feel that he should go to his mother at Tapeley. On 11th May she wrote to him:

> I will tell you frankly why you must not return to Tapeley. Your mother wrote to me telling me she could not stand any scenes of roughness from you and begging me to keep you away from her as your temper frightened her so last time. She has had another attack of illness only a little time ago and is I know very weak. Oh if you would only master your temper, if you could only learn to check and curb it, it would, dear Gus,

make you yourself so much happier and all those about you . . .
I hope too you will think over what I wish and strongly urge,
that you should go abroad again with Dr Howard . . . He is
cultivated, prepossessing in manners, would agree with you in
politics and other tastes and I am sure would do his best to help
you to cure this terrible temper. Think gravely yourself and you
will see how impossible it is for any woman to live with you
until you have learnt to master it . . .

And yet it would appear that Mrs Christie, Augustus's mother,
although herself frightened of her son's outbursts, attempted to
persuade Lady Rosamond to return to him; for Lady Rosamond
wrote to her mother-in-law on 15th July:

My dear Mrs Christie,
    I am most reluctant to give you pain but I am obliged to tell
you my resolution is as fixed as when I wrote to you last . . .
    When your son went abroad I thought and anxiously hoped
that his repeated insults and cruelties were caused by mental
derangement, and this belief was also shared by my parents. I
anticipated that travel and change of persons might remedy
this ill health, as I then firmly believed it to be. On those grounds
I had forgiven him the wretched life he had made me lead and
from pity I laid aside the remembrance of his cruelties. But now
I know it was only deliberate hardness and cruelty that prompted him to offer me foul insults and horrible treatment and to
repeat them after frequent pardons and while I was working
hard for his interests and consulting and deferring to his happiness
and wishes in every way. This knowledge came to me with a
very painful shock and for long I refused to be convinced; but
now I feel how dangerous it would be to put myself and the
child ever in his power again, and how necessary for our safety
and my reputation it is that I should abide by my resolve . . .

★　　★　　★

In February 1885, more than two years after the separation,
Augustus was still attempting to persuade his wife to come back
to him. Direct appeal having failed, he turned to his brother-in-
law, Lord Lymington, begging him to approach his sister on the
subject. Lymington replied very coolly, addressing Augustus as

"Mr Christie" and saying that it would be "worse than useless" for him to intervene. "If you would permit me to offer you advice," he continued, "it would be that you should learn to exercise such control over yourself, and to prove yourself by your conduct and interests worthy of regaining the confidence and trust, which you have forfeited in the past."

Unable to prevail upon his brother-in-law to act as an intermediary, Augustus was obliged again to appeal to his wife. His letter is missing, but on 3rd March she replied to it in one that has no conventional opening and which ends with a bare signature:

> Your letter has pained me much; and while I am thankful to believe that you have at last come to understand to some extent your cruel treatment of me and are sorry for it, I fail to perceive that you at all realise that you have rendered it impossible for me to look back on those terrible days of my married life without shuddering, or to regard your suggestion that I should return to you as anything but an impossibility. I cannot forget that month after month your treatment of me was one cruel system of persecution, or how hoping against help [*sic*], in a burst of tears my mother wrung from me the confession of my wretchedness, and I obtained my parents' protection at a time when my condition of itself ought to have appealed successfully to you to discontinue a course of conduct endangering my life. I cannot forget how you have disillusioned me of life—yes, wrecked my happiness and taught me to look upon a separation as the only melancholy alternative open to me.
>
> And now, after two years, you ask me to return to you! I cannot do so; it is impossible. The Past (my married life) you have forced me to contemplate as some terrible nightmare, to remember it with a sense of loathing. You, with a disregard which shows your utter want of appreciation of what I bore in silence for so long, describe it as "not a happy one". I had a right to expect, and you know full well had never done any one thing to forfeit my right, that kind of loving treatment which was my due as your wife.
>
> The child is happy with me and I am content to endure this maimed life (your work) and with him and for him to live the life you have condemned me to.

Augustus felt—and probably not without some reason—that his wife was treating him unfairly. He wrote again at once:

My darling Rosamond,
    I am very sorry to hear that my letter caused you pain; I am sure that I had not the least intention of doing so, and after this expression I hope you will feel satisfied that such a result was very far from a wish of mine . . .
    It is not true that I have "*at last* come to understand" etc. I have written to you several times expressing my sorrow, and asking you to hear me, and since my return to England I have taken every means to let you know how sorry I am. It was because I was sorry that I refused your earnest entreaties to come to Eggesford before I left England in '83, and because I was determined to be able to control myself before I again saw you. Look at the letters which passed between us between the time I last saw you and the time whilst I was abroad even up to my return home; are they in accordance with your letter of March 3rd? Remember how during that time I have learnt to control myself, and there are many who will be only too glad to speak on my account should you wish it. Is your letter in accordance with the promise which was held out to me that after I had been abroad up to the middle of May [1883] we were to have a fresh start? What then have I done since to deserve the tone you now adopt? . . .
    I repeat, nothing was further from my thoughts when I last wrote, than to cause you the slightest pain; on the contrary, I endeavoured to express my sorrow for the past . . . I only now ask, and I sincerely beg you to give answer, whether you are willing to hold out any hope that at some future time it is possible you may not be adverse to take into consideration the matter of your returning to me, or whether you have already made up your mind never to return to me. I think you will allow that this is but a fair question . . .

The letter, which concludes with an illegible scrawl, drew from his wife a reply that offered him no encouragement. She begged him to spare her further correspondence. It was clear, she said, that he was quite unable to understand how completely he had shattered her trust in him, or to realise her mental torture when she discovered his true nature. She closed: "I cannot return to you, therefore I beg you to cease from reviving the bitter memories of a past that were happier forgotten."

★   ★   ★

For another year husband and wife continued to live apart. But for Victorians it was important at all costs to keep up appearances; finally, in 1886, a conclave was held in London of various members of both families (but not including Augustus), to see whether the marriage might yet be saved. After a discussion in which Lady Portsmouth is said to have played a decisive part, Lady Rosamond—a woman with the highest sense of duty— agreed to go back to Tapeley. At the same time Agnes Christie, Augustus's mother, left Tapeley and went to live in Wales.

Augustus seemed at first to be better; but it soon became clear that he was not. In fact he was worse. His outbreaks of temper returned, and what might formerly have been mistaken for eccentricity, now became indistinguishable from mental instability. He was insanely jealous of his son, who had to be kept, so far as was possible, out of his sight; he would not even allow his wife to give the child its bath. But Lady Rosamond had made up her mind: it was her duty to remain with her husband. In the intolerable position in which she now found herself she was much helped by a Miss Robinson—known affectionately as "Dobbie"—who came to her as a companion. Dobbie, a remarkable woman, some years older than Lady Rosamond, stayed at her post in most trying circumstances for thirty years; she contrived not only to be of the greatest help to Lady Rosamond, but also to exert a salutary influence on Augustus.

Augustus hated his wife's going away from Tapeley, even for a single night. So did the staff, who, during her absences, were the victims of his temper. She herself, after one of his outbursts, would collapse in tears and cry, "Poor, *poor* Augustus! He can't help it." In her misery, all her affection was lavished on her son—an affection that the boy found irksome. He was rather like the wretched child in Mörike's poem, *Selbstgeständnis* (Self-confession).* He could not then, and did not for a long time after, understand that he was the one outlet for her emotion; he did not fully appreciate how difficult life was for her. But much later he was to say, regretfully, "If *only* I had realised. . . ."

★   ★   ★

Such was the unhappy background of John's childhood, and it is hardly surprising that, brought up in this atmosphere of discord, he proved a difficult boy. Various stories of his childish peccadilloes have survived. Lady Rosamond, in her Reminiscences of Tapeley Park,† wrote:

> Jack‡ was a most troublesome child, and I recall with horror one of the very long railway journeys of those days . . . and the little boy, still in petticoats, swinging from the rack in the railway carriage. I have also a remembrance of the child escaping from my side, swarming like a monkey up one of those ragged larches in front of the dairy building, reaching nearly to the top clasping the tree and swaying it to and fro, mocking meanwhile the anxious mummy below. In a temper he threw a stone at the groom, and when I had birched his hand he stretched it out again with, "Mummy, do it again, it doesn't really hurt."
>
> When, however, it came to an attempt on his part to let the bull out of the yard, I decided that school discipline and the companionship of other children might be safer, and we sent him to a tiny school of little boys attached to the bigger one at

---

* "I am my mother's only child, and as no others came after me—there might, after all, have been another six or seven—I got their share of everything. All her love and affection were poured out on me; I got enough for half a dozen . . ."

† Unpublished, but presumably somewhere in manuscript in the library of Tapeley or Glyndebourne; I have only seen the typescript copy of a page from it. Lady Rosamond wrote a novel, *His Private Life*, which was published under a pseudonym (H. Smith) by Philip Wellby in 1905. The manuscript of two further, but unpublished, novels are at Tapeley, and a few lines from the opening chapter of one of these, *God is Love*, will give a fair idea of her style:

> Twining her fingers in the tangled sprays of clematis, Gertrude leaned close by, languorous with the warmth and fragrance of the night, while Frank's musical laughter glided into song. With head slightly thrown back, he sung with all the passionate sweetness of the nightingale wooing in summer nights . . .

‡ His family called him Jack.

Ellerslie, Fremington [near Barnstaple]. Jack was then six. The first complaint I received promptly. On his first night everyone was roused by terrified howls from the dormitory. My little boy had waited till the other children were asleep, then slipped out of bed and hurried along the dormitory stripping the bed-clothes off the sleeping children. We paid a bill of nineteen shillings for broken windows after his first term.

These and other childish pranks that have been recorded were no more than naughtiness that came from a sense of adventure—a foretaste of the complete indifference to danger that he was later to show in the trenches in the First World War. But he was, as one of the neighbours recalled, "a poor, lonely little boy" and Lady Rosamond was obviously wise to send him, even at so early an age, to a boarding school. Fremington was near—but not too near —to Tapeley, and it was easy for her to visit him there. At Ellerslie he was beaten more than once, but was not on the whole un-happy; he had his own pony, and he found no trouble with his work. One or two of his letters to his mother and one or two school essays, written when he was about eight years old, have sur-vived. To his mother he wrote:

Will you please get me a big garden because I want to build a hothouse in it because I want to get some money for the fruit and I shall give some to you and I can take some back to school with me may I have some matches and can I please smoke.

Lady Rosamond was presumably in Florence, which she often visited in the spring, when he wrote:

Will you please bring me back an olive tree. . . . Have you been to see many churches. Are the pictures as big as ours at home. Are there many boats on the river Arno. What do they sell in the shops which are on the bridge. . . . Do not the mules look very funny with their red blankets over them. Do you pick the anenomes that grow wild. . . .

His essays have a naïve charm. He was always fond of animals, and writing on *Birds* he said: "Birds are very pretty and people often by them for pets. It is a great shame to shut English birds up in cages, any one could shut foreign birs up because they do not mind it, and English birds do not like it at all. . . ." A cruder script and orthography suggest that *Horses and Dogs* is an earlier production: "they have long nearx horses have long tails horses have beg bodeyes when horses put there eyers back there are cross. . . ."

In 1890, when John was eight years old, Lady Rosamond began to make enquiries about a suitable preparatory school of a more conventional kind. In the draft of a letter beginning "Dear——" she wrote that the boy was "a very strong child for his age and very headstrong and difficult to manage. I want to place him under good regular discipline, and, as he is an only child and has no brothers to counteract the influence of bad companionship, where the tone and moral supervision is excellent."

But it seems that John remained for two more years at Ellerslie before going, at the age of ten, to St David's at Reigate, a school of some seventy boys and in the charge of a Mr Churchill. Lady Rosamond, innocent of the ways of boys at a proper preparatory school, despatched her son there in Little Lord Fauntleroy clothes; it was not a propitious start. Many years later John wrote:

> I fought a lot of the older boys, and any who commented on my clothes; my darling Mother did not understand these things and my Father didn't help. I don't suppose it was a bad thing. Perhaps it developed my character. On the other hand, I wonder whether I should have learnt to fight on more important things. At any rate, boys who laughed had to defend themselves, and it did not disturb me.

Mr Churchill believed in the cane and apparently used it for very trivial misdemeanours. His methods in general were rough; Sir Charles Ponsonby, also at St David's, recalls that Churchill, when coaching a batsman, would stand beside him and lash out at his right foot with a stump if he moved it; and John remembered the headmaster throwing the ball at his head after he had made a bad stroke: "So I hit the ball out of the net, whilst the other boys ducked." Mrs Churchill, a relation of Ruskin's, was a charming woman who brought a touch of kindliness into an establishment which had otherwise been unbearably austere, even barbarous.

It seems that the cane, which was to pursue John throughout the whole of his school career, had very little effect on him. In spite, however, of the beatings to which he was subjected at St David's, he enjoyed his time there. He learned to play cricket and football, and finally captained the football team. Before he left he became Captain of the School, and a report on his work at the age of ten certainly suggests that he was an able boy. Mr Churchill also praised his "fearless honesty"; the boy never lied to get himself out of a tight corner.

*   *   *

John may have been happy at school, but how did he fare during the holidays?

He seems to have spent them partly with his father at Tapeley, partly with his mother wherever she happened to be. No wonder that his parents, when writing of him, referred to him as "the Orphan". Not fully conscious of the tragedy of his mother's life he could not share her sorrows and anxieties with her, though he can hardly have been unaware of the tension when his parents were under the same roof—a tension that his presence always aggravated. No doubt he owed a good deal to the invaluable Dobbie, and presumably at Tapeley he spent a large part of the day in the outdoor pursuits that he always enjoyed; this taste, which he shared with his father, for a time served to bring the two of them together.

And perhaps now, and certainly later, he was much with his uncle and aunt, Vernon and Lady Margaret Watney. Lady Margaret Wallop, Lady Rosamond's younger sister, had married Vernon Watney, for many years Chairman of Watney's Brewery—a cultured man with a good library and a collection of pictures ranging from the Florentines* to the Pre-Raphaelites. Lady Margaret was a charming, witty woman, less highly strung than her sister and very happily married; she kept an excellent table and had no puritan strain in her. John soon came to compare the atmosphere of his home very unfavourably with that of his uncle's house.

* His Botticelli fetched a hundred thousand guineas at Christie's in 1967.

(*Above*) Three generations at Glyndebourne: William (seated), Augustus and John Christie, *c.* 1895. (*Below left*) Lady Rosamond and John Christie 1888. (*Below right*) John Christie 1895

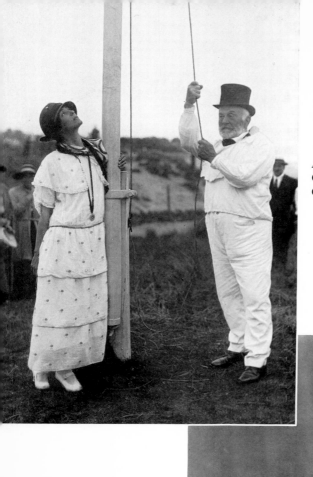

4   Augustus Christie at the Centenary of the Instow Cricket Club

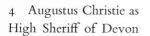

4   Augustus Christie as High Sheriff of Devon

The Watneys had a London house and a sporting estate in Ross-shire; but in 1901 they bought Cornbury, until recently a Churchill property and a dower house to Blenheim—a fine Tudor, Jacobean and Renaissance building standing in a splendid park. Cornbury was to become for John a second and a far happier home.

Meanwhile relations between Augustus and his wife remained strained, and she now spent much of her time away from Tapeley. In October 1889 she saw her doctor, who said it would be a great risk for her to have another child and that she ought to have a separate bedroom. "I am afraid this will vex you," she told her husband, "but I felt it right to be open with you."

Then there were difficulties over Dobbie, of whom Augustus had grown jealous. And difficulties too over servants. No doubt the presence of Augustus in the house made it hard for Lady Rosamond to get good servants and harder still for her to keep them, but she appears to have been more than unlucky, especially over "that perfect fiend" Harriet who made trouble at Tapeley while she was in London. She thought that the woman had some kind of a hold over Augustus (who was warned to beware of exposing himself to the danger of blackmail and libel), and that she spent much of her time inciting the other servants to rebellion. When another servant was taken ill, Augustus told his wife that she had better not return to Tapeley yet. Lady Rosamond replied indignantly that it was absurd to keep the lady of the house away because of a servant's illness. "My dear," she added, "it is a *very* great pity that you let bad friends influence you and put all kinds of silly notions into your head."

She had given up her house in Berkeley Square; when in London the Christies therefore sometimes made use of 117 Eaton Square, the town house of William Christie, Augustus's father. On 1st November 1890 Lady Rosamond—who was what today would be called "very county" by the charitable, and by the less charitable "a snob"—wrote from that address to her husband at Tapeley:

The china your father has left out for us consists of four more or less cracked kitchen cups and saucers (the same as those left out for his caretaker), a pair of broken kitchen jugs, and a few kitchen tumblers. I have written to complain of the caretaker's impertinence and have trounced the woman down well myself. Of course she has not a stroke of work to do for us, but makes Lizzie's life a hell downstairs and speaks most impertinently of our presence here. We are turning out on Monday to an hotel or lodgings. I am surprised that your father imagines that I and my friends can use the *kitchen* china, etc. I think sometimes he forgets the birth and rank of his daughter-in-law. I cannot help contrasting the difference between Mr Evans's treatment of Henry and the bearing of your family towards me. I should be sorry to allow the Wentworths or Lady Manners to see our tea-table. . . .

In short, she was sick of servants, and servants were sick of her: "It will be a good side to this poverty and depression," she told Augustus, "if it knocks some of the nonsense out of them."

Meanwhile a great change had been taking place in Augustus's attitude to his wife. Whereas formerly he had hated her being away for a single night, he now no longer cared whether she was at home or not. This angered Lady Rosamond, who, even if she found life with her husband far from easy, did at least want to be needed. On 24th July 1891 she wrote to him saying that she regretted to find that he was happier without her; but that since she had given up her London house when she returned to him, she had no homes other than Tapeley and her father-in-law's house in Eaton Square. They could go their own ways when they were under the same roof, meeting only at meals; or would he prefer that they should even eat apart? She must continue to insist upon separate bedrooms. She must insist upon a more social life. "But when man and wife can't get on, they had better make the most comfortable and convenient arrangements to see nothing of each other—or at any rate as little as possible." If he did not agree to all this, then she would take another house of her own.

If this was meant as a threat, then it singularly misfired. For it would appear that Augustus was only too willing to accept her conditions. He had learned to manage without her. She could come to Tapeley whenever she liked, but he showed no pleasure on her arrival and no sorrow on her departure: he simply ignored her. Two more years passed, during which the misery and the humiliation of not being needed grew steadily more unbearable. In despair she took to writing to ask his advice on every conceivable subject. Sometimes he replied in a formal letter; usually he did not even trouble to answer. "I really feel", she wrote to him, "as if I had not got a husband to turn to. . . . How nice it would be if I could get you to be different, and how painful it is to me to feel that though I have been away so long you do not seem to mind."

That was the trouble: he did not mind at all. Inevitably their relationship was desperately difficult, but by her unwise handling of it she had made it hopeless. For nearly forty more years, until the death of Augustus relieved her of this intolerable burden, Lady Rosamond was to endure a married life which at its best was a mockery and at its worst a deep tragedy.

3

Eton Boy

IN JANUARY 1896 John went to Eton, taking Remove*; he was just thirteen.

It was the Eton of the great Dr Warre, of Percy Lubbock's *Shades of Eton* and of Sir Lawrence Jones's *A Victorian Boyhood*. It was the Eton of Hornby as Provost, of Warre Cornish as Vice-Provost and of his almost legendary wife, of Austen Leigh ("the Flea") as Lower Master, of A. C. Benson, and of H. E. Luxmoore as champion of aesthetics. It was also the Eton that had just emerged—was perhaps still emerging—from the bad old days of a narrow classical education, of largely unorganised games, of fighting with bare fists, of bullying and excessive flogging.

The Public Schools Commission of the 1860s had inaugurated long overdue reforms, which had to some extent been implemented by Hornby and were carried further by Warre after his arrival "like a breeze from the sea" in 1884. Mathematics, modern languages and history had become an integral part of the curriculum. Science had recently been introduced, and music was advancing. Games, from being casual and amateur, were assuming the regrettably dominant position that they have ever since held in the Public Schools. "Divisions" (classes) had dropped from an impossible hundred boys to around thirty. Of the Dames who had formerly run the boys' houses only one—the invincible Miss Evans—still remained.

John went to White-Thomson's house, which with only eighteen boys was one of the smallest in Eton; it stood on the site of the present School Library. Two years later White-Thomson moved

* Being placed with the cleverer boys.

to a larger house, the newly built Waynflete, and the number of his boys was doubled. The choice of housemaster was not a very fortunate one. White-Thomson was a man of narrow interests, with little sense of humour and little imagination. He was conscientious, but he was unnecessarily strict. Many years later John was to say that he had deeply felt the lack of sympathy shown him by his tutor, and the absence of an unsentimental affection—that kind of affection that life at home also failed to provide.

Certainly White-Thomson never seems to have appreciated, though he was ultimately forced to recognise, John's unusual qualities. But John was still a difficult boy. His reports all told the same story. He was—and he remained—childish for his age. He was always impossibly unpunctual. His conduct, even when he was quite high up the school, continued to provoke unfavourable comment. He would work for masters whose teaching stimulated him; for others he would not make the least effort.

Of the initial impact that Eton made on John, there is no record. Like every new boy fresh from a preparatory school he will at first have enjoyed the greater freedom and the possession of a room to himself. He can hardly have been unaffected by the beauty of the place and its surroundings, then still untroubled by the roar of traffic. He liked games—football, cricket and later rackets—and was a reasonably good and a plucky athlete; in due course he played football for the house, and was also a "stylish bat". In White-Thomson's Athletic Book (which has strangely come to rest in the bookshelves of Glyndebourne) John, playing "post" in the Field Game in the 1897 team, is described as "a very uncertain player who has done well in the last few matches. A neat dribbler but sometimes rather shy of charging. Too small to have much command over the ball in the bully." At this time he was only fifteen. One contemporary recalls that John could sometimes be heard strumming the "Valse Bleue" on the piano in the pupil-room, but that was as far as his interest in music then went.

Of how he spent his holidays from Eton almost equally little is known. Tapeley was at this time let, and it seems that he was much at Cornbury; he became greatly attached to Lady Margaret Watney and during the First World War was to write her a number of long, interesting and affectionate letters from France. No doubt life at home—the Christies now had a London house and a fishing cottage in Hampshire—remained difficult and at times embarrassing.

At Eton, John early showed an interest in science, and his scientific curiosity was on one occasion to get him into trouble. In 1898, after electric light had been installed at White-Thomson's, an injudicious experiment of John's fused the lights of a section of the house. White-Thomson retaliated by removing John's lamp. Not long after, John, wanting to work late, installed himself with his books in the lavatory. He was caught, sent up to the headmaster and duly flogged. Apparently this was by no means the only time he was thus punished; in later life he recalled that he had once been flogged without (he alleged) discovering what offence he was supposed to have committed. On another occasion he nearly received a second flogging because he stooped to gather some fragments of the birch as a souvenir.

When he was sixteen it was decided that he should make his career in the Army. In order to help boys to pass into Woolwich and Sandhurst, Warre had recently started an Army class; John now joined this. It was a happy choice, for it brought him into contact with the Rev Dr T. C. Porter, one of those stimulating teachers and fine eccentrics to whom Eton at various times has owed so much.

Dr Porter—"that rubicund, unbelieving parson" as Sir Lawrence Jones called him—was the first scientist to make science a reality at Eton. A myth in his own lifetime, he enjoyed his reputation as a magician and miracle-worker. It was said that he had raised a dog from the dead. It was said that in a fit of temper he had nearly killed a boy. It was said that he had been unfrocked for preaching a sermon proving that Shadrach, Meshach and Abednego had survived the fiery furnace thanks to asbestos suiting—whereupon he had held his asbestos-gloved hand for half a minute in the flame of the pulpit candle. He would have denied none of these stories. His end-of-Half "good-boy lectures",* which were

* At a later date Porter also gave "good-master lectures" to his friends on the staff.

preceded by an enormous tea, were famous and might include a home-made volcano or other such sensation; there was always the thrilling element of danger, and casualties were not unknown.

Porter was also an artist, a musician, a photographer and a long-distance cyclist. He was mildly interested in spiritualism (perhaps inspired by Sir Oliver Lodge) and foresaw, at a time when E.S.P. was still outside the scope of scientific investigation, that one day Science would make psychic discoveries. His pupils during the First World War maintain that he invented the atom bomb then and also predicted television. He remained at Eton for forty years, and his brilliance as a teacher is shown by the fact that in 1930 no fewer than six of his former pupils were Fellows of the Royal Society.

Most Etonians, at some point in their career, find a master who becomes an important influence in their development; John found Dr Porter. He had always had a taste for science, but henceforth it was to be his greatest interest, both at school and during the holidays. Unhappily, at a later date there was some kind of a quarrel and John, though always ready enough to laugh at Porter's foibles, was never again heard to speak of him with affection or with the gratitude that he undoubtedly deserved.

There was also Dr Lloyd, organist and precentor, who was putting new life into the music of the school. On his return to Eton as a master John was to form a firm friendship with him, and Lloyd's passion for playing the organ was a contributory cause of opera finally coming to Glyndebourne.

House tutors' reports are a great feature at Eton, where they take the form of a long personal letter to the parents at the end of each Half. In March 1899 White-Thomson wrote of John:

> His unpunctuality is a constant source of annoyance, and although he is so high up as the first Army Class, his conduct is still not above reproach. . . . He has taken to racquets with great keenness and has wasted, I fear, a great deal of his time as well as his money in pursuit of the game. He is really interested in science for its own sake I believe—I often find him reading science instead of a novel or a paper. I mention these facts

because I think they show how complex his character is and out of the common. I trust he has understood his preparation.* It certainly has sobered him and I have been very glad to see him attentive in chapel since that preparation began. As far as I can tell he is absolutely straight-forward and clean-minded; like many boys, however, he had never thought for himself and religion has never been any reality to him. I hope his change of mind in this respect may last; he is bound to feel his responsibility sooner or later and I want him to do so now. He has done very poorly in Trials†. . . . His Latin marks are despicable.

These sentiments—which, incidentally, seem to suggest that White-Thomson had sized up the boy pretty well—were more or less echoed by all those other masters who taught John. One described him, rather neatly, as "a strange little boy—very flighty but with plenty of ability. . . . He is everything by turns . . ." "Little" he certainly still was, although now over seventeen; not until the very end of his time at Eton did he attain the five foot four inches which qualified a boy to discard his jacket and don the more dignified "tails".‡

At the end of the summer Half of 1899 White-Thomson repeated the criticisms he had made in March and added: "He is always very friendly and pleasant to my wife and me . . . and is always amenable to reason, but if he does not work better in school in the future it might be unwise to let him stay on at Eton. . . ."

But John did remain at Eton,—and for another year. On his return there in September he tried to persuade White-Thomson to allow him to take additional "extras" in chemistry. This, wrote White-Thomson to Augustus, could not be arranged at so late a stage. "I fancy," he added, "he would really like to do his chemistry with Dr Porter instead of Mr de Havilland. This of course is not now possible."

R. S. de Havilland, a highly successful rowing coach and quite a good housemaster, was a most incompetent teacher of mathematics and science. Though John apparently, and understandably,

---

* For confirmation, taken at Eton by the house tutor.
† Examinations held at the end of each Half.
‡ Jackets were abolished in 1967.

did not wish to be taught by him, he came to like and admire the man; in later years he used often to relate that de Havilland had been largely responsible for his wanting to return to Eton as a master, and that he "had never had a hard word from Havvy".

In December John went to London for an interview in connection with his entry into Woolwich. On such occasions it was customary for a boy to be given some form of extended leave; but since John had been annoying Mr Allcock, the senior mathematical master, this leave was refused. Allcock was evidently one of those masters for whom John would neither work nor behave. He was, reported Allcock, disobedient and babyish, a waster of his own time and everyone else's. He *could* work—when he wanted to —but he mainly indulged in futile scribbling.

This state of affairs evidently brought Augustus Christie to call upon White-Thomson, for at the end of the Half White-Thomson reported to him:

> We have discussed John's character and his prospects so recently that I feel there is little to say in my report this time. . . . He has been doing well in Science, I believe. . . . He is so perfectly satisfied with himself in all circumstances apparently that he does not realise the bad impression he produces. Were he to go a little farther in his disobedience it would become impossible for him to stay at the school; but so far he has just stopped short, and on two occasions this Half I have been able to avert a catastrophe by persuasion. There is so much that is good in him, and he is such a likable boy in himself and so much liked by others, that it is a great pity he will not do himself justice.

A letter written that autumn by John to his mother shows the extent to which science was getting a hold on him:

> I want to see you badly about my laboratory which I am going to get at Baird and Tatlock's. Will you please tell me the full extent of my assets. I have about £12 in one bank which Grandpapa gave me, and some with Lewes Savings Bank. I want also to know what Dad has taken for the bicycle. Without that I should have about £23, which sum would just about buy the laboratory if you can fit up a room. Every day I get keener

on science. I want to see you about giving up the Army and doing science. It is such a waste of time going into the Army.

But Woolwich had been decided upon; provided that he passed the entrance examination a military career now appeared inevitable. He seems to have made the best of a bad job, and his various reports at the beginning of April suggest that he was turning over a new leaf. "He is liked by the best boys in the house," wrote White-Thomson, "and that is a very good sign." In May, now for the first time dressed in tails, he began his last Half at Eton. He had become a reasonable member of society, aware of his responsibilities as a senior boy in the house. A single lapse is recorded: he attended the Eton and Harrow match wearing a very unorthodox kind of collar known as a "Roddy Owen". One of John's few surviving contemporaries still remembers the expression of resigned disapproval on White-Thomson's face when he learned of this.

John's career at Eton had not been particularly glorious; it had been much the same as that of hundreds of other boys. He had arrived undisciplined and somewhat rebellious. He had been admonished; and admonition having failed, he had been flogged. He had sometimes worked hard and sometimes idled. But finally he had begun to put his childishness behind him, coming to realise that some degree of discipline had to be accepted. He never became captain of his house or achieved the eminence of "Pop"*; and it is doubtful whether any of his contemporaries at White-Thomson's would have foretold a future for him other than that of a normal country squire, enjoying his hunting and his shooting and adding little to the common weal.

Certainly no one would have connected it with music.

* The Eton Society, whose members are the equivalent of school prefects.

4

Woolwich, Cambridge and Cars

THE EXAMINATION was successfully taken, and in the autumn of 1900 John went to the Royal Academy, Woolwich.

Of the first year he spent there we have little information except for what is to be found in a single and brief letter; in later life, beyond commenting that he had received "a pretty boring and utterly useless and rotten education" there, he was rarely to refer to his time at "the Shop". Then, during his fourth term, he met with a bad accident in the riding school; his horse slipped when taking a jump and fell, crushing his foot. "It was my own fault," he said; "I ought to have got clear." He was taken to the Military Hospital, where his foot was put in a cradle but left unexamined for ten days by "the criminally incompetent Army doctors". Finally his mother sent the carriage and brought him to London. There he saw Sir Thomas Barlow, the Royal Physician, who X-rayed his foot and discovered a serious injury. The bones were set, but John was to remain slightly lame for the rest of his life.

It looked like being, and was in fact to prove, the end of his military career—a career that he had accepted without enthusiasm and was now ready to relinquish without regret. Perhaps a future in science lay open to him. On 24th January 1902, while he was convalescing in London, he wrote a careful letter to his father:

> It will be some time before I shall be able to go back to Woolwich and I shall lose a good deal towards getting "Field"* by missing so much riding. It will take some time for my legs to get strong on a horse owing to the little

* Qualifying for the Field Artillery, rather than being posted to a "heavy" battery or to Garrison Artillery.

exercise they have had. . . . To ensure my getting "Field" I should have had to get very good marks in riding, which I should have done but for this accident. Sir Thomas says that I should have a perfectly valid excuse for leaving the Shop. My own tastes lie and always have done in experimental science and original research. My only liking for the Artillery was the outdoor life, i.e. riding, etc. . . . but fighting and the science of tactics do not interest me. I should do a certain amount of science in my spare time in the Army but should not have time for much. If I went into the Army my interests would lie only in the sport attaching to it; if into Science, in that itself. Once started in Science, games and sport would come second. Going into the Army would never lead to my being more than a major or colonel probably; Science I hope would. If I went into Science I should not merely dabble in it but work at it.

These things ought to be settled fairly quickly as notice would have to be given at Woolwich . . .

The case for not doing what had never appealed to him, and for doing what he had really wanted to do since he was sixteen, could hardly have been better put. How a decision was reached we do not know; probably his mother supported him and his father finally acquiesced. At all events, in the summer we find John preparing for Little-go* and the entrance examination to Trinity College, Cambridge.

At that time the Classics figured prominently in these examinations. John had done no Greek since he was fifteen, and Latin had never been a strong subject; he needed some coaching, and was therefore sent to Antony Vicarage, near Devonport. In this rambling Victorian house lived the Vicar and his wife, their large family, and two female cousins. The eldest son, a young man of twenty-nine and his father's curate, was to be John's coach.

In August he went for a short visit to his grandfather at Glynde-

* The Cambridge University Entrance Examination.

bourne, and after his return to Antony Vicarage wrote a long letter to his mother:

> I returned here on Saturday from Glyndebourne where I enjoyed myself very much indeed. I drove a good deal and turned one corner at which there was not more than 8 inches on each side of the wheels with the waggonette at the gallop, one of the horses shying at a wheelbarrow. . . . Grandpapa made two speeches at the Flower-show and exhausted all his information at the first, had nothing to say at the second, so he commented on the ladies' dresses, etc. . . .

William Christie is still remembered as a generous and kindly old man, much loved by the villagers of Ringmer. One of Ringmer's oldest inhabitants recalls the Jubilee mugs given to all the local children in 1897, and the jerseys and warm red capes with hoods which he distributed at Christmas, one for every year of his age, among the various families. Each year two waggons were sent to bring the children to Glyndebourne for a summer treat.

Into John's letter, and into others of about the same time, there creeps a slightly peevish tone which was to grow with the years when writing to his mother: "Please do not go on about . . ."; "Of course you got hold of the wrong day," and so on. There was the implication that she fussed him, that she muddled things, that she was silly and unreasonable. On 7th September, after partridge shooting for six hours, he wrote to her: "My leg is all right. I am not bothering about it, why should you?" The fact was that he found her affection for him stifling. Poor woman! with her home life a perpetual misery, what else had she to live for but her only child?

His letters to his mother also contain endless requests to send him various things from home that he needs. He never hesitated to make her fetch and carry for him. He asks for his scientific books, his prints, his trouser-press, the X-ray photographs of his ankle, his shirts, his shooting boots, his cricket boots, his collars. . . . Soon after, he is demanding his Eton tail-coat and trousers, his great coat, his top hat and the remainder of his bottle of hair-wash. When these things did not arrive by return—and they rarely did, for Lady Rosamond was dilatory—he wrote again, petulantly.

At the end of September John went up to Cambridge to sit for his examinations. He wrote that he thought he had passed; and he had. There was now the question of his allowance to be settled —and here again it was to his mother, not to his father, that he wrote: "R. V. Buxton is having £300. His elder brother started with £250 but could not do [on] it, and so they have had £300. This is the usual thing I believe. This includes fees and living." What John finally received is not told; there are grounds for believing that he was not too generously treated by a very rich father, but he expressed himself as satisfied and grateful.

There was also the question of furnishing his rooms, and once again he relies on his mother for advice. He had very clear ideas as to what he wanted, and sent her a long list of his needs. He would prefer the bedroom suite to be white, and to have oak or chestnut for the sitting-room. He observes that his predecessor's furniture was fake antique and that he had doubtless been "done" by the local shops. If his mother can provide some chairs from Tapeley, they should not have monograms, "which would be very queer here". His mother was also summoned to Cambridge to inspect his rooms. "Mind you come down well dressed", he added.

Virtually no letters survive from John's first winter at Cambridge. In the early spring, however, his pen suddenly becomes extremely active. He wants to buy a car. He wants one passionately. He had his eye on a 6 HP Regal, costing between £200 and £210, but how was he to raise the money to pay for it? His mother was not at first enthusiastic about the project; but she seems to have helped him, for on 20th February he wrote to her:

> I am very grateful to you for raising the money. It is really most good of you. I hope my father will consent to it. I could also add the £10 given me by Grandpapa when a baby, which by now will be £20. I am going to sell my induction coil and everything I can spare. I have not mentioned

the coil to my father; I think I may make £1 over it. I could raise about £50 in this way I think and possibly get £10 from Grandpapa. . . . If you could raise £150 over the shares I could thus manage it. If necessary I could sell my furniture and go into lodgings, buying my furniture again with what I could get from my car if I go to Eton.★ I would rather not do it but I would if necessary. Perhaps my father would buy 22 bottles of whisky and 10 bottles of claret which is not drunk here. Can you send me all the boots in my bedroom; I could get several pounds for them. I think Grandpapa would give me a pound or so to make it up to the right amount. . . .

Presumably he was still short of the money he needed, and it would seem that his mother was still wavering about the wisdom of the purchase, when he wrote to her again on 9th March to stress the advantage of keeping a car:

> I have a good many arguments for it. It would be most use-ful to have a certain amount of practical knowledge of the petrol motor. I can't see any reason against it. There will be a great many other motors up here soon, a lot of new ones are coming up next term. The garage is going to be enlarged. I want to try and bring out some patents. I am thinking of two at present. I should also be able to take my lecturers out. They would be most anxious to come. It would make me much more fit for my work as I should have something definite to do for recreation. I should also save all my railway journeys. . . .

His mother now agreed to help him with money, and his uncle, Vernon Watney, also made his contribution. He wrote to his mother to thank her and to tell her the kind of car he had in mind; he had already ruled out the Regal. Three days later he reports that he has made his choice; and the letter almost seems to imply that his mother has decided that the car should be a present to him, for he thanks her for "this magnificent gift". He continued, "I shall now have some object of definite interest, which I had not

---

★ It is interesting to note that he already had in mind the possibility of returning to Eton as a master.

before. There is no fear of an accident as I shall drive most carefully, as the driving makes a great difference in the expense of upkeep".

The car he had chosen was a Georges-Richard, and he proceeds to give her the minutest details of the design of the body (which will be of steel instead of the customary aluminium), of the tyres and manometer and lamps, and of his ingenious alterations to the placing of the petrol tank and accelerator lever. The letter, which runs to sixteen pages, was written from Cornbury, where the car was in due course delivered. How much experience John had previously had of driving is not known; what is known, however, is that he immediately took his Georges-Richard on the road and drove it to Birmingham and back, a distance of about 120 miles—"just to make sure that I can", he wrote.

He soon established himself as a skilful and dashing, if rather alarming driver. One of his Cambridge friends, now Sir Edward Duncombe, recalls John arriving at his rooms and saying, "Duncombe, it's a lovely slippery day; come out in my car and we'll do a bit of skidding". A sixth sense, John would often at a later date assure his terrified passengers, enabled him to *know* that nothing was coming round the corner in the opposite direction.

Psychiatrists today recognise that for many young men a car is a sex substitute; undoubtedly it was for John some kind of sublimation. He was in love with his Georges-Richard. He was incessantly tinkering with her, taking her to pieces, fitting new lubricators, encasing her belly in zinc to exclude the dust. He changed the brass gearwheel to a fibre one, replaced worn ball-bearings, fitted new exhaust valves. He adjusted the gear-box and stripped down the engine. Then, when everything was to his satisfaction, he competed in a hill-climbing competition. To his mother—who could not have understood a word of it—he wrote incessantly and in enormous detail on motoring matters. The car had become his mistress.

A second interest which was making itself apparent about this time was music—and music, for John, was more or less synonymous with Wagner.

5 (*Above*) Tapeley as it was and (*below*) as reconstructed

6 John Christie (*left*) *c.* 192◦ and (*below*) in his motor a Ringmer in 1911

John could do no more than strum upon the piano; it has been alleged that he could only play a single tune, and a dance tune at that. But he joined the Cambridge Music Club, and also "learned his notes" from Hylton-Stewart, the organist of St Catherine's. He had a piano in his rooms, on which his more musical friends came and played, and incorporated with it an "Angelus"—an early form of pianola—which John played in his shirt-sleeves, a towel round his head to collect the sweat. Very briefly, towards the end of his time at Cambridge, he took lessons on the 'cello— "a much better instrument for me than the piano"—but apparently he soon gave up. He did not, at this time, appear to be really very musical.

But where Wagner was concerned, this hardly mattered. For Wagner was a religion, and his worshippers were to be found among the non-musical as well as among the musical. John began to attend Wagner concerts at Queen's Hall and also heard the *Ring* at Covent Garden. On one occasion he took his grandfather with him to Queen's Hall: "Music is not very much in his line", John told his mother. "However, he did not talk."

In the long vacation of 1904 John had the felicitous idea of harnessing together his two current hobby-horses, Wagner and the Georges-Richard, to make an audacious expedition to Bayreuth. The party consisted of Dr Lloyd from Eton, George Lyttelton, R. H. Longman and John. But the car was an open two-seater, and room had to be found not only for two extra passengers but also for tins of petrol and luggage; further space was therefore improvised by "nailing" to the back of the car an enormous crate that had originally been made to transport cheeses. In this crate, it must be presumed, sat Lyttelton (among other things a heavy-weight boxer) and Longman, for Dr Lloyd, an elderly man, will almost certainly have been given the seat of honour beside the driver. It says much for John's mechanical ingenuity that this strange contraption did not fail him.

Cross-channel steamers had at that time no facilities for transporting cars; a barge was therefore chartered and the car, together with its complement of passengers, towed behind the steamer to Calais. The journey through Germany was hardly less adventurous.

4

Mr Longman recalls that there were frequent halts to allow the over-heated engine to cool; and once, when in an arid and uninhabited stretch of country, the radiator ran completely out of water, they were obliged themselves to supply it. The roads were bad; the dust was worse, and Dr Lloyd's beard was often white with it. Lyttelton most reluctantly agreed to help push the car up the steepest hill they encountered. It was something of a miracle that they arrived at Bayreuth in time for the start of the Festival.

They stayed a short distance outside the town; thus they came to miss, when the car failed to start, the first act of *Parsifal*. But they heard the last two acts and, besides the *Ring*, *Tannhäuser* and *Tristan*. No letters survive to record the impression that Bayreuth made on John, but his enthusiasm for Wagner continued unabated. He had become the complete Wagnerite.

Though motoring and music figured prominently in John's letters home, there is no doubt that he was working, and continued to work, conscientiously. During his three years at Cambridge he read physics, chemistry and mineralogy; and in later life he always spoke with gratitude of his time under Sir J. J. Thomson in the Cavendish Laboratory. Even when the first part of his Tripos was still some months distant, he reports that he is studying seven hours a day; and in the vacations there were often reading parties, with a coach, at Lowestoft or in the Isle of Wight. For recreation, besides motoring there was golf and shooting; and one winter, dressed in a fur coat given him by his uncle, John sat to John Collier for his portrait.*

In short, but for the apparent absence of social parties and of dancing, John was leading the normal life of an undergraduate of his day. But his mother was still fretting herself about him. Was he looking after himself properly? Was he taking care of his health? In the Christmas vacation of 1904 she wrote to her brother-in-law, Vernon Watney, with whom John had just been staying, telling him of her anxiety. Watney replied in terms that must certainly have reassured her:

He has now come and gone; and I can only . . . repeat

* Now at Tapeley.

what I have said before, that he seems to me (and I think to everybody who meets him) to be an unusually good and able fellow.

You say that you are fidgeting yourself about what he eats, and the amount of exercise he gets. I shouldn't allow myself to do that—if I were you; for you might fidget him, which would be unfortunate, and also there does not appear to be any reason at all why you should be anxious.

He is reading hard, and will have to continue to read hard till his examinations are over; (after which I should—if I were you—give him anything from £50 to £100 and let him go abroad for a holiday with a friend). He is reading hard; but he seems to me to be very sensible about it, and I should say that he took as much exercise as his lameness would allow him to take. Whatever class he may take does not really matter very much, because it is obvious that he is doing his best, and no one can do more. . . .

My dear Rosamond, I have never met a lad about whom a mother need have less anxiety. May I alter one word in Rosalind's words to Phebe, and say: "Down on your knees, [and] thank heaven, fasting, for a good son's love?"

At the beginning of his last year John moved into lodgings in the town. Again his mother helped him, and between them they seem to have made some shrewd bargains. He also hired a Blüthner grand piano. He mentions in his letters to her the famous hoax "performed by friends of mine", when the Mayor of Cambridge received with great ceremony the alleged Sultan of Zanzibar and his suite. The organiser of this and many other practical jokes was Molar Cole (who was, rather surprisingly, a brother-in-law of Austen Chamberlain). John was himself the victim of one of Cole's more macabre jests: he awoke one morning at half past three to find Cole plunging a dagger into the pillow on either side of his face. John also told his mother of the attempt at this time to have Greek made an optional subject in the entrance examination; "the place," he said, "was swarming with persons who have been voting for Greek. They reached 56 per cent at one time."

It has often been said that John's father made it a condition of his eventually leaving Glyndebourne to him, that he should work for his living until he was forty or until his grandfather died. This is not certain; but it is clear that his parents at this time wanted him to do some kind of a job, and that he himself did not wish otherwise. At one moment he thought of scientific research. He was offered an engineering post in one of the railway companies, but refused it. At the back of his mind, for some time past, had been the possibility of returning to Eton as a master. In view of his chequered and undistinguished career there as a boy, this was rather surprising; but a week spent at Eton coaching a boy may have helped him to decide to write to the Head Master to ask for an interview.

It was perhaps fortunate for John that Dr Warre had retired; his successor, Dr Edward Lyttelton, would be less well informed of the various troubles of his Eton career, though no doubt he wrote to White-Thomson.* Not realising that the Head Master alone was responsible for the appointment of his staff, John also wrote to a family friend, Sir Henry Roscoe, a Fellow of the College. In addition he did a little canvassing among his friends on the staff, among whom will no doubt have been Dr Porter and de Havilland.

A fortnight later he told his mother that he had seen Lyttelton, who had as good as promised him a job within a year or two. But in March he heard that he would probably be needed in the following September; this was in one respect disappointing, for he had been hoping to go for a year to a German university to take a Ph.D.

A new laboratory had recently been built at Eton. He learned that he would be given charge of it, and £50 to purchase equipment; but enquiries that he made at Cambridge convinced him that such a sum was quite inadequate: £200 was the minimum needed for a start, and £1,000 would be necessary to do the job properly. He therefore decided to contribute £150 himself; "Aunt Lizzie's money will here be very useful", he told his

---

* White-Thomson, finding that schoolmastering was not really his métier, had left Eton in 1904 and become a Civil Servant.

mother. It was a generous gesture, for he was at this time far from being a rich man.

John's appointment was confirmed and he set to work to prepare himself for the second part of his Tripos, which he was to take in the summer. But he still found time for his car and for his beloved Wagner. On 30th April 1906 he wrote to his mother:

> I am coming up to town on Friday to hear the first cycle of the *Ring*. . . . I think you will like the new car very much. It is a great improvement on the old one. I got £140 for the latter from an acquaintance up here. The new one cost £300 and is an extraordinary bargain. I could realise this sum on it with the greatest ease. . . . I am told that there is a probability of the salaries of the science masters being raised. At present they get £450 from the school and £10 from each pupil. I imagine that in two years time I could have about 50 pupils if I want. I should at any rate get £50 from pupils in the first year. I go down to Eton on Sunday partly to look for rooms. I believe this is a matter of considerable difficulty.

Thus in the autumn of 1906 John became a master at Eton where, except for an interlude in the Army, he was to remain for the next sixteen years.

5

Eton Master*

JOHN WAS often heard to say that his time as an Eton master was
the happiest in his life, and often to recount to suitable, and sometimes to unsuitable, audiences anecdotes of that period.

His satisfaction with his Eton life was not surprising. He was
young and carefree. He had a comfortable private income which
enabled him to live well and entertain freely. There were congenial
colleagues (though it took him a little time to discover the fact),
and he made a number of close friendships which endured. He
was teaching a subject that interested him. He had plenty of opportunities for playing the games he enjoyed—cricket, football and
rackets during the Half, and long holidays in which he could shoot
and fish, play more cricket and travel abroad. The world was very
good, in the opening years of the century, to those who were
young and eager and affluent.

But there was one thing that he lacked: a happy home life. He
went to Tapeley as little as possible. Almost all his letters to his
mother at this time contain criticism of her, and in not a few of
them there is abuse; and since John apparently kept none of her
letters to him, we do not know to what extent she earned these
constant reproaches. We do not know how unwisely her letters
to him were worded, nor how she defended herself against his
charge of an inefficiently run house. But what he failed to find at
Tapeley he fortunately found at Cornbury. Poor Lady Rosamond!
The tragedy of her marriage was hardly of her making, but it is
difficult to believe that she was wholly blameless for the strained

* This chapter deals with John's career as an Eton master both before and after
his two years in the Army, which are discussed in the chapter that follows.

relations with her son. Clearly John was intolerant; but clearly also she must have handled the situation very unwisely.

At Eton John seems first to have lived by himself, probably in a house in the High Street. In view of his constant criticisms of the staff at Tapeley, it may seem surprising that he invited his mother to help him to find servants. But this he did, and moreover he wrote to her afterwards a very amiable letter thanking her for the trouble she had taken over this and in assisting him to settle in. Dobbie also kept her eyes open for him at local furniture sales and made several purchases on his behalf. In January 1909 he moved into another house, but that autumn he was offered a place in what at Eton is called a "colony"—a house occupied jointly by a small group of bachelor masters who are not housemasters. His housemates at first were Dick Durnford and G. W. ("Tuppy") Headlam.

Colonial life at Eton before the First World War was comfortable, even luxurious. By comparison with other public schools the staff—though more especially the classical masters—were well paid; not a few of them had private means; and several—for example, "Bunny" Hare—were land-owners. The colony which John now entered—2 Common Lane—had formerly been a small "boys' house"; it was soon christened Liqueur Cottage in honour of the formidable array of bottles on the sideboard in the dining-room—bottles that were there (contrary to Gibbon's well-known sentence) more for ostentation than for use. The staff consisted of a housekeeper (Mrs Child), a parlourmaid and a boy, and John had his own manservant, Frank; he also had a groom for his horses, and later a chauffeur as well. Young masters would usually find themselves dining out on at least three or four nights a week —generally with one or other of the bachelor housemasters—and the Common Lane Colony also did a good deal of entertaining on its own account.

John liked his companions, and they will certainly have liked him or they would not have extended an invitation to him to live with them. Dick Durnford (wrote Mr A. S. F. Gow, who later joined the colony and became a close friend of John's) was "a genial and friendly soul of whom most people were fond, and with (and sometimes at) whom they enjoyed laughing"; he was to fight at John's side in Flanders and there lose his life.

Tuppy Headlam, wrote Mr Gow, was

> a much more individual character, an Eton Colleger, a Balliol scholar and a friend at Oxford of remarkable men such as Raymond Asquith. He was able but not much interested in scholarship (though he once wrote a book) or teaching. Boys, however, enjoyed being "up" to him. Later on he had a good but somewhat unusual house, taking more interest in the character than in the brains of the boys in it. Temperamental, liverish and somewhat saturnine; extremely amusing with a whimsical turn of wit; excellent company among friends, but a caustic critic and not given to concealing his criticism, consequently not universally liked. . . An able but idle man with a wide circle of diversified friends, some of whom later abused his abundant hospitality.

Tuppy became an enthusiast for the harpsichord and a close personal friend of Violet Gordon Woodhouse, one of the finest performers of her day on that instrument. At his invitation she played from time to time to selected masters and boys. Although this was by no means John's favourite type of music—and certainly it was a strange pabulum for a Wagnerian—he caught the enthusiasm which these concerts engendered.

There was, however, at any rate one contemporary of John's on the staff who did not approve of the extravagance of the occupants of Liqueur Cottage; but allowance should be made for the fact that he was a very untypical Eton master, a man of many prejudices, and with a chip on his shoulder. "John and his friends", he wrote,★ "lived in a different world from mine, a world of money, wines, operas and motors." He considered Headlam "the world's first snob", that he exerted in this respect a bad influence on John, and that John became "friendly and approachable" after Headlam left Eton.

★ In a letter to John Gwynne. He asked that his name should not be given.

There was much opposition to Edward Lyttelton as Head, and J.C. took his full share in that. The difference in pay-scales between Classics and Modern subjects was much discussed. At a meeting of Maths and Science beaks* Duckworth, a new Classical beak said to be getting more pay than we got, was mentioned as a grievance. You can guess who said, "I understand that Lyttelton has imported Duckers so as to improve the standard of Eton beaks; in that case the sooner we get rid of him the better." Duckworth was a friend of mine; but I was much too young and insignificant to raise a voice.

After John's return from the War

a senior beak, possibly P. V. Broke, asked him if he would be going out again: "But Christie looked over the top of my head and talked to me as to a very small child." And that was how he talked to many of us. I think it was Broke also, Senior Maths Beak, who told me that Christie was going to teach Maths because he was offended at being "passed over" for Head of Science. When I asked, "Does he know any Maths?" he answered simply, "No." Later, when Conybeare was Senior Maths Master, and I had to make up the Fourth Form Divisions, he said, "Don't put any boy up to John twice running."

At first, as so often happens with a young schoolmaster, John found himself closer to the boys than to his colleagues, many of whom were old enough to be his father. (Colonel) Arthur Lloyd-Baker, a contemporary of John's at Eton as a boy, visited John at Eton in July 1907 and recorded in his diary a full account of an interesting conversation that they had together. The gist of it is as follows:

John believed that the moral tone of the School had been low in his day. He had since been told that it had then been impossible for a boy to become popular or to get into Pop without adopting "the bad life". Now that he was a master, he determined to try to put matters right; and to do this he decided upon a rather perilous course of action: he set about making himself "a confidential friend" of a number of boys at the top of the School, mostly Pops,

---

* Masters.

with whom he discussed quite openly any problems that they cared to put to him—including, of course, sex. He well realised that he was playing with fire: that there would be a "huge row" if this came to the ears of some of the housemasters, and that he was also laying himself open to a charge of snobbery; but so far as snobbery was concerned, he knew that it was only by influencing influential boys that he could hope to get results.

John believed that many housemasters made no attempt to become friends of or advisers to the boys in their houses, and that in any case a housemaster might not be the kind of man to whom a particular boy felt he could turn in a crisis. If a boy can then turn only to his housemaster, often he will turn to no one. Lloyd-Baker agreed that it might be mortifying to a housemaster to have to admit this, but thought that the man ought to be above petty pride; he ought not to be so conceited as to imagine himself the most sympathetic counsellor of forty different boys.

"John has certainly carried his 'friendship' theories to extraordinary lengths", Lloyd-Baker noted. "He calls his friends by their Christian names. On one occasion he said to a boy in school, 'Now then, get to work, Harry!' whereupon the answer was, 'All right, John.' This is certainly a novelty for Eton! During the holidays he had the various captains and keepers to stay with him, six or eight at a time; they 'raised hell' in a small village and were known as the Christie crew."

It was Lloyd-Baker's opinion that John was "on the whole doing good work in his way; but this way is very personal and individual, so that I doubt whether he will be able to continue it successfully in a community where so much depends on co-operation".

In brief, John was, as one of his pupils wrote later, "more like a school chum than a master"; indeed John went so far as to admit that he thought the generality of beaks "rather rotten", though he did not dislike them personally. He annoyed them unnecessarily in a variety of ways, as, for example, by driving his car noisily into Cannon Yard when he had to "call absence" there, and by departing afterwards even more noisily. Lloyd-Baker thought that John's colleagues had been rather easily shocked, but that John had been silly to play into their hands in ways such as this. Housemasters at Eton have great power.

Presumably in the course of time John grew up and became, as do most young reformers, more discreet and more tolerant of evils which they cannot hope to eradicate; at all events we hear little more of his campaign for the improvement of the morals of Eton. Ten months later, after another visit to Eton, Colonel Lloyd-Baker noted in his diary: "John Christie . . . says he is getting on excellently now, with very little friction. I should fancy he has slightly modified his method."

"To the last", wrote John Gwynne, who was up to John at the very end of his time as a master, "John continued his practice of making friends with the boys, but I think I was one of the few of the younger ones who struck up a friendship with him. On one occasion I invited him to tea, a meal which was eaten in one's own room and began at 6 p.m. He accepted but added that he did not want much to eat." He was however, provided with the gigantic spread that was customary—a spread to which he did full justice until he had to leave to dine with a colleague.

Of the capacity of John as a teacher, his anonymous colleague has already given a hint. Mr Gow develops the theme:

> John was seriously interested in the Physics that he taught at Eton, contemplated and even started a text book on the subject, and bought a lot of expensive apparatus which he subsequently presented to the school. I remember a vast rheostat and a liquid-air pump which never, I think, manufactured liquid air but was useful for inflating the tyres of John's car. I should doubt if he was a very good teacher for his expositions whether of relativity or, in later days, of the organisation of Glyndebourne, were noticeably lacking in lucidity; but his pupils, like his colleagues, were fond of him and enjoyed such incidents as the arrival in early school of John's Jeeves-like butler, Childs,* to announce that Captain Christie† had overslept but might be expected shortly.

Mr Gow's reference to relativity concerns an occasion when

* See p. 82.
† John attained the rank of Captain during the First World War.

John had been attempting to explain to Headlam and himself Einstein's newly propounded theory—a theory which John maintained to be "perfectly simple". After ten minutes of incomprehensible exposition John suddenly uttered the first words which seemed to make a certain sense: "Draw two lines upon a pig's bladder."

One who was taught by John in school wrote: "He was quite unpredictable to be up to. You never knew when he was going to turn up and you often wondered whether he knew anything about his subject at all; and suddenly you realised that he was, in his vague way, most knowledgeable." He was apt to write on the blackboard some teasing little problem and then append the solution. When asked how he had arrived at this solution he would say with a chuckle, "I did it *by a dodge*," and leave it at that.

Mr Quintin Hogg said that the only time he nearly "failed in Trials" was when he was up to John. Mr W. N. Roe, who was a King's Scholar as a boy, and who later became Senior Science Master at Eton, wrote* that John's teaching of science was "largely incomprehensible":

> His real contribution to science at Eton was that he brought with him a young man to act as his personal laboratory assistant (having got to know him, I believe, in the labs at Cambridge) who stayed for some fifty years. This was Bertie Wolf— a superb chap who was of immense value to us. . . John, characteristically, made a very large contribution to the sum we subscribed on his retirement.
>
> The other thing John is remembered for in the science department is his purchase of several expensive items of apparatus which—at that time—they certainly wouldn't have screwed out of the School Fund. One of these was an enormous induction coil. According to Wolf, he earthed one end of this on the water pipes, which resulted in people all over Eton getting sparks out of their taps while he was working it. . .
>
> John did a splendid thing at Glyndebourne, but his time at Eton was a sort of harlequinade—except that it came before the real stuff of the performance instead of after it.

* To Mr John Gwynne, 15th August 1963.

In fact, John was one of those delightful, unconventional, easygoing schoolmasters which no school should be without, provided that they are reinforced by a good supply of orthodox teachers who get through the curriculum to time and who stuff their pupils' heads with what is needed to pass examinations.

Before going to Eton John had told his mother that after two years he would be able to have about fifty pupils if he so wished. But in September 1910 he reports to her that the number of his pupils has dropped from twenty to ten.* This was a clear sign that his housemaster colleagues, however much they liked him personally, had little confidence in him as a teacher.

Eventually there was real trouble. The science teaching of the school was examined and reported on unfavourably. Dr Lyttelton, anxious to reduce the size of the staff and looking to find a master who could be dispensed with, and preferably one who would not thereby suffer financial hardship, informed John that his services were no longer required. John's colleagues, in spite of their doubts as to his teaching ability, immediately rallied round. They discovered that, owing to an oversight, he was the one member of the Science staff whose Division had not been inspected. A deputation approached Lyttelton and the dismissal was rescinded.

Lyttelton did not always command the support of his staff and there was a good deal of opposition to him, especially later, during the War, when his attitude towards the Germans and his desire for peace were considered too Christian to be patriotic.

★   ★   ★

A number of Old Etonians and colleagues recall John's athletic activities while a beak. As a bowler he used to lumber up to the wicket, where he delivered the ball in such a manner that it appeared to emerge from behind his head. His bowling was quite innocuous, but he took the wickets of those who anticipated something dangerous. Cyril Butterwick, a colleague of John's,

* At a later date, George Orwell was for a time his pupil.

mentions two "dodges" by means of which John attempted to make additional runs:

> He had a theory that if a batsman called "No" and then ran, he would catch the fieldsman napping. That it certainly did; but it caught his partner napping too, however carefully he explained that "Yes" meant "No" and "No" meant "Yes". The second and more complicated theory was that in running between the wickets much time was lost by turning. So his plan was to spin round three yards before reaching the Popping Crease and complete the run backwards so that the next run could be started without delay. This plan was for a time quite successful, because the fieldsmen were so helpless with laughter at the sight of a massive baldish man spinning round like a teetotum that they failed to take advantage of the fact that each run took several seconds longer than the normal procedure.

John Gwynne, writing (from a boy's point of view) of the closing years of John's career as an Eton master, says that his enthusiasm and vigour on the cricket field were remarkable in a man of nearly forty; his mighty swipe at the ball left an indelible impression on a fifteen-year-old boy, even after an interval of nearly fifty years. "Then there was the intense interest he took in boys' play and the animation with which he would discuss a particular match, however unimportant: 'Mott [a junior boy] took an *absolutely superb* catch!'—and the word 'superb' would be uttered with just the same emphasis as he would later use to describe an outstanding operatic performance."

On the football field John was "always a formidable opponent, charging about pretty heavily". Another Etonian remembers him there as "a terrifyingly violent figure—on one occasion in a pink silk vest; and I seem to recollect that, as a Rugby footballer, he destroyed several members of his own side." (Sir) Rex Benson recalls that when playing rackets John "was extremely dangerous with his gammy leg. I used to take cover in the court whenever I got the chance."

John was also an officer in the Eton College Officers' Training Corps until he resigned in 1918. The best-known episode of this

phase of his military career occurred after his return from the
War when, during a Field Day, he sent a boy* disguised as a
hurdy-gurdy man to reconnoitre the enemy's position and then
landed troops in their rear from a launch on the Thames.

In January 1910 John canvassed on behalf of his friend, Aubrey
Herbert, who was standing as Conservative candidate for the South
Somerset division at the General Election. William Christie, delighted to learn of his grandson's new interest, now wrote to
encourage him to leave Eton and take up politics. But John could
give him no encouragement: he found, he said, "the whole
business [of electioneering] extremely strenuous and almost de-
void of humour"; he was happy at Eton and intended to stay
there. In later life he professed to despise politics, saying that he
did not think it mattered which party got in.

At the same time that William Christie was advocating a poli-
tical career, Lady Rosamond was advocating matrimony. She
consulted John's friends on the subject and from time to time
plied her son with photographs cut from the pages of the *Tatler*.
These he would discuss with Mrs Whitworth, the wife of one of
his colleagues; but he could never find one that took his fancy.
He demanded perfection. Mrs Whitworth said to him:
"You expect too much of a wife. What should she expect of
you?"
"I've never thought of that."
"Then don't get married."
But with his mother John was not yet prepared to discuss the
matter. "I am afraid", he tells her, "I cannot give the idea of
marrying any encouragement at all." However, Lady Rosamond
would not let the matter drop. Four years later she was still
nudging him. On 20th February 1914 John wrote again, principally to complain once more of what he considered her incompetent running of Tapeley, and added: "You and father talk

* The boy was Wogan Philipps, now Lord Milford.

about my future wife. Do you not understand that this hypothetical person is likely to disapprove of the culinary and other deficiencies just as strongly as I do? What is the point of it all? I think you are being very unwise."

But John was by that time well over thirty, and possibly he had begun to feel that he ought in fact to get married. At all events, the following month he reports to his mother that he has been having a dancing lesson from his cousin Silvia Watney at Cornbury, and found that as a result he did not wholly disgrace himself at Lady Cavan's ball. But he realised that he still had a long way to go: "I don't think really I dance very well at present, and the dancing is so much easier than the 'jaw'. There is really so little to say to these women whom one meets for the first time and for two or three minutes. They all look exactly alike and very few of them are at all attractive, at any rate under the conditions when they are seen at dances. Fortunately I am fairly tolerant."

In the spring of 1910 there occurred an event which at first sight might hardly seem worth the recording, but one which was in fact to have an enormous influence on John's life. Finding his manservant, Frank, to be idle and incompetent, John dismissed him and engaged in his place a man named Childs. A month later he wrote to his mother, "My new servant is I think very successful and at any rate is highly intelligent". This remarkable man upon whom P. G. Wodehouse might well have modelled his immortal Jeeves, this devout and simple Christian who was one of nature's Boy Scouts, we shall meet again in the pages of this biography.

★   ★   ★

One day in the summer of 1910 John was hit in the left eye by a ball while playing rackets. (Many years later he told his wife, "I could have been an outstanding rackets player but for this".) His uncle Vernon urged him to see a specialist, and in August he went to Elmore Brewerton, who was acting as *locum tenens* for the distinguished ophthalmic surgeon, Walter Jessop.

Brewerton said that in his opinion there was only one possible treatment: to puncture the eye behind the retina. The chances of

7 Glyndebourne (*above*) as it was and (*below*) as it is today, with the organ room and opera house added

8   The organ room at Glyndebourne

success were very small indeed, and he advised John to consult Jessop when he returned from his holiday in September. But Jessop (John told his mother) was "strongly against any kind of treatment. It would appear that if any operation of incision was made on the bad eye there would be a tendency for the other to go wrong. . . So there is the end of this affair." Many years later, when the eye had become quite useless, John had it removed.

*   *   *

In March 1911, when Lady Rosamond was about to go on a Greek cruise, John wrote to tell her that several of his colleagues would also be on board:

> E. L. Vaughan, a man of nearly sixty, is anxious to make your acquaintance. You will find him pleasant but he is quite devoid of any sense of comfort. He is besides possessed of extraordinary bravery. He does not know what fear is. He sails all round England in any weather by himself. In any wind everything is done with full sail flying including casting anchor, a process he adopts after reducing headway by bumping into everything else in the harbour. I think he is taking one of his pupils with him.
> Wells, I expect, you will not meet. He is an extremely able man and an extraordinarily strong man in every way but he never has anything to do with women. I like him very much as I also do Churchill. They are both men who work all day here and most of the night.

This is the first mention by John, in the letters to his mother, of a very remarkable Eton figure, C. M. Wells, brilliant both as a scholar and as an athlete. John had, however, got to know him as soon as he joined the staff. Wells, he said, "took me up. The very first time I dined with him a bargain was struck: if I taught him to fish, he would teach me about wine." It was the beginning of one of the most important and mutually advantageous friendships of John's life, and it was to endure unclouded for more than fifty years. There were several fishing holidays together in Ireland, Scotland and Norway, and no business, however important, was allowed to interfere with the annual celebration (on no less

5

than forty-two occasions) of Wells's birthday with a dinner served with memorable wines. John was a man capable of hero-worship, and Wells was the greatest hero of his life.

Wells was an acknowledged expert on wine, winning praise from even such a fastidious critic as André Simon. As recently as the middle fifties the *imprimatur* which he gave to a new type of Hock grape (the Scheurebe) resulted in bulk buying of the wine by the London clubs. He was already in his forties when, after damage to his knee put an end to more energetic forms of sport, he began to fish, using tackle generously presented to him by John. This new activity surprised Wells's friends. "I cannot imagine Wells fishing," wrote one of them to John; "did he ever catch anything?" He certainly did, and indeed the pupil soon outdistanced the master; Wells's astonishing record culminated in his killing, on his eightieth birthday, his eightieth salmon of over 40 lbs. He was also a philatelist, and his stamp collection contained such rarities that that great collector King George V on one occasion summoned him to Buckingham Palace to show it to him.

John's holiday before the War continued to be spent mostly away from Tapeley. He was often at Cornbury, where he was always happy; at Glyndebourne, though he was fond of his grandfather, he soon became bored. And there were, as has been said, many expeditions with Wells. In the spring of 1910 he told his mother that he was "contemplating a trip to the Cape, or to Uganda, in August and September, but nothing is fixed yet. Possibly the West Indies would be more suitable." But September saw him deer-stalking with Vernon Watney in Scotland, from where he wrote to his mother, "Next holidays I hope to go to the West Indies and I shall certainly go to Bayreuth and to Munich in the summer if the festivities are on." It seems clear that no trip to Africa or to the West Indies was ever made, but John was certainly at Bayreuth for the Festival in 1908, and probably on at least one subsequent occasion in the years before the First World War. No doubt it was his interest in Wagner that prompted him in 1912 to take German lessons, first from a colleague and subsequently from a niece of the brothers Grimm who wrote the fairy tales.

Other stray facts emerge from John's letters to his mother. He mentions that "Wednesdays at the bench at Slough take up a good deal of my spare time". He was often in London to hear lectures at the Royal Institution or to go to the Opera. He saw a flying display and immediately received a letter from his mother begging him never to go up (which he immediately did). He started a collection of etchings by Muirhead Bone and other artists, which he subsequently sold for a small profit. He wrote more than once, and at great length, about the advantages to be gained by installing electricity at Tapeley. He sold his Angelus and had his own piano sent up from Devonshire. And of course he bought a better car—a 1909 "Ariel".

★   ★   ★

A correspondence between John, his father and his grandfather, on the subject of the Saunton estate in North Devon, throws some light on the character of all three men.

The Devonshire property of the Christies consisted of two separate estates—Tapeley, about six miles to the south-west of Barnstaple, and Saunton, on the coast about seven miles to the west of the town. Within the two estates were approximately twenty farms, some good freehold and leasehold properties, and a large number of cottages. Tapeley Park stands on high ground overlooking the estuary of the Taw and Torridge rivers, about a mile from the village of Instow where the Christies also owned the Marine Hotel and the Quay, a Sailing Club, Cricket Ground and Pavilion, and the greater part of the foreshore. The two estates, though lying some distance apart, had always been closely associated.

Augustus had also purchased Lundy Island (from a Mr Heaven, and so known locally as "The Kingdom of Heaven"). The island had once belonged to the Clevlands, but Augustus's main reason for buying it was that he could not bear to see from his house any land that he did not own. It was sold in the twenties.

In November 1911, John's grandfather, William Christie, wrote to John saying that he proposed handing over Saunton to him now, and not, as he had originally intended, when John came to marry. Since the estate would bring in at least £700 a year, he would therefore at the same time discontinue the yearly allowance of £200 he had previously been giving him.

John wrote at once to his father to ask his views on the matter. "I feel that you have a prior claim to his land," he said, "and I therefore write to you to ask exactly what you think on the subject. I should not like to take over Saunton unless you entirely acquiesce in the transfer." Augustus replied:

> I appreciate highly the good and proper feeling you extend to me with regard to my father's proposal to you about the Saunton estate. You ask me my opinion. I have no hesitation in saying that the offer is unprecedented, and that only a fool could make it. It is unfortunate that my father's vitality has long outlived his brain.
>
> The Saunton estate has for a very long number of years been part of this property [Tapeley]. The whole became my father's property *for life* as a solemn trust, and he has no right to dismember it. My father also has no right to ignore me, and make you offers of this kind. You and I alone must deal in these matters ourselves.
>
> In the meantime I will tell you in private that in my opinion my father and the ex-governess are secretly married. . .

John was taken aback: he had assumed that his father would be delighted at the news. "I had not expected any opposition from you," he replied, " and it comes as rather a surprise." " 'Comes as rather a surprise' !" Augustus retorted. "My dear Jack, what are you thinking ! You express surprise because a man does not wish to see his estate broken up before his very eyes by an old fool. My father in his old age does not understand these matters, and I may add never did."

Possibly William Christie was in fact becoming rather muddleheaded; when he informed John that until Saunton was his he would double his annual allowance (of £200) and send him £200 annually, it took five letters from John before he could be made to see his mistake.

The matter dragged on for more than a year. Augustus continued to maintain that this proposal "of an old man in his dotage" was "most mischievous" and not in John's real interests. He told his son: "I am sorry to say your grandfather's mental condition is so bad that the doctors are surprised no steps have been taken to get him declared incapable of managing his business matters. I went over to see him a few days ago, and it was painful to see how weak he has become both mentally and physically. Cases of this kind are always difficult to deal with. . ." Less than ten years later Augustus was to provide John with the same problem in a more acute form.

But John had made up his mind to accept Saunton, though he offered to hand the estate over to his father on his grandfather's death; in April 1913 he wrote to tell Augustus of his decision. Augustus replied, more in sorrow than in anger, that he had done his best to prevent John making a fool of himself; but—"so be it. I accept your decision." He had, of course, no alternative, for William had established that he was entitled to dispose of Saunton as he wished. Three days later, however, Augustus wrote again to John to implore him to change his mind.

The summer passed, and John had not yet received Saunton when, in November, William died, leaving him the estate in his will. On 3rd December Augustus wrote to his son:

> I hear that my father has left you the Saunton estate. If I can help you in the management, dear boy, I shall be very glad. The main thing is that you and I shall pull together, and be at one, and do our best for the estates, and our duty by them. Bring us a good daughter-in-law soon. Your mother and I want to see you happily married, and grandchildren to succeed us.

A year later John sold Saunton to his father for £32,000.

★   ★   ★

In 1912 came, temporarily, a welcome and a marked improvement in John's relations with his mother, and the following year he went so far as to suggest that she needed a holiday and that they should go abroad together. But when the time came he found that Wells wanted him to fish, so she went to Paris without him.

Before long, however, the bickering starts again. He tells his mother that her letters are illiterate (which comes strangely from one who had recently reported to her his pleasure in "a Brahm's symphony".*) When she mentions 1913 as "a memorable year" he hastens to tell her that *he* can see nothing memorable in it whatever. When she reports that Augustus, who has been ill, is "better in himself", he replies that she uses "such curious expressions that it is not always easy for me to understand exactly what you mean. I gather that my father has been quite ill but that he is now getting rapidly better. . ."

By 1914 John has remounted his hobby-horse—his mother's inefficiency in running Tapeley—and is riding it full tilt again. A few lines of a twelve-page letter devoted wholly to this theme will suffice:

> I have read your letter with disappointment. It appears that you intend to do nothing. Your servants are quite incompetent. The cook is not worth training. . . There is a complete absence of "joie de vivre" in your house and I think you will be very wrong if you do not try to alter this. . . I am very glad I did not take a friend down to Tapeley the other day; he would not have enjoyed it. . .

John was always strangely insensitive to the feelings of others. But can he really have believed that he was simply offering his mother helpful advice? He must surely have been aware, however vaguely, that he was deeply wounding her.

★   ★   ★

In December 1912 Lady Rosamond had written her son a letter in which, apparently, she had urged him to consider a future as a country squire. Old William Christie had at this time been still

---

* There are a number of spelling and grammatical mistakes, which I have in general corrected without comment, in John's letters.

alive, but over eighty and rapidly failing; presumably therefore she envisaged her son leaving Eton after his death and living at Glyndebourne. Her letter is missing; but we have John's reply, which offered her no encouragement:

> I am afraid my interests lie in a somewhat different direction from those about which you wrote. Perhaps it is just as well. Your views about the possession and keeping of wealth may be all very well for those who possess it. I do not think I am quite in sympathy with them. My view is rather that so long as there is sufficient for the moment, no further attention need be bestowed on such a matter. In fact, if it requires attention it is rather a nuisance. Fortunately I have interests which can easily absorb my time. I don't really want to become a "country gentleman". I have sufficient to do already. Such a mode of living, though no doubt coveted by many people, does not appear to me to be any more attractive than my present one.
>
> Furthermore, if it were one to which I were looking forward, I should not be here [at Eton] now. I am satisfied with my life here, and there seems nothing more to be said. Wealth in itself does not produce happiness. It is quite unnecessary to have more than is sufficient for present purposes. Of course one's views change, but I do not want to alter mine. They may alter of their own accord. They must take care of themselves. I have accepted the life of the ordinary working man. Anything which comes along and is of assistance is welcome, but I do not think it is necessary or desirable to receive anything further. . .

But just as John believed that by persistence he could eventually get his mother to make Tapeley by his standards habitable, so Lady Rosamond believed that if she persevered she would in the end persuade John to leave Eton. Eighteen months later she was still working on him. He replied:

> I am afraid we approach these matters from different points of view. At present I have had no experience of being wealthy. I have rarely had a balance in the bank and I have had nothing but the plea of poverty at home. This talk of riches then leaves me cold. I don't really take much interest in them. They do

not seem to affect the near future. Anyhow I do not wish to make myself a slave to them. I want to make use of them, rather than they of me. At present I cannot entertain the idea of giving up my work here. . .

When writing the letter to which John had thus replied, Lady Rosamond had been in possession of fresh ammunition; for by this time William Christie had died, leaving Glyndebourne to John's father. Augustus, satisfied to remain at Tapeley, handed Glyndebourne over to John, though it was not until seven years later, in 1920, that it became his *de jure*.

Glyndebourne was at that time a Victorian house concealing, except from the back, all traces of a much earlier building which it embodied. The interior was both ugly and uncomfortable. For those who know it only in its present state it must suffice to say that the south and west fronts were presently to be completely remodelled and that at the east end, where now stands the Organ Room and the Opera House with its dependencies, there was nothing but an Eton Fives Court.

Mr Spike Hughes has traced in detail the history of Glyndebourne. The original house probably dated from the first half of the fifteenth century, but it was virtually rebuilt in Elizabethan times. It seems likely that Glyndebourne was given by the Morleys, of the nearby Manor of Glynde, to Mary Morley on her marriage in 1589 to John Hay of Herstmonceux; certainly their son Herbert came to live there in 1616 and his descendants continued at Glyndebourne for many generations. In 1803, there being no direct heir on the death of Frances Hay, the estate passed to her cousin, Francis Tutté. When Tutté died unmarried in 1824, Glyndebourne came to another cousin, James Langham. In 1833 Langham succeeded, as 11th baronet, to the Langham baronetcy and the Northamptonshire estates, and Glyndebourne, as we have already told, passed under the wills of Frances Hay and her sister to Langham Christie, son of Daniel Christie and Elizabeth Langham.

John at once made Glyndebourne his holiday home, and even during term-time he often managed to get over there at week-ends. He was soon busy with schemes for reconstructing the house. It was, perhaps, fortunate for Glyndebourne that before he could take any action the War put a stop to all building operations; for when they again became possible his plans for the house had had time to mature.

PART II

6

Active Service

IN JUNE 1914 Augustus had a serious attack of pneumonia and for a time his life hung in the balance. He just pulled through; but he had been thoroughly frightened, and on his doctor's advice never again touched alcohol, in which he had previously indulged rather freely.

While he was recuperating, war broke out and he learned that John was about to join up. His own narrow escape from death, and the possibility that his son might not survive him, turned his thoughts to the future of his estates. By the will he had made in 1901, his wife was to have them for her lifetime if John predeceased her without issue; but Augustus felt very strongly that in such circumstances the Devon estates should ultimately pass to a Clevland. He had taken a great fancy to his nephew, Edward Le Marchant, the son of his youngest sister, Mary; Edward had been much at Tapeley, where he had always received a far warmer welcome than had John, being invited to shoot and receiving expensive presents from his uncle. After some discussion it was agreed that Edward should eventually succeed to the Devon estates if John died without issue.

Lady Rosamond did not much care for Edward, and still less for his background: "I thought his mother's set a very common and vulgar one", she wrote later to a friend. She considered that it would be wise for the young man to spend as much time as possible at Cornbury, where he would have the privilege of "mixing with more refined and desirable people". But Edward was never to inherit Tapeley and Saunton: he too enlisted; and it was he, and not John, who was to be killed.

*   *   *

When war was declared, John's first thought was how to get into the Army as quickly as possible. He still limped as the result of his riding accident; he had a damaged knee; he had lost most of the sight of one eye; and he was nearly thirty-two. But nothing deterred him. It was, however, surprising that he did not apply to join the Royal Artillery, in which he would at least have been mounted, but the 60th Rifles (the King's Royal Rifle Corps).

His knee trouble, and his limp which he had long since learned to live with, he managed to conceal from the medical officer. As for the eyesight test—that he survived by what he termed (and it was still a favourite word of his) a "dodge"; a dodge that was worthy of Nelson. His good eye was examined first. Told to transfer the pad to the other eye, he contrived, without being detected, to replace it on the same one. So they passed him as fit, and early in September he joined the 9th Battalion of the 60th at Farnborough, from where he was soon transferred to Aldershot.

Those who knew John, both before and after the War, found it hard to picture him as a soldier; yet it is clear that he soon became a keen and efficient, though always an unconventional, officer. On 9th October he wrote to his mother from Aldershot:

> There are about 50 officers and there will be over 60 in these barracks. There are only two baths and a small stove which just heats the water for one small bath. This to my mind is typical of military matters. . . . At first I was fearfully bored with this work, but it is getting better. We are supposed to be getting on, and we have now got about two thirds of our rifles but no machine guns. I am a First Lieutenant and second-in-command of a company of 267 men, but I hope soon to become a Captain. . . .
>
> My private laboratory assistant* is being taken on at South Kensington with small wages. I am proposing to put him up at

* At Eton—the invaluable Bertie Wolf (see p. 44). It is difficult to imagine anyone else in those days accommodating a laboratory assistant in a house in Belgravia.

Eaton Square and let him get his food there if you agree, and in addition I shall give him some financial assistance if necessary....

In November the Battalion was moved to Petworth, where they were Lord Leconfield's guests at Petworth House:

> We are most comfortable here [he told his mother]—500 men in the house and stables and 20 officers and their servants as well as the wives of two of them. It's like a first-rate shooting party. We dine off silver plates and all the waiters have white gloves. . . .

He adds an interesting piece of information about his present financial position and his prospects. "The disentailing deed has arrived, and as far as I can see everything becomes mine absolutely if I survive my father. In the meantime the £60,000 comes to me, and that at once."

His mother's letters to him have not survived; but it is clear that he disliked the tone of them and found her affection cloying, for he wrote: "I think it would be well if you were to eliminate the sentimental strain from your letters." Poor Lady Rosamond! She would have been less than human if she had not felt, and superhuman had she not shown, any emotion under the circumstances; but the least sign of it in her letters, any hint of heroism, was to invite a snub. John could not bear sentiment or emotion of any kind.

Over the New Year he had a week's leave and then returned to Petworth. His ankle had recently been giving him trouble; but now he found himself promoted to the rank of Captain, in command of a company and so entitled to a charger, which was a great help. He was, however, far from satisfied with the standard of training reached. "The N.C.O.s", he told his mother, "are very incompetent and hardly any of them know anything. We are short of officers, and those we have know nothing. None of them can pass a message. It will be much worse under fire. I am providing all my men with notebooks and pencils and hope to improve this. . . ."

Towards the end of January (1915) came what was afterwards always referred to in the Battalion as "the retreat from Moscow".

On the 21st of that month, after an early dinner, the Battalion paraded and marched to Witley camp, a distance of about sixteen miles. What followed is described in the *Chronicle* of the King's Royal Rifle Corps:*

> Witley was only in course of construction then, and we spent the night (a frightfully cold one) in huts, without doors or windows. The next morning we woke to find the ground white with snow, which was still falling. An early parade and a five-mile march brought us to Hawkley, where the whole of the 14th Division was drawn up in mass for an inspection by Lord Kitchener and the French War Minister, M. Millerand. Owing to the state of the roads, the War Ministers were late, and the Division was kept waiting for five hours in a blinding snowstorm. The inspection over, we marched five miles back to Witley. As the accommodation was so bad, and the men wet through and perished with cold, the C.O. decided, after the men had had their dinners, to march straight back to Petworth. We moved out of Witley at 4 p.m. (the Battalion having already marched ten miles that day), and began a march which none who took part in it will ever forget. The snow lay two feet thick on the roads, horses and men slipping and falling every other step, and a pitch dark night with snow falling, and sixteen miles to go. . . . The Battalion did it. Not one man was left behind, and Petworth was reached just before midnight.

In March the Battalion returned to Aldershot to undergo final training before leaving for France, and on 20th May John wrote to his father to say that they were leaving at last: "We are just off; our luggage went yesterday morning. We cross tonight. My cob is at Camberley. Possibly C. H. Blakiston, a master at Eton, will use it; otherwise can you send for it? . . . Childs is arranging my clothes at Eton. . . . He is, I think, going out to France with Boy Scouts." And to his mother: "I have made a will leaving everything to you absolutely, with the exception of various legacies."

*   *   *

Next day the Battalion, with Captain Christie in command of

* (1916), p. 154.

"A" Company, landed in France and after a crowded journey in cattle trucks, followed by a hot and exhausting route march during which sixty men had to fall out, reached Zeggers Kappell—a point well behind the lines in the Ypres salient. All John's active service was to be passed in this sector of the front.

An uneventful week was spent in billets at Zeggers Kappell. John told his mother that he had Charles, the Cornbury footman, as his batman and that he was proving a great success. To his aunt he wrote: "I hope I don't get any gas. I don't much mind the idea of bullets; they are so small. . . . Very hot weather. We feed out on planks and boxes in a hay field. Fortnum & Mason's and Tiptree are a great help."

From Zeggers Kappell the Battalion marched to Terdeghem, and three days later to Dickebusch, four miles south-west of Ypres. Next day they marched three miles nearer to Ypres, to a point on the Yser Canal, and soon after were moved up to the front line. The author of the K.R.R.C. *Chronicle* describes it vividly:*

We had heard a lot about the trenches; was the life anything like what we had pictured? For myself I can honestly answer "No!" and I believe it is absolutely impossible to imagine, and nearly as difficult to describe. . . . I have heard it described as blood, mud, noise and stench, and that cryptic phrase certainly sums it up, but hardly describes it. . . . If you multiply all the greatest discomforts you can imagine a hundredfold, all the vile smells and noises you can think of a thousandfold, you will then only begin to realise what it is all like. Death is there, too, everywhere, always. . . .

I don't pose as being a brave man, but I can honestly assert that the feeling uppermost in my mind . . . as we doubled over the ridge, was solely one of interest. . . . Then came a feeling of pity. The first trench we struck was full of the wounded who had been hit in the early morning attack, stretcher cases which could not be moved until dark: the dug-outs and trenches were packed with them. . . . One poor fellow, quite young, with half his face blown away, asked me for a cigarette. . . . Of course he could not hold it in his mouth; he had no mouth left to hold it

* *Op. cit.*, pp. 158–9.

in. Another man with a bayonet thrust through his thigh, was calmly pouring filthy water from a stagnant pool over his wound with an empty bully beef tin. Without a murmur they waited patiently for the night. . . . But alas! when I passed that dug-out nine hours later, I found it blown to pieces. . . .

So June passed: in trench-digging, in digging dug-outs, in more trench-digging—interrupted, for John, by an attack of food poisoning from which he was sent to recover in a nearby monastery. Sometimes there were bombardments lasting several hours, but casualties were surprisingly few. Periods of intense activity alternated with long stretches of boredom, and it was now that John began the curious practice of reading Spenser's *Faerie Queene* to his men. One may wonder what his audience—or indeed the reader himself—made of that far from simple poem, and how John coped with the questions that he invited at the end of each reading. There is also mention of Plato's *Dialogues* and of *Alice through the Looking-Glass*; but it would appear that Spenser best suited his mood. At no other time in his life did he show much interest in poetry, except perhaps for Housman's *Shropshire Lad* and *Last Poems*.

On 29th June John sent his mother a long letter. After mentioning that he had been suffering from food-poisoning, he continued:

My impression is that the Germans are losing far fewer men than we are. Their machine-guns take the place of men. They have every advantage: if we fire five shells, they fire fifteen back. Their trenches are, I suppose, greatly superior to ours. Better system, the outcome of all their military work in the past, and the great advantage that they could prepare their trenches in advance. Unlimited ammunition and guns, and good staff work. Every trench I have been in has necessitated wading in places up to the knees after dry weather; in wet it is of course higher, and the whole is a quagmire in which one goes slipping about. The Battalion we relieved the other day had been in the trenches for twenty-six days on end and were very glad to get out. In this period they had lost three-quarters of their strength.

Well it's very dull here and no one likes it. So it will go on until we get ammunition and guns.

Then he describes the conditions of Ypres itself, a mass of rubble with not a single house intact, even in the outskirts. Two days later he wrote to his mother from a relatively comfortable billet in a farmhouse, where he was sharing the loft with two brother officers:

> Most of my men were out last night with other companies digging within a hundred yards of the firing line. Very bad place. Many bodies ten days old. Impossible to bury them. Poor place to dig owing to those which had been buried. Like the Crimea. Had a bad account of it from my subalterns. Very few casualties. None in my Company last night. I was not out.

In the middle of July he received a slight wound—so slight that he "couldn't get up any enthusiasm" about it. He remained on duty. On 24th July he wrote to his mother:

> Thank you for your letter. It was less gloomy than some of the others. The trouble is that you don't take my father in the right light. If you had any humour you would manage him without much difficulty. What does it matter if a lot of things do turn up for which there is no sensible use? If you took them as a joke and didn't care how many arrive, wouldn't it be much better? . . .

This was very sound advice—but advice that Lady Rosamond was never to succeed in acting upon. Augustus was of course difficult; but had he been rightly handled, how many outbursts of temper might have been avoided! It was her complete failure to understand either her husband or her son, that added unnecessarily and enormously to the unhappiness of her life.

A fortnight later John described to his uncle a sharp engagement in which he had taken part:

> Next morning we left our dug-outs and advanced under a pretty hot shell fire. Very fair trench and perhaps three-quarters of a mile of it. Several very bad places, one where we had to cross the road. Never thought I should be hit, though they were bursting very close, a few yards. Wounded about. Had to push on, then we crossed another devilish hot corner, did this at the

double. . . . Then we had three-quarters to one hour of bombardment, with fairly heavy stuff, eight inch and six inch. Trench badly damaged, and men killed and wounded quite close. . . .

At a certain time had to move up to occupy and fire on other trenches. Poor fun waiting for the moment. Then had to run about setting [*sic*] various lots going up. Men will get in the way. They always lose the connection, and you never saw men so stupid. They don't think at all. . . . Then went up with the rear half. . . . Shell burst quite close, got me behind the right ear, and in front of the right shoulder, seems as if the bits didn't go straight. It blew a sergeant over while we were talking together. Rather pleased at being hit; it didn't hurt. . . .

We moved on again into another trench. Then the first half of the Company advanced again and took possession of a trench which had previously been taken by another Company. This had charged from its parapets and been wiped out. Sent up two men to find out whether there was room for the remainder. No answer after a long wait. Had to go up myself. Bad ground to cover. Dead and wounded about. Bound up a dying sergeant-major and sent for the rest of my men. Brought them into the trench. My second-in-command here dashed out, as I got up to bring in a wounded man. We had already brought in one wounded officer. He was shot by an expanding bullet in the right breast and lung. Bound him up and began to arrange the trench. . . .

Just before dawn a spectacle quite indescribable. Coloured rockets, and the German trench immediately in front of our trench, and on the horizon a glowing red line of flame. Thought they were going to try liquid fire. Immediately all their guns and rifles went off, and as far as I could tell ours followed suit. There appeared to be no interval—a wonderful spectacle. . . . Noise quite continuous. Most of the shells were going over our heads. . . . We had our heads over the trenches most of the time. . . .

The Germans came out on our right and left, but had to go back. Don't know how long it lasted. Then I heard that Dick, our Colonel, and Faber (an Eton boy) had been killed, and others. Felt very sad. Stayed on for two days more and were relieved on the third night. Had had no sleep. . . . The condition

of the wounded was appalling. Got in some after lying out in
the sun for two days. Wounds undressed, could not get them
down to the ambulance stations. No stretchers. . . . It was light
before I could get my last wounded away. . . . I had promised
them that I would not leave before they did. This much the
most horrible part. Just think of these wretched fellows, badly
wounded, lying in the bottom of the trench, one of them hit
twice again, for three days and nights, officers and men continually climbing over them. I did not know what to do. . . .
Thought it would be better to leave them till the stretcher-
bearers arrived at dusk. The stretcher-bearers did not come. . . .

Half the Company hit. My face black with smoke. Only had
bread and jam to eat, and this only at nights as the flies were so
awful. My Chartreuse however saw me through. Such is life out
here, or such it may be. It is not often as bad as this; one gets
used to it, and really I did not mind the prospect of not being
relieved on the last night. They had failed to do so the night
before, owing to an attack. Hope now to have a rest. . . .

Yet to his mother, the following day, he could write: "In spite
of all, the thing that satisfies me almost more than anything else is
German music." On 1st September he wrote again:

I am not sure yet when I am coming on leave. Possibly on the
18th or 23rd. I shall stay in London the first night and get a good
dinner and go to a play. I shall also probably spend a couple of
days at Eton. . . . Your letter makes me nervous lest I may find
the cooking and general household management as beastly as
usual. You speak of more economy.* There must be no sign of
it when I come home. . . . I have had months of wretched food
and drink and, quite frankly, I expect it to be good when I come
back. I think you had better engage a good chef from the Café
Royal for the few days. . . .

We went into the trenches about a fortnight ago. . . .

And he describes again in detail his daily life in the trenches.

In complete contrast are his letters to Cornbury, where his uncle
and aunt, and his cousin Rosalind, are constantly sending him the

---

* Lady Rosamond had for years past been deflecting a large part of the housekeeping money to the reconstruction of Tapeley (see p. 86). The War provided
her with a splendid excuse for further economies in food and drink.

luxuries that he so much appreciates: "So delighted", he wrote, "to think that there's somebody who's not always economising..."

John did not, however, get his leave. On 21st September he became second-in-command of his Battalion—"but I stick to my Company". Two days later the Battalion was inspected by Lord Kitchener, and the same day the Battle of Loos began. Their role was to capture Bellewarde Farm. This they succeeded in doing, but were subsequently thrown out by a strong German counter-attack. John describes the action in a letter to his mother:

> We came out of action and returned here yesterday [26th September]. My Company lost about sixty-five men. No officers touched. One officer I had lent to our sister Battalion in our brigade was killed. They had four officers left; all the others killed.
>
> We had a hard time. Horrors much worse than before, but I don't mind them. . . . We were shelled from 3.50 a.m. till 6 p.m. Trenches flattened. A whole network of trenches without a sound bit amongst them except the one we were in. . . . We hardly fired a shell in reply. Suppose we hadn't any. Our gunners say we had forty-eight batteries on us. Shelled again all the way home as far as Ypres. I went a different way, a bit longer, and never had one [shell]. They passed overhead and burst all along the road most of the men were using. Very lucky to get out.
>
> The Brigade didn't take its trenches. Took many and had to give them up again. Very few came back. Enemy in large numbers. Apparently we fulfilled our object in drawing and holding large German forces and guns. . . .

A young Etonian in John's regiment—Lt G. Holloway—described, in a letter to a cousin, the attack on Bellewarde Farm and John's bravery on that occasion:

> I had meant to write to you before to thank you for your letter and also to tell you how splendid Christie was in the battle of the 25th. To begin with I must say that the horrors on that day were something which defy all description—quite unimaginable, luckily.
>
> Christie took the Company, which was reinforced, up to the

front German line, where there was a large crater caused by the explosion of our mine. Shelling was thick and continuous—and after a few hours, shell fire is pretty demoralising and seems to paralyse every initiative. Christie was absolutely calm, leading out a reconnaissance in one direction and ordering entrenching in another and sitting down to write reports. At one time he stood on the edge of the crater to see what calibre the shells were. . . . In the afternoon, when we were sitting in the battered trenches under the same relentless shell fire—one man was blown to bits five yards from us—he produced from his pocket the *Faery Queen* and read it aloud to cheer us up.

The shell fire must indeed have been demoralising: it came from British guns.

After this engagement John was recommended for the D.S.O. He saw his name on the list and himself struck it off; but in spite of this in due course he received the M.C. A. E. Conybeare, an Eton colleague who later became Vice-Provost, clearly knew his man when he wrote to John, "I suppose you will be fearfully fed at getting the Military Cross, but you must let me congratulate you all the same." Lady Rosamond was of course obliged to conceal the full extent of her pride and joy when writing to her son; but she could at least tell her friends, one of whom replied, "How proud you must be! What courage! What modesty! The beauty of it all brings tears to one's eyes. . . ."

For the rest of the year the Battalion was constantly on the move. Sometimes the billets were relatively comfortable and the food reasonably good; at other times John lived in filthy, flooded dug-outs, with food that was "simply disgusting". It grew bitterly cold too. Often they endured heavy shell-fire; but sometimes he was, he said, grateful when firing relieved the monotony.

At the end of October he was at last given a week's leave in England. He spent two days of it at Eton, where, as well as playing his usual ferocious football, he gave a talk to some of the senior boys on life in the trenches. It proved to be a detailed account of how to make oneself as comfortable as possible there and behind the lines, what food to have sent from home, and so on; he stressed the importance of not overlooking the breadcrumbs if game was despatched. He did not mention the fighting. At Victoria Station his last words to those who had come to see him off were, "Be sure to tell Fortnum and Mason's to send the breadcrumbs!"

Back in Flanders he wrote to his mother:

> It has been very cold. The ice on the water in parts of the trenches has been strong enough to bear. My boots—the spare pair I take up—were frozen in my dug-out one morning and had to be thawed before I could get them on. However the trenches have been comparatively dry. When we came in, the water in the communicating trenches was up to our thighs. Since then, though, we have had fairly dry weather. I prefer the cold to the wet. This life is very dull. . . .
>
> About 6 p.m. now. Shelling all over. Has been quite strenuous. One or two in the water near us. Dining shortly. Fried pheasant, bread and honey.

But now, though he little knew it, John's active service was drawing to its close. As far back as July at least, Lady Rosamond had been intriguing secretly at high level, and on 13th July, at her instigation, her old friend Sir Henry Roscoe had written to Lord Fisher in the latter's capacity as President of the Board of Inventions at the Admiralty. John Christie, said Sir Henry, was

> a man of definitely original type, with a keen interest and also ability in scientific discovery. . . . He is at present a Captain in Kitchener's Army in the trenches. His mother, Lady Rosamond Christie, explains that he is blind in one eye, lame in one foot and has a damaged knee, and it seems extraordinary that he has been able to pass the medical examiner. He is an only son and heir to a large property, and on that account felt it incumbent upon him to go into active service as an example to the men on his future properties, though in fact he is altogether physically unfit for his present post.
>
> He is just the man to be of service to your Committee, as he is a level-headed man with plenty of common sense as well as scientific knowledge. May I ask you to use your influence to place this man in a position in which he would probably be of greater service to his country than he is at present?

What action Lord Fisher took is not known. It seems certain that he, or someone else in high places, did act, but it took many months before there were any tangible results. To Lady Rosamond, waiting anxiously and guiltily, terrified that her son would learn of her part in the plot, this must have been a worrying time.

Meanwhile, however, little though she guessed it, John too had growing doubts as to whether he was really fit enough for active service. There was a rumour that his Battalion was to be sent to Serbia, and he doubted whether his knee would stand up to the marching there:

> I am a rather ridiculous soldier [he told his uncle]. I fall into every hole on the trench boards, and go lurching along. I think anyone who takes these matters light-heartedly—the only way —must be rather amused. So far my knee has not gone out once. On my way out from the trenches the other night I walked into a mound of earth and fell with a mild oath flat on my face. . . . There were a number of men standing by at the time and no one laughed. Dull fellows. . . .
>
> I don't know which is the better plan: to get passed unfit for Serbia—I suppose we shall have a medical—before going, or to break down after getting there. I am not anxious to get sent to some other battalion out here, and wonder whether that might be the result of the former course. . . .

But the decision was one that John did not have to make. A month later he was recalled to England to attend the first of several medical boards. This time his "dodges", if he attempted any, were unavailing, and he was finally invalided out of the Army.

7

Glyndebourne Manor

DURING THE spring and summer of 1916 John remained in England on Medical Board leave. He did some temporary work at Eton during the Lent Half, and a part-time job there in the summer; in the autumn he returned as a full-time master—"rather against my wish as it hangs up my book so much". He is here doubtless referring to his textbook on Physics, which was never to be completed.

He was much at Glyndebourne at week-ends and during the holidays. Mr Gow recalls visits there "when on a warm evening one could sit on the terrace talking of what might presently be done to the house and listening, when the wind was in the right direction, to the guns in Flanders". Mr Gow also remembers various expeditions that he made with John, some of which were associated with a small green two-seater Napier that John then owned:

> I remember in particular one during the War when John, lately returned from active service, decided to go and investigate a strike on the Clyde. We set out from London one Sunday morning with Childs in the dickey guarding a small barrel of oysters and a large jar of caviare, pausing in Bond Street for John to surprise a group of pedestrians by asking whether anyone knew the way to Edinburgh. After various incidents, including an altercation in a hotel in Edinburgh which wished to charge corkage on the caviare, John interviewed the labour leaders in Glasgow* seemingly without much profit and we made our way back to Cornbury.

* Exhorting them to end the strike.

Another more venturesome expedition was in 1919 when, the doors of the car having been removed to make more room and the party reinforced by Tim [now Lord] Nugent and Childs (armed with boxes of chocolates from Charbonnels), we set out to view the battlefields. Among many episodes I recall Amiens where John, who had lately taken up badminton, astonished a shopkeeper in whose window he had noticed some shuttlecocks by ordering a gross, and our arrival late at night in the ruins of Arras where we should have had no hope of finding beds if John had not recognised in the street an Old Etonian officer who put us up in his prisoner of war camp. There we spent three not very comfortable nights while our springs, which were suffering both from overloading and shellholes in the roads, were reinforced by German prisoners. Our ultimate return to Glyndebourne at 3 a.m. was unheralded and we might again have had difficulty in finding supper and beds if Childs, a man of much resource, had not effected a burglarious entry and produced a meal of oxtail soup and honeycomb.

Several hundred letters from John, almost all addressed to his mother, survive from the years 1916 to 1922, during which time he continued as a master at Eton. Four themes predominate: his plans for the reconstruction of Glyndebourne and the reorganisation of its estates; the problem of his father and his increasing mental instability; his constant concern over the family's properties and finances; and his endless bickerings with his mother.

Anyone who reads this long correspondence might not unreasonably come to the conclusion that John was perpetually brooding over his mother and her alleged shortcomings. In fact, said Mr Gow, "when John received from her a letter which annoyed him, he wrote an offensive answer at once, tore up the letter and thought no more about it until he got another".

George Christie says:

My father was obviously on the one hand driven mad by my grandmother's affection for him, her sentimentality and her efforts to coddle him: he was a desperately independent person who hated the cloying relationship she wanted with him. He was on the other hand maddened by her lack of humour and wit, and there seems to have existed all the way through their relationship a considerable lack of understanding of one another's character.

In a letter which John wrote to his mother on 4th January 1916 he puts his case clearly and sensibly, not denying his share of the blame:

My dear Mother,

I know that I am much to blame, but it is difficult for us to get on if there is no mutual influence. I feel that I cannot influence you at all, that you do what you think is wise and right but ignore what I suggest. Take the case of your late cook. I said at the start that she was grossly incompetent, but against my advice given repeatedly you insisted on training her. In the end, who was right? My father I know is very difficult at home and at times does not behave as a gentleman; but then he is really not quite right in the head. You, on the other hand, seize innumerable opportunities of irritating him—trivial little things which annoy him and which really make no difference to you, yet you *will* do them or say them. I know what upsets him and I urge you to say or act otherwise, but entirely without effect.

Can two people get on if neither has any influence over the other? You don't seem to understand what has for long been my impression of my home. My father is very difficult, which no doubt makes the domestic régime abnormal. But it is exaggerated by bad cooking, bad servants, and great economies. . . . I think you have always striven after economy rather than efficiency. The same is the case when I have been with you away from home. Latterly certainly there has been no need for it . . .

I write in a friendly spirit. I lose as much as you do by our strained relations, and I think I am as anxious as you are that we should get on well, but I doubt whether it is possible if you never listen to what I say or advise. Don't you think you can do so? I am not a child, nor am I unreasonable . . .

I am anxious to try to get on well with you. Let us try . . .
Your affectionate son
John Christie

But in general he pounces upon anything in her letters which he can attack. If she tells him about her domestic troubles, he hastens to inform her that they are all the result of her stupidity and inefficiency. If she offers, at his request, advice about gardening (where she is very knowledgeable), he answers that she is ignorant of Sussex soil and climate. If she discusses estate management he replies that all women are fools in such matters. When she suggests that he is self-indulgent and luxury-loving he is (not unnaturally) indignant; but when she reproves him for having massage he becomes "really angry" and writes pages about Greek athletes and the care they took of their bodies. His letters were, he believed, "blunt but not hostile"; they do not read like this today.

Yet she kept them all.

*   *   *

Though extensive alterations to Glyndebourne could not be undertaken until after the War, John was soon beginning to consider what could now, and what might eventually, be done to modernise the house. In August 1916 he told his mother, "This house should be put in order as soon as possible. We don't live for ever"; and in December he wrote more fully on the subject. At this time Glyndebourne was not yet legally his property; no doubt he therefore felt obliged to submit his plans to his parents. His mother obviously raised objections, for he tells her:

> I should like to see Glyndebourne put into order within the next two or three years. It should be a capital expenditure. At present it is quite impossible. It is quite unpleasing. I don't agree with you about modern pictures.
>
> I am expecting a railway waggon of furniture any day, things I have bought at Eton. But it won't go far. I should like to get rid of most of what's in the house and now is a very good moment to do it. All the drawing-room furniture and much of the bedroom stuff. Also all the modern pictures my grandfather bought ... Furniture will fetch a better price now than later. I should do it at once. Will you let me know? ...

For a time, only minor improvements and relatively small purchases were made; but by 1919 John had embarked in earnest on his scheme for the modernisation of Glyndebourne, for which he employed as architect Edmond ("Bear") Warre, a son of Dr Warre of Eton. This included the building of an organ room for a fine organ by William Hill & Son and Norman & Beard. John's old friend Dr Lloyd, formerly Precentor at Eton and at this time Organist of the Chapel Royal, was about to retire, and John had expressed the hope that he might come with his sister to live in Ringmer. Lloyd stipulated that John should build an organ for him at Glyndebourne. This he therefore did, and Lloyd's advice was of the greatest assistance to him over its design; it was therefore a tragedy that Lloyd's death was to occur, in the autumn of 1919, before the organ had been completed. John felt his loss very deeply; to his mother, who had sent her sympathy, he replied:

> Thank you very much for your letter about Lloyd. He was a dear old man and everyone was fond of him. All the tradesmen, cabmen and others turned up at his funeral [at Eton] as they all felt indebted to him for his organ recitals. He was old in years but young in spirit. Only two years ago at Glyndebourne he rode my hunter though he hadn't ridden for twenty-five years and never rode much. When we were sawing wood he carried as many logs and as large as any. He is a great loss at Glyndebourne. The organ was designed by him and he took the most immense trouble about it all. The Glyndebourne variations were finished and were to be played on the day he died. His powers of accompaniment on the organ were quite unique . . .

In three letters to his mother, written in February, April and November 1919, John describes his general policy with regard to Glyndebourne and defends himself against her repeated charges of extravagance. He had decided, he told her, to take down the additions that had been made to the house around 1800 and to replace them by a rather larger building to contain kitchen premises and various bedrooms and bathrooms. The fives court, which was as ugly as it was useless, would go. He was installing electric light. He was improving the drives and hoped in due course to make a hard tennis court. The flower garden was being extended, and "I may perhaps make more kitchen garden in order to feed my boys' house which I get shortly".

But what excited him most, and what also most exposed him to his mother's charge of extravagance, was the construction of the organ and the large room to contain it. He explained to her that the organ would prove invaluable "for musical education and for raising money for various purposes by recitals . . . I feel it will be a source of great intellectual pleasure to me for the rest of my life, and to many others. It will not be expensive to keep up, like the deer forest. I am now a comparatively young man and I cannot see the point of waiting until I am an old man before I set out on these undertakings, or of having the house upside-down for several years in order to do it gradually." No doubt he was remembering Tapeley, and the confusion that had resulted from renovation carried out over a number of years.* He continued:

> Therefore I make the plunge now, believing that, though things now cost twice what they did, they will not come down appreciably for some years. Besides, when the sales of land † are completed we shall have sold about a quarter of a million pounds worth and lost only land which was no use to us and which produced very little income. Then there is the point of view that my Father, or rather that we for him, can entertain the prospect of a much limited activity, and that in consequence his expenses are not likely to be very heavy. I think that on reflection you may be thankful that I am not wasting money on expensive pleasures of the moment.
>
> I have spent and am spending a good many thousands on Glyndebourne. What I have spent so far could be got back with interest if I were to have a sale; what I am now spending might do so, though it would not be in such a ready form. At any rate I do not wish to take on a heavy annual expenditure. I would point out that I have not charged the estate or my own pocket with the expenses of even one keeper. At present I have one old horse and have not looked for a second. A second-hand car at Eton, another here and no chauffeur—or at least my mechanic has much else to do and I may not have him at Eton. I think you take too narrow a view of these matters . . .

* See p. 86.
† Chiefly of land in Lincolnshire, but of some in Sussex also.

My expenditure at Glyndebourne is roughly as follows:

Furnishing	£15,000
Alterations to offices, etc.	£4,000
Shell and floor of organ room	£6,000
Ceiling	£1,000
Panelling and organ case	£3,000
Organ	£6,000
Electric light	£2,000
Sundries	£1,000
	£38,000

To some extent I admit that I am anticipating my prospects after my Father's death, but this is only in the distribution of capital. Apart from the expenditure of capital in a way which, unless Glyndebourne is let, will produce no income, I do not live at an extravagant rate. This must be obvious. I have plenty to show for my expenditure, which is the chief thing. There is, I suppose, some advantage in being able to see during your lifetime what your successor will do. This my Father can now see.

It is in connection with his various activities at Glyndebourne that John's letters first make evident his great interest in detail. Even after the house and estate had become his *de jure*, he continued to supply his mother with the most minute particulars of the improvements he was making. Brick by brick, nail by nail, she was enabled to follow their progress. If a coat of paint was applied to the banisters of the servants' staircase, she was promptly informed of its colour and its cost. She was told the price of every picture, every rug, every *objet d'art* that he purchased, every bottle of wine that he laid down, and was assured that each successive purchase was a sensational bargain. The Victorian "junk" that he sold invariably fetched far more than anyone had dared to hope, yet only of course a fraction of what it would fetch today. In the choice of books for a small lending library designed to promote good literature among the villagers of Ringmer and Glynde, he was much helped by Mr Gow.

This same passion for detail, and for passing detail on to Tapeley, was evident in all John's letters about other activities at Glyndebourne. These activities included various sales and purchases of land, farming matters and finance generally. There were also at this time several commercial enterprises which foreshadowed yet greater ventures to come: the Glyndebourne Motor Works, the Ringmer Building Works, a home-grown timber business in Plashett Woods and, at a later date, the Ringmer forge. Of the first-named John wrote to his mother on 5th March 1919: "I am becoming a motor trader and shall have a garage at Ringmer whence I shall let out lorry and tractor and perhaps sell machines of this type and cars." The Glyndebourne Motor Works, which were probably started to fetch and carry materials in connection with the reconstruction of Glyndebourne, subsequently came to include an electric department and traded—indeed still trades—under the name of Ringmer Motor Works.

The Ringmer Building Works (R.B.W.) had their origins in the old Estate Yard, but were developed when the house was being rebuilt; from these humble beginnings they grew until they became one of the biggest building concerns in the south-east of England. Many of John's letters, of this time and later, deal with the contracts he has obtained, or is hoping to obtain.

Of course there were difficulties at first. In May 1923 John gave his mother his reasons for starting businesses and put on record his conviction that his initial losses would soon be wiped out. He was the eternal optimist, but where the R.B.W. was concerned his optimism was to be justified:

> Our family fortunes contain no business and offer no business training. I think this should occupy part of my time and therefore I have endeavoured to create business and to enter a business. I started at the wrong moment and was let down by the Government.* But had my Father or my Grandfather started the same things, as I think they should have, we should have done very well in them. I started as soon as I could. Under the circumstances I do not think I have done badly. In the future I think I shall recover what I have lost and also earn a larger income than I should by investing in Trustee stocks ... And I certainly think I have done good to this neighbourhood by

---

* By the cancellation of the subsidy for corn.

developing as far as I can the opportunities which have offered themselves.

I might take up politics presently, but I think some business training is an essential preliminary and also that developing one's resources is probably of more use to the world. My Father and Grandfather have offered no opportunities of meeting other men who are doing something in the world, and I have to create these opportunities in the first place by doing something myself.

On 6th May 1920 John informed his father:

I have made good progress in reorganising the estate. The old Powells are more or less handing over the management of the Glyndebourne estates to a nephew, Humphry Powell, aged about twenty-seven—a big, active man with a good head on his shoulders ... I have got Craig as head of the farming, with Veness local foreman. This is the most important branch. My accountant [Edwards] is excellent, in fact exceptional.

Under Craig were twenty-five men. There were also a mechanic and four men; a builder in charge of the estate yard, with ten men; five gardeners; three keepers, and an agricultural machinery expert. A man named Smith ran the brickyard with half a dozen or more men under him. John was at this time farming nine hundred acres; but he expected that figure to be doubled within a year, and later it was to be further considerably increased.

John's method of appointing a man to work at Glyndebourne was unconventional. He reacted very strongly to people. The applicant might be interviewed quite briefly and then appointed on the spot if John happened to take a liking to him. On occasions this had unfortunate results; but his judgment was good and some of his most loyal men came to Glyndebourne in this way.

There was, for example, Harvey, who applied for the post of head gardener in 1924. The interview lasted only half a minute:

"I do not want a Victorian gardener. Can you grow grapes?"
"Yes, Sir."
"Can you grow peas and celery?"
"Yes, Sir."
"Very well. You are engaged."

Harvey proved to be a genius, and the gardens which today

give so much pleasure to visitors were largely his creation, though he obtained advice on their design; for many years the Glyndebourne Opera programmes regularly carried a tribute to him. John, having decided to trust a man, always gave him a free hand, and Harvey made the best use of the confidence placed in him. He had strong views and was prepared to fight for them. Perhaps his greatest hour of triumph was the occasion when he succeeded in preventing Warre from erecting a summerhouse where it would have interrupted a view of the downs which Harvey had just laboriously opened up.

Other admirable men came in due course to work at Glyndebourne. After an inauspicious start, a man named Sharp was appointed to take over as Managing Director of the Ringmer Building Works. He had been employed at the Works in a more humble capacity for some years, but John saw his potentialities and promoted him. Sharp remained with the R.B.W. until his death in 1953.

W. E. Edwards, who came as accountant in May 1920, was indeed "exceptional". One of John's most loyal and devoted assistants, he continued at Glyndebourne until 1953 and is today still a Director of the R.B.W. Edwards recalls John saying to him when he engaged him: "I don't yet know *what* I am going to do, but I shall find out. I want to make the world a better and a happier place, and I want someone to help me to do the things I want done." John said that "the salvation of England" must be sought in "work", and he was to provide work at a time when unemployment was growing at an alarming rate. Like William Morris he wanted the men who worked under him to have the opportunity of becoming skilled craftsmen. He added that he did not believe that a man with money should just live on his wealth. An idealist himself, Edwards was impressed; though concerned at first with what might seem to be the dullest side of the enterprise, he eventually became the cornerstone of the whole undertaking, and responsible for the administration of all John's enterprises.

After Sharp's death, Jenkins, who had run the R.B.W. office for nearly thirty years, succeeded him as its Managing Director. John would consult Jenkins at all hours of the day about contracts

7

and building procedure and often have long telephone conversations of an evening. John would frequently argue a point; but if Jenkins remained unconvinced he would finally say, "I am sure you are right, Jenkins", and yield with a good grace.

Tom Veness had come from the East Sussex family estates after their sale in 1919. As Reeve and Manager of the timber business in Plashett Woods he built up the new enterprise and remained at Glyndebourne till his death. His son is still there.

It was men such as these—and there were many others—who served John faithfully for the rest of their lives. He won their loyalty by becoming their friend and by taking a personal interest in every detail of their work, as well as in their private lives and their families. They were made to feel that they "belonged" to the estate, and they fully repaid his trust in them. Whenever an employee, his wife or a child, died, John invariably attended the funeral dressed in a morning coat and top hat.

It has been said that John was rather ruthless in dismissing old hands on the estate whom he considered inefficient or lazy, and for a time this made him unpopular in some quarters; and of course he made his mistakes. Also it might happen that a man who had long been unsatisfactory would finally be dismissed for a quite trivial offence which chanced to arouse John's wrath. But generally his outbreaks of anger were soon over and without aftermath. It was also noticed that he sometimes tolerated a high degree of inefficiency in a man who amused him.

Within the house there was of course, first and foremost, the indispensable Childs, who in addition to his household duties ran a troop of Boy Scouts and sang lustily in the Ringmer Church choir. He was not only the perfect servant, who understood his master's wishes before he could voice them, and who would pack suitcases for a journey that had never even been mooted; he also became his closest friend, and was later to act as best man at his wedding and as godfather to his son. Childs never presumed upon the familiarity with which John treated him. Many are the Jeeves-like stories told of the various occasions when Childs came to the rescue of his master, even to directing him to the Book of Ruth ("Try further back, sir! Try further back!") when John failed to find it to read the first lesson in Ringmer Church. In the house there was also Georgina, who had been housemaid at Glyndebourne since 1902 and who by this time had married a mason named Daniels. In due course she came with her husband and daughter to live in the house itself—an unusual arrangement for those days. Georgina was a sterling character who did much for the smooth running of the establishment and for the comfort of guests. John provided Daniels, who besides working at the Ringmer Building Works also helped in the house, with a sawn-off 12-bore shotgun intended, so John informed him, "to wound, but not to kill" burglars. Georgina still lives in Ringmer in a little bungalow which John built for her and her husband after their retirement.

Hardly less important than Childs or Georgina as a member of the household was John's pug, George, who accompanied him everywhere—even on his visits to London. George used to be taken out shooting on about fifty yards of string—which of course got tangled up in the bushes (loud cries from the beaters: "Where's the Captain's dog?" etc.) He often figures in John's letters to his mother:

> George is the most bloodthirsty dog. He rushes at rabbits and tears them to pieces. . . . He was beaten again twice yesterday for "running in", but it has little effect as he is so keen. Brambles don't stop him.
> George was wounded out shooting yesterday. Another large dog attacked him because George had bagged his rabbit, and bit him over the heart. George now walks about like Amfortas wounded in the side. He carries a large red splash just where you shoot a stag. He took no notice and never uncurled his tail.

It was the absurd in George that appealed to John, who would urge him on to growl and bite, sometimes quite hard; whereupon John would exclaim, "George, you *ludicrous* dog!" George and his successors—Sock, Bimperl and others—were very familiar to all visitors to Glyndebourne, where once John gravely shocked the hunting men of his house-party by stoutly maintaining that a pug was far more beautiful than a thoroughbred horse. John sometimes went too far and teased his dogs—and Sock in particular—rather unkindly. This unkindness was not intentional: it was aimed at getting a "rise" out of the dog, whose reaction was interpreted by John as "showing character".

Pugs are endemic in the Christie households. The first recorded pug, another George, belonged to Augustus; he died on 6th November 1905 at Tapeley, where his tombstone records that he was "POSSESSED OF IMMORTAL VIRTUES: CONSCIENCE, LOVE, CONSTANCY". Today George Christie and his wife have two: Vino and Bertie.

★   ★   ★

Mention has already been made of the big sales of property in Lincolnshire and East Sussex. In addition, John was constantly buying and selling farms and smaller plots of land. Details of these transactions were duly reported to his mother, as were also the day-to-day affairs of the farm.

Farming developed until about 3,000 acres were under cultivation or being used as pasture. But those were difficult years on the land, and much money had been invested; in spite of the great successes scored at shows by the Glyndebourne Friesian herd the enterprise did not pay, and gradually many of the estate holdings were allowed to revert to tenant farming. The losses on farming might have been recovered eventually if John had persevered, perhaps with less emphasis on the show-ring; and if he had had more time to give to the affairs of Glyndebourne, for it must not be forgotten that until 1922 he was still a master at Eton. But the real reasons for his deciding to cut his losses were that farming had ceased to interest him, and that he had become convinced he would always lose money over it. Market gardening, another venture of this time, also miscarried and was soon abandoned.

It was fortunate for John that, unlike many smaller farmers and market gardeners, he had the capital to stand these losses.

8

Augustus Christie

A CONSIDERABLE CORRESPONDENCE between Augustus Christie and Lady Rosamond survives from the early years of their difficult married life; but of a later date than 1893 only two letters from Augustus to his wife have been preserved, and from her to him there is none.

The first of Augustus's two letters is dated 15th November 1901 and deals chiefly with the redecoration of Tapeley Park, to which he and Lady Rosamond had just returned after having let the house for some years. Augustus writes:

> In my opinion you have VERY EXCELLENT taste for decoration etc. and FAR ABOVE the average knowledge of what is good. Do you wish my bedroom to be got on with at once? My study is finished, and I think will look well when the prints are hung.

He adds that he hopes his wife will become "known in the district" and that he is thinking of becoming a District Councillor. "I am anxious that Tapeley shd. take its position in the County, as it did years ago. . . . P.S. I always consider myself a very humble pupil of yours in love and knowledge of pictures and art."

Tapeley, when Lady Rosamond first saw it shortly before her marriage, was externally unimpressive though containing fine pictures and some good rooms; during the next fifteen years, with the help of an architect named John Belcher, she transformed it into an agreeable and dignified house with a splendid garden. On a slip of paper she jotted down the following note:

> Mr Belcher became a close friend and our business intercourse

was charming. We could only do these alterations bit by bit, spreading the work over years. Much of the cost was defrayed from my savings out of housekeeping* and pocket money, and I used to go to the office with a "dear Mr Belcher, I've saved so much; what can we do with it?" Unfortunately the result was that for long years we lived in a perpetual muddle.

In the beautifying of Tapeley, and in the writing of pious and sentimental novels, Lady Rosamond found some kind of an escape from the unhappiness of her married life. Tapeley today has enormous charm, and its gardens (open in summer to the public) are beautifully designed, finely maintained and planted with many interesting sub-tropical trees and shrubs. Against the south wall of the house, mimosas, presumably of her planting, climb to nearly forty feet and have survived several severe winters. There are formal Italian gardens, a shell grotto, and magnificent views over the estuary of the Tar and Torridge rivers. Though the more important pictures have been removed to Glyndebourne, the house can still show some interesting examples of Morris and Burne-Jones furniture and a remarkable collection of *pâte-sur-pâte* ceramics.

Lady Rosamond loved Tapeley, and the Tapeley of today is largely her creation. But unfortunately there was little chance of the house playing, as Augustus had hoped, its part in the county: "The ladies of Instow",† Lady Rosamond informed her husband, "are beneath my position." It was hardly surprising that she was soon very unpopular in the neighbourhood.

The second letter was written on 2nd June 1913:

My dear Woman,
    I am a very happy man. I enjoyed so much your week-end stay at Tapeley. After you left me I got the two dogs, and we all went for a long walk over the estate. We came home by the reservoir and your dear Child‡ had his first bathe. . . .

---

* Devonshire neighbours recall to this day that Lady Rosamond's teas were always so meagre that if they did not arrive punctually they got nothing at all to eat.
† The local village, about a mile from Tapeley Park.
‡ One of the dogs, no doubt.

I beg you will not overtire yourself at Epsom. Please drive to
the course from the station and also back. I *beg* you will not
think of walking either way. I will willingly pay. I must, of
course, leave it in your hands; I can only ask you to carry out
my wishes. . . .

I often think, dear woman, that you do not in the least
realise how many tastes we have in common. I want so much
for us both to be utterly devoted to each other. At one time I
think you feared my [lack of] fondness for Jack. You have
recently seen how well we understand each other. I do, indeed,
however, resent the interference of outsiders. If we are left to
ourselves we shall be all right. All that I want is to be allowed to
tend on you, and take care of you. How surely is your good
mother's vision of a happy middle age for you coming true. I
love you, my darling. Let me take care of you, and be everything
to you.

Yours,
A. L. C.

Nothing could be more affecting than this loving letter. Or
indeed more rational. Why have his other letters to her dis-
appeared? Is it mere chance that these two have survived, or were
they the only two that Lady Rosamond cared to keep? That seems
most unlikely, and it is worth remembering that she did keep
many unkind letters from John. Doubtless Augustus's outbreaks
of temper alternated with calmer periods when, oblivious of what
his wife had sometimes to put up with, he felt that she did not
understand or appreciate him. That he came to be appointed
High Sheriff of Devonshire in 1911 is surely evidence that, in
public at any rate, he could be relied upon to behave.

Some kind of a *modus vivendi* must presumably have been established when Augustus and Lady Rosamond were together at
Tapeley; but in December 1918 there was a new cause for anxiety:
Augustus had a slight stroke which temporarily affected his speech
and the movement of his right arm, and a month later a more
severe stroke which left him for several months to a large extent
incapacitated. John wrote to his mother saying that he thought
his father ought to sign a power of attorney. This was done, and
various small sales of property transacted by John and his mother.

Augustus slowly recovered, but one effect of his stroke was to make his outbursts of temper more frequent. It was as John had feared: "I am afraid my Father will recover sufficiently to be very tiresome about things. My alarm is not, of course, that he *will* recover, but that recovered he will be irritable and difficult. He cannot share anything, and he cannot manage anything." Life for Lady Rosamond became very difficult indeed.

It had long been clear to John that his father ought never again to manage his estates. But John had no confidence in his mother's business capacity either; what he really wanted to do was to run the Devonshire estate himself. He had gone down to Tapeley soon after his father had been taken ill; in April he went there again and more amicable relations seem to have been established between father and son. The following winter, Augustus, to save the family from crippling death duties, agreed to hand over to his son his Sussex estates and the moneys received from the sales of houses and land in East Sussex and Lincolnshire; the sum involved was in the nature of a quarter of a million pounds. John wrote him a grateful letter: "It is very kind of you. . . . I am glad to find that I am completely trusted and I can assure you that your trust will not be misplaced. . . ."

The matter was arranged in the nick of time. In May 1920 Augustus was again taken ill, and the following August he had a third and serious stroke which left him slightly paralysed. He could take in what was going on and think reasonably clearly, but his power of speech was now permanently affected and the frustration of not being able to express or carry out his ideas often enraged him. Sometimes he was just pathetic, uttering a few words and then explaining, "Hard luck—can't speak."

As usual, bulletins from Tapeley on this fresh disaster had been vague and frequently contradictory. On 28th August John wrote to his mother:

I am afraid you are having a difficult time. I am of course very sorry to hear that my Father is ill again; at the same time it was becoming impossible to go on as before and something had to happen. Life under those conditions was little joy to him and intolerable to others. . . . I cannot make out how bad he is, but

I gather that for a time at any rate he will be in bed, and I suspect that he will gradually get better but will lose his speech, perhaps entirely.

I am sure that we must now take this opportunity of getting control of all business and finance . . . and also of getting proper attendants for him. You cannot go on as before or you will become as bad as him. It is really no good your thinking you can nurse him; you will only break down. . . . Of course it is awful [for him] to be unable to express his wants; but you must remember that his mind under these conditions is not healthy, and that one of its weaknesses may be to aggravate and bully. . . .

Under these circumstances he must submit to some restraint —supplied by others as he is unable to supply it himself. He will get used to it and it is better that it should be exercised by someone who is accustomed to such cases. We have given him full opportunity of trying to manage his own affairs and you can see the result: a life intolerable to everyone. . . . Your efforts have been quite noble. But you must realise your limitations and please listen to advice. I shall be ready to return south and go to Tapeley if I hear from you. Can I do anything ? . . .

In the course of the next two or three days he wrote to Dobbie and again to his mother; but the news that reached him from Tapeley was confused and on 5th September he wrote yet a further letter to his mother:

I cannot make out how my Father is, or what has happened to him. Has he had two strokes, and what kind of fit ?

I was rather nettled when I wrote to you last time. I feel that you will take upon yourself too much of the control of my Father. He is quite intolerable. Of course he does not mean to be, but he has never been put in his place. You haven't done it, and as he is surrounded by toadies no one else has done it. Now that his intellect is impaired and he has lost control of himself, he is unbearable. . . .

He never has any money because he muddles everything. Therefore take this out of his hands and run his affairs properly. This is what he really wants, though he has cranky ideas which must be put on one side at once. When he sees that there is money to spare, then he can't say much. His mind is now childish and naughty. It is bad for him to be allowed to have his own way. . . . He must trust us. There is nothing more to be said. . . . Anyone with character would realise the position and accept it, instead of making everyone else miserable. . . .

It would seem that things were allowed to drift for a time. In March (1921) John drew his mother's attention to one of the basic difficulties in dealing with his father: the very different image that he created in the neighbourhood and at his club in Instow, from that which he created in his own home. "My father", he wrote, "earns the character of being a kind, genial, generous old gentle-man in public—a character he doesn't live up to in private." In June there is for the first time mention of the possibility of having Augustus certified:

> I am afraid there are difficulties ahead. It is obvious that my Father's secretive nature will not be satisfied by his affairs being managed by others, especially by you and me, since of you and me for some inexplicable reason he has always been intensely jealous. It seems to me fairly obvious that he is not fit to manage his own affairs. He cannot read or write and can only at rare intervals understand us and cannot at any time follow an argument. . . .
>
> I do not think there is any chance of my Father giving up the idea of cancelling the power of attorney. There is the prospect of bad rows and of his getting an Exeter solicitor or other solicitor to give him the deed to sign. He could get someone to get it for him. Then we are done or at least forced at a dis-advantageous moment to get him certified.
>
> We must choose the occasion for battle. This means prepara-tion and the collection of evidence. You cannot rely on the doctor being able to persuade him not to do what he wants. He wants to fool about with his things much more than he wants anything else.
>
> I have little doubt that he will have to be certified. His con-trol of himself will get worse and he may easily become danger-ous. There is always a tendency for the wife to put off certifying a husband. . . . I should like Doctor Toye to listen to some of the rows unknown to my Father. He behaves himself if he knows the Doctor is about.

Could you not come away again for a bit and we could settle some plan of action? . . .

It would seem, however, that for some reason or other the idea of having Augustus certified was not for the moment pursued. Perhaps Lady Rosamond could not bring herself to do it; but in any case she soon learned that his illness was not as yet sufficiently advanced to make certification possible. In the summer of 1922 Augustus was persuaded to go to London to consult Sir Thomas (later Lord) Horder, John and Lady Rosamond accompanying him. Horder diagnosed advanced hardening of the arteries, and a slight paralysis as the result of damaged blood vessels in the brain due to the stroke. He did not consider him certifiable, but agreed that he was unfit to manage his affairs and that his condition could only deteriorate.

John had suggested that his father should visit Glyndebourne and see the improvements that he had effected there. This visit, which he now made, had been under discussion since January, when John had written to his mother:

I wrote to my Father asking him to come to Glyndebourne in February. I shall of course be delighted to see him there. If he comes, I think we must make him keep to the rules of the house, i.e. no quarrelling. I don't want to start scenes at Glyndebourne, and we should make the occasion the opportunity for stopping them. Also he must give up his cranks there and take things as they are. I don't want work going on round or in the house interrupted because he doesn't like seeing people about. In fact he must expect to see strange faces. I do not imagine he will want to interfere with the farming. I expect him to be an interested spectator. I am ready to discuss anything with him and am anxious to show him everything. I will do my best to make him comfortable and welcome, but it will make it easier if he comes in this spirit. I shall be there for the week-ends. . . .

Apparently the visit was a success. Augustus admired the organ room, and there is no mention of any scenes. It seems that Lady Rosamond did not come to Glyndebourne with her husband; no doubt the best holiday she could have was a brief respite from his continual presence.

9

Glyndebourne Host

"PLEASANT SURROUNDINGS of an artistic nature, tennis, fishing presently, motors, golf, books, organ, etc., and a general atmosphere of freedom and happiness"—such, John told his mother, were his ambitions for Glyndebourne and the attractions to be made available to his guests.

All who stayed at Glyndebourne, both at this time and later, remember John as a most hospitable host. At first the parties were usually small and often consisted of colleagues from Eton. From time to time, when she could escape from Tapeley, his mother paid him short visits. But once the reconstruction of the house had been completed he began, during the holidays and even at week-ends in term-time, to entertain on a larger scale.

Week-end parties soon became the rule in the holidays. There were parties for tennis on the new hard court, for dancing, for organ recitals, for agricultural shows. John was an excellent shot and there were frequent shooting parties (during one of which a guest recalls being offered, at the picnic lunch, a choice of '87 or '97 port). The atmosphere was informal and unconventional, the hospitality lavish but without ostentation beyond the serving, when there were large parties, of meals on silver-gilt plates. There was only one defect: the cold in winter. John, like so many people who are themselves impervious to cold, had no conception what others suffered in this respect. And like so many rich men he had his strange little economies: hating to see fuel wasted, he would carry a small electric fire, attached to a long wire, from room to room until someone plucked up courage to ask whether proper fires could be lit. He loved turning out lights that he considered unnecessary, sometimes thereby leaving a guest in total darkness.

Conversation at meals was stimulating and often bizarre. It was John's habit to start the ball rolling by making some preposterous pronouncement which he defended vigorously and in the face of all reason. He was a good actor and warmed to a large audience. Then, when the whole company had become involved, he would sit back in his chair, silent and beaming, contentedly surveying the scene. When an expert on a particular subject was present, he liked to lead him on and pick his brains.

As a rule the daylight hours were spent out of doors. There was always some innovation on the estate to be seen, some alteration to the gardens to discuss, some prize animal to admire on one of the farms where, armed only with a small switch, John would enter the enclosure of the fiercest bull and proceed to pat it. "Bulls", he used to say, "are quite safe if you're not afraid of them." John's cricketing days were now virtually over, but he was still always ready for an energetic game of tennis. After dinner, and after lunch if it was wet, the company would move to the organ room where Mr Potter, his tame organist, might be on hand to play; and one guest recalls with distaste an organ recital during breakfast.

John no longer went to London dances; but he continued to dance in Sussex with great enthusiasm, sometimes taking parties to the Metropole and other hotels in Brighton. He practised assiduously, even at Eton where (in 1921) a boy recalls having seen him and a colleague, Edward Bell,* through a window of Liqueur Cottage "dancing round the room to the gramophone, each clasping a cushion to his bosom. Bell cannot have been keeping very good time because John continuously admonished him: 'You're late, Bell; you're late!'" However, in spite of all his efforts, John remained a clumsy performer, finding the brisk foxtrots and one-steps of the day ill-suited to his short legs and stocky figure. But he enjoyed dancing. Moreover, for all that he had formerly

---

* Bell, an eccentric but charming historian who professed to be a socialist, was a brother of the later famous Bishop of Chichester, George Bell. He had joined the Common Lane colony in 1921, replacing Tuppy Headlam who had taken over a boys' house.

told his mother to the contrary, he had by no means resolved to remain a bachelor; and at a dance one might perhaps meet a partner for life.

In fact, there begins at this time to be observable in his letters to his mother a change in his attitude towards matrimony. Only a few months earlier he had written to her: "As regards marriage, I have never met anyone whom I want to marry and I believe I am too cautious to get engaged. It seems to me to be impossible. Besides I cannot imagine myself having any respect for anyone who consented to marry me." But now, even if he was still "not hopeful about marriage, as I am rather old to begin and also very particular", yet he could also write: "I agree with you about wives. I am not standing out against marriage."

Potential brides also began to be included in the house parties at Glyndebourne, but he could find little to say to them beyond, "Are you quite happy?" After their departure, their merits and defects were discussed with his more intimate friends, and points awarded for looks, charm and intelligence. It always seemed to be their defects that predominated: "Her voice is too loud." "Very pretty; very dull." Yet at some moment—we do not know when —he got so far as to propose during a visit to Scotland. But he was rejected: "My first attempt has been unsuccessful," he said afterwards, "perhaps because it was made under an umbrella in the pouring rain." It appears that he was not much put out by his failure.

In 1922 he gave a ball at Glyndebourne to raise funds for the Red Cross, with a house party of sixteen to stay for it. His aunt, Lady Margaret Watney, acted as hostess, and her daughter Silvia invited most of the girls. John asked the men—his much older friends and contemporaries. He told his mother:

> We had just over a hundred people and there was plenty of room. Could get no waiters, but Childs preferred to manage with his own men rather than with strangers and I had six men in the house for the week-end. . . . I hired an extra cook and that was all as far as I know. We drank eighteen magnums including the band and dinner. Ran the electric light engine all night. . . . We danced in the organ room and all the furniture

was stored on the terrace on planks and covered with a tarpaulin.

And characteristically he added: "We used 35 units of electricity during the evening. The wine cost me £12.10.0. and was thought to be particularly good. The band was £15.15.0. So the whole cost was low. The band was quite admirable. I shall probably have another dance. . . ."

★   ★   ★

Oscar Browning, who was always rather ashamed of being a schoolmaster (at Eton), when asked on one occasion where he lived, gave his holiday address but added that he spent "a few months every year in the neighbourhood of Windsor". John was not in the least ashamed of being an "usher"; but anyone reading the letters he wrote to his mother during the period between his return to Eton after leaving the Army and the year 1922, must find it hard to remember that they are those of a schoolmaster and not of a country squire. His Eton life is hardly mentioned in them.

Lady Rosamond, perhaps realising that his heart was more at Glyndebourne than in schoolmastering, intensified the campaign she had begun many years earlier, to persuade her son to retire and live at Glyndebourne. But his views were unaltered, and as late as November 1921 he had written to her in terms that made it clear that he still had no thought of leaving Eton. Yet on 5th June of the following year he tells her, without a word of comment or explanation, "I have more or less decided not to take a house here and to retire at the end of this Half". What had occurred to make him change his mind so suddenly?

We may safely assume that he had not been influenced by his mother; yet if the decision was his own, why did he not give her his reasons? Also he had already known quite well, in November, that he was almost next in succession to a boys' house, and that if he accepted it he would be under some obligation to remain at Eton for a number of years. How had the situation altered between November and June?

For some time past John had been spending every leisure moment at Glyndebourne, which had become the centre of all his thoughts and ambitions. But as a housemaster he would no longer find himself able to slip away at week-ends and on holidays during term-time. Therefore it is possible that he suddenly realised, at the eleventh hour, that he had come to the end of schoolmastering, and that if he were to leave he must leave now. It was characteristic of him to pursue an interest with feverish concentration and then to drop it almost completely when a new one turned up: cricket, lawn tennis, golf, blue-and-white china, oriental rugs, fishing, are examples. Perhaps schoolmastering was another, and Glyndebourne the interest that replaced it.

There is also reason to believe that all was not at this time well with his teaching. His work was now largely with the less intelligent boys, and he did little in the laboratory; further, he was made to teach, in addition to Physics, a certain amount of Mathematics, for which he had small enthusiasm. One who was up to him at this time remembers a note of exasperation sometimes coming into his voice when a boy failed to grasp the point he was trying to make, and he was apt to deal out unreasonably severe punishments without warning.

But there is another possible explanation of his sudden decision to leave Eton. It must have been obvious to Dr Alington, now Head Master, that it would be something of a gamble for John to take on a house. Wells, who had the best house in Eton at that time and who knew John intimately, believed he could succeed. Alington will certainly have discussed the matter with one or two of the senior housemasters, and he may have decided to advise John that his outside interests had grown to such an extent that it would be wisest for him to retire. If this was so, then it would appear to have been advice that could more kindly have been given sooner.

We are forced to the conclusion, though without any proof, that this is the more probable explanation. At all events, Mr Gow, John's friend and colleague, had no doubt that the decision to leave Eton was the right one. But he and many others on the staff were very sorry to see him go; as (Sir) Henry Marten, later Provost of Eton, wrote: "You gave us a whiff of fresh air by coming to Eton, and I shall miss you." Not a few parents who had boys entered for John's house were, however, disappointed, and one at least was indignant, that John had, as they saw it, "let them down".

John realised how much he would miss Eton, but he took his departure philosophically and turned his face towards the future. He still did not know *what* he was going to do; he was, however, confident that he would one day find the answer to his quest for an ideal.

*   *   *

When John left Eton in 1922 he was forty, still in the prime of life. To outward appearance all signs of youth had vanished. His frame had become heavy; much of his hair had gone, to reveal a large domed head with a high forehead. He was blind in one eye and noticeably lame; but his appearance was very deceptive, for this rather Pickwickian figure was bursting with energy, teeming with ideas and strong as a horse. ("Whenever there was anything large to be moved," said one who worked on his estates, "Mr Christie always took the heavy end.") He seemed, like Don Quixote, to be perpetually tilting at windmills; but with him it was the windmills that ultimately fell.

John disliked all pomposity and snobbery and useless conventionality. It is true that he was to "recommend" (i.e. virtually make compulsory) evening dress for those who came to his Opera House; but this he did in order to train his audiences "to show respect for our work". If the artists took trouble, then so should the audience (though heaven knows that the pilgrimage from London to Glyndebourne might have been considered trouble enough). For the same reason he adopted an admirably firm line with what the Germans jokingly call "Spätlinge";* he also had the foyer left in darkness for several minutes at the end of performances, to discourage "Frühlinge" from failing to give the applause that was the artists' due.

Yet though Glyndebourne audiences were urged to dress conventionally, John's own dress was at times highly unconventional.

---

* Literally, animals born late in the season—i.e. late-comers.

8

He is usually remembered as wearing those odd combinations of garments generally associated with foreigners who have failed to master the English rules. On one occasion he had to go to London on some business involving a frock-coat and top hat, but wanted also to have a net at Lord's. After having this he decided not to change back, but found his top hat would not go into his cricketing bag with his frock-coat, etc. So he decided, quite logically, that there was no reason why he should not wear it, but startled two elderly ladies by throwing himself (and cricket bag) into their already moving carriage at Paddington, wearing top hat, Eton Rambler blazer, flannels and cricket boots.

Miss Belshaw, Managing Agent of the Devon estates, remembers him on Exeter platform, complete with pug, wearing a brown coat, very baggy trousers, white tennis shoes, and that favourite hat of his, a hybrid between a top hat and a bowler which was known as a square bowler or Coke hat. Yet he could write of an acquaintance:

> I met him recently in Regent Street wearing a top hat, hunting stock, Gladstonian collar, silk waistcoat, cheque [sic] trousers, spats, two sticks (one in each hand), and feet turned out at 180°. No lunatic could look more lunatic.

Impervious to cold, he would come to Eton on St Andrew's Day (30th November) wearing a tropical suit and no vest—a fact that he would embarrassingly demonstrate at dinner to the lady placed next him. But towards the end of his life, when his circulation was less good, he would appear at the Wall Game in a tweed frock-coat, black evening bow-tie, and on his head his celebrated square bowler, thus sometimes providing the only excitement during the game. When suffering on one occasion from lumbago, he travelled to London with a hot-water bottle tucked in the back of his trousers, and emptied it on the platform at Victoria. He finally cured himself (he alleged) of this painful complaint by kneeling to say his prayers instead of saying them standing up.*
The son of a colleague at Eton, Mr Lawrence Impey, remembers

* See p. 4, footnote.

"his dancing gloves in London that were always two sizes too big, and the eiderdown in which he wrapped himself on the London pavement after a dance, to drive back in his huge two-seater Daimler to Eton".

John was a *gourmand* rather than a *gourmet*. He had a passion for cream and milk puddings, especially for that peculiarly revolting kind called tapioca, of which an Eton housemaster, Mr Nigel Wykes, once saw him eat seven helpings at boys' dinner. In Common Lane he always had a separate rice pudding for lunch and ate it out of the dish. His over-indulgence in cream no doubt helped to produce his heavy figure and probably caused the jaundice and liver trouble from which he often suffered in later life. Though interested in and knowledgeable about wine, a subject which bulks very large in his letters to his mother, he himself drank little.

Something of the mischievousness of a boy was never to desert him, and he never tired of the same old jokes. He loved pulling people's legs—for example, pretending when he was driving his car that he did not know where the brakes were, or that they did not work. It amused him to introduce his guests to one another by the wrong names. He loved making provocative statements. This was not mere childishness (though some insensitivity may have been involved): it enabled him to judge the character of the person concerned, particularly if that person was a stranger to him. In fact, he teased people for much the same reason that he teased his pugs.

On one occasion, after a rather dull dinner party, he found himself seated in the drawing-room beside the silent and boring wife of an admiral, a woman he had never met before. On the floor at his feet a boxer bitch lay on its back. John studied the bitch and, pointing with his forefinger, counted the nipples; then, turning to his companion, he said: "Six. And how many have *you* got?"

John, like many of his generation, was a curious mixture of generosity, and of that kind of thrift that is almost indistinguishable from meanness. He rarely supported charities, and understood poverty so little that he could not see how anyone could get into financial difficulties without being "a dishonourable man". He would grudge the spending of a penny, and nothing pleased him more than to rescue and use again a stamp which had escaped the postmark; yet the next moment he might give away fifty pounds. And of course he was always enormously hospitable. "Why must we pay X so much?" was a cry frequently heard. He never gave a tip if he could possibly avoid it. After Opera had restarted at Glyndebourne, he was to grudge Rudolf Bing, his General Manager, the rail fare to Edinburgh to investigate the possibility of a Festival there, and when Bing was about to sail to America he begged him to remember not to have his shoes cleaned on board since they would not get dirty. He was obsessed by electric light wastage, and after every opera performance at Glyndebourne would go round turning off the lights—a job for which a man has now to be specially employed.

To the end of his life he always travelled third class. When his friend Rhona Byron pointed out to him that this was very selfish since he kept not only one seat but, because of his bulk, a part of another from those who could not afford the extra for first class, he said, "I don't want people to think that I can have anything more than they can". He genuinely believed that he was thus showing public spirit.

He had an apparent modesty which cloaked a fundamental conceit. For instance, he always thought (and said) that other land-owners were incompetent and did not "contribute anything"—a favourite phase—to the world. But without a firm belief that he could win battles against seemingly insuperable odds, he could never have succeeded in establishing Opera at Glyndebourne.

Various eccentricities are remembered by those who were his guests at Glyndebourne. At one time knitting was provided for all female visitors. The bathroom doors had, at first, no locks: "What does it matter," John asked, "if someone does come in?" Mr Lawrence Impey recalls an occasion when two visitors to Glyndebourne—"The General and his wife, who had been invited to lunch" received a rude shock. John (who had quite forgotten they were coming) and Impey were "catching fish by hand in the first lake, naked, as it was being emptied", when Childs let the unsuspecting guests down through the garden. "Even Childs permitted himself a smile."

John liked purchasing in bulk. To Edwards, who asked if he might buy a typewriter for the office, he replied, "Oh yes, buy half a dozen, we shall need them". Mr Wykes remembers John "doing a little shopping" when staying with him at Eton, and returning with three umbrellas and seven suits of silk pyjamas. Audrey Christie reported that at one time her husband possessed 230 shirts. He took seven copies of *The Times* so that all his guests might have something to read at breakfast, and there were always at least two dozen balls on the tennis court.

Shortly after the last War John had two thousand pairs of cheap plastic dancing pumps made, costing about 10s. 6d. a pair, which he unsuccessfully attempted to persuade a large London store to sell for him. He then tried to dispose of them himself, even considering the possibility of advertising them in the Glyndebourne Opera Programme. Brooks's Club was at one time littered with these pumps when he carried on a private sales' campaign there—with little result.

Many of the Christie stories are associated with railway carriages. Nothing riled him so much as a man smoking in a non-smoking compartment, and if someone lit up a cigarette he would ask him to put it out. Once, when he met with a refusal, he knocked the cigarette out of the man's mouth, and finally blew out the matches one by one when he attempted to light another. He would sometimes put up an umbrella to shield his eyes from the electric light; and on one occasion, and in spite of the protests of the woman who was the only other occupant of his carriage, he removed the bulbs. His terrified companion rushed out into the corridor to fetch the guard and was duly transferred to another compartment.

How much of these eccentricities was pose, how much was natural? It is probably fair to say that, though he obviously enjoyed surprising people, John was not as a rule calculatedly eccentric; often the perfectly logical solution of a problem—for example, that of how to dispose of his top hat after a net at Lord's —resulted in apparently abnormal behaviour. He would not have been his father's son if there had not been a fair strain of whimsicality in him. We must, however, be thankful that in him it did not take a more extreme form; and grateful too to his wife, who was later to curb his excesses or by her charm to make them seem excusable.

10

Organs and Big Business

SOON AFTER the end of the First World War, Messrs Hill, Norman and Beard had begun the construction of the organ at Glyndebourne.* This new interest of John's was to lead in due course to his embarking upon one of the largest of his many business ventures.

While the organ was being built, he had interested himself in every detail of its construction. He knew what he wanted: "the rolling diapason quality heard in cathedral organs"; and he instanced the organ in Eton College Chapel, also built by Messrs Hill. He wanted, said Mr Herbert Norman, the firm's chief designer and tonal expert, "an organ with brilliant but soft tones, especially in the treble, because he had an ear extraordinarily sensitive to high pitch". The fashion was then for weight and volume. John's requirements seemed perverse at the time, but the trend today is in the direction of the very qualities that he demanded.

Though the Glyndebourne organ was theoretically more or less complete by Christmas 1920, alterations and improvements continued to be made over the next two or three years. John was never satisfied. "At every week-end house party", said Mr Norman, "he would consult 'experts' and on Monday would want changes and further refinements. So the workers would often deliberately leave an improvement unfinished on the Friday, knowing that if they finished it then it would probably have to be altered on the Monday." One improvement that did get carried out was the

* John also presented an organ to Ringmer Church in memory of his grandfather.

addition of pipes of sub-fundamental pitch, the lowest of which vibrated eighteen times to the second. Such pipes were suitable only for a cathedral or very large church. John was delighted when, on their first being tested, the vibrations brought a large piece of plaster crashing down from the ceiling.

In the end, and not surprisingly, the instrument, which had of course become something far more elaborate than that which Lloyd had planned, "lacked all distinction". Mr Donald Beard, son of the senior partner of the firm, wrote: "It was never a success. It was far too big for a room of that size and I will not dwell on the countless number of hours wasted and the amount of money spent in trying to remedy matters. In my opinion the scheme was wrong and ill-advised from the very start. . . ."

Gradually the popularity of the organ waned until finally it had to be dismantled to provide the additional space needed, on the side of the stage adjoining the organ room, when in the early fifties the proscenium arch of the Opera House was widened. Today, of the organ only the handsome shell remains.*

John had soon come to the conclusion that it ought to be possible to produce cheaper and better organs than those built by Hill, Norman and Beard. When, in 1923, Dr Hill died, he purchased his holdings in the firm and became a director. Shortly after this he also bought the remainder of the shares, which were owned by various members of the Norman and Beard families. Donald Beard returned from Ceylon about the time that John acquired the business; he has some entertaining recollections of John's management of the firm:

> I remember thinking that probably the new Mr Christie would remain in the background, happy to leave the day-to-day running of the business to my father and myself and the works staff. . . .
>
> Well, one morning John Christie duly arrived at the office, dressed in full morning kit and driving a large two-seater grey

---

* John issued a brochure on the organ, which gave an account of its construction and potentials and was illustrated by a photograph of the organ. It also contained, for no apparent reason, a picture of a Friesian cow.

Daimler coupé with a spotlight on the roof and fitted with balloon tyres on the rear wheels. My father introduced me, and John Christie said: "So you are Donald, are you? Well, from now on I'm John, you are Donald, and", turning to my father, "you are 'Old Beard'."

Donald Beard soon discovered that his assessment of the role John would play was about as wrong as it could possibly have been. Within a few minutes John was pouring out schemes for improvements and modernisation. He proposed new offices and new lavatories. He wanted a restaurant which could also be used for meetings and entertainments. He found a site suitable for cricket nets to provide recreation during the lunch hour (though in fact they were never erected). It was clear that the firm was going to see a great deal of its new Chairman:

> His exuberance and energy were terrific; all who came into contact with him felt the force of his character and were compelled to fall in with his schemes. From the moment he arrived in the office—and he was there almost every day—all routine work came to a standstill; indeed, it never seemed to occur to him that such work was really necessary. He used to stand with his back to the fire, his hands in his trouser pockets, and pour out ideas until one became quite numbed, deprived of all power to fight back. I found that the only way to get any work done was to disappear into another office, leaving my father to face the onslaught which sometimes lasted for hours.

After a time John came to the conclusion that the Beards were in a rut, that they were impervious to new ideas—"though heaven knows we did our best". He began to go into the works and pick the brains of the workmen and the works manager. He would buttonhole a man who already had more than enough to do, and cross-question him or, more often, attempt to indoctrinate him with his own ideas. Then he would return to the office and inundate the wretched Beards with more of his fantastic schemes.

Sometimes he would single out one of the workmen, make a tremendous fuss of him and propose that he should be promoted to works manager or even made a director; then, as abruptly, the man would be dropped. This sudden turning against, and even discarding, of people who had served him well was unfortunately by no means limited to the employees of Hill, Norman and Beard, and a number of those who were to work with the Glyndebourne Opera also became the victims of John's capriciousness.

Donald Beard was an astute observer of John, especially of John at the wheel:

> A few months after John had taken over the reins at York Road he bought two T model Fords—one a two-seater which he used, and the other a four-seater for the firm's use. . . . It was a comic sight to see him in morning kit and top hat sitting bolt upright driving his car through London. He seemed to be quite oblivious of the fact that he was in any way unusual, and gave a beaming smile to anyone who was rude enough to stare, or sometimes even to laugh, when he was held up in traffic.
>
> One morning I called for him at his house in Hyde Park Terrace to take him to the office, and I was surprised—and very thankful—when he asked me to drive. As usual he had his attaché case with him. As soon as we had started he placed this on his knees, opened it, drew out several old collars and some socks and proceeded to throw them into the gutter of the Bayswater Road. "It's the easiest way of getting rid of them", he said.
>
> He was a most alarming person to be driven by. He drove at great speed, cutting in and out of the traffic and shaking his fist violently at taxi drivers or pedestrians who got in his way. The other chap was always in the wrong. However, I cannot remember, in all the years that I knew him, that he ever had an accident.
>
> Later on he bought a second-hand Singer which was a dreadful machine; he used to drive up to the works in it from Glyndebourne each morning and back again at night—why I could never understand. One night on the way home the car caught fire, I believe on Blackfriars Bridge.

A whole book could be written about John and his innumerable cars, one of which he had licensed as a taxi though, so far as is known, it never actually plied for hire. Childs described an occasion when John, with great presence of mind, saved both

master and servant from a serious accident at a corner by swerving
off the road and into a field of stubble:

"Sir, sir—you're off the road, you're off the road!"

"Yes, Childs, I know. I've seen another gap further on and I'm
going back through that."

★   ★   ★

John always had grandiose ideas. He was soon planning to get a
monopoly of the organ-building trade in the British Isles, and
hoped in time to make about £50,000 a year profit, only a portion of which would be his. The principal difficulty, he told his
mother, was the number of dishonest men in the trade. "As a start
I have in mind to purchase five or eight businesses all over the
country. . . . I am having Boy Scout and Girl Guide camps at
Glyndebourne next summer for the organ trade. . . . It is as much
as anything a dodge on my part for attracting workmen from
other firms. I think these firms will have to feel the pinch before I
take them over; but it is obviously a good thing to do for one's
men."

But though John was now "thinking big", he still attended to
the smallest details. He was, for example, in touch with Khartoum
where he hoped to get ivory organ-knobs made at half-a-crown
less apiece than they cost on the English market.

Meanwhile Ringmer Building Works had completed the new
restaurant at York Road, which was managed by Mary, the cook
from Glyndebourne. The food was considered excellent. John
had a passion for scallops, which therefore appeared on the menu
at least two or three times a week, as did also of course the milk
puddings of which he ate such huge quantities. Various members
of the inside and outside staff—nine or ten of them in all—were
in due course made salaried directors, and it was observed that
these were almost always to be found lunching in the restaurant:

At lunch [wrote Donald Beard] John would sit at the head of
the table and pour forth his ideas on all sorts of subjects. One
pet ambition of his was to modernise the construction methods

of organ building by introducing mass production of as many parts as possible. . . . He bought several very expensive wood-working machines which mass-produced certain parts in quantities far in excess of our requirements. He liked to see rows of organ consoles (keyboards) stretching the length of the workshop floor.

One of his favourite arguments, often produced at lunch-time, was that an organ could be broken down into hundreds of small parts which could be mass-produced and then, as he put it, "stuck or screwed together to make up any machine you want". This was practical up to a point in the construction of certain types of organs—e.g. cinema organs or church exten-sion organs—and was in fact largely applied; but it was not possible in all cases.

These mass-production methods were mentioned by John in a letter to his mother in March 1924. He had just returned from a visit to London to settle the purchase of two small organ firms, one of which was defunct:

I am aiming at being responsible for £100,000 a year in the organ trade and I think I shall be doing it by the end of the year. . . . We have become the fashion. . . . I ought to get £10,000 a year clear profit and really more from the turnover. My new machinery is creating a most favourable impression and the organ builders are coming round to my views of mass production. . . .

I am sure my methods are right, and I have good men behind me. Beard is supposed to be the wisest man in the trade. His eldest boy, who is with us, has done very well, and besides I have some practical organ builders who were at the head of the business I have bought. At present I have every reason to be optimistic. . . .

It seemed he had. By 1929 his combined companies had sup-plied new organs to, or renovated the existing organs of, the Chapel Royal, Glasgow University, Peterborough Cathedral and Lagos Cathedral. There were also many private commissions, especially from France and Germany.

In the mid-1920s, the heyday of the silent films, the cinema organ became popular. To supply the new need, Hill, Norman and Beard produced the Christie Unit Organ. This remarkable instrument, which could be bought in various forms at prices ranging from £1,145 to £4,594 (for service in the tropics), was produced with "Twenty Selective Stop Keys producing special combinations of tone colour" that ranged from "Sleigh Bells" to "Crockery Smash". The first organ was completed in 1926 and scored a considerable success. More than fifty of them were sold in England, and representatives of the firm, despatched to sing their praises overseas, disposed of many more—particularly in Australia and New Zealand. Then came the "Talkies" and a rapid falling off in orders.

The financial collapse of the cinema organ trade coincided with John's loss of interest in organ building, and with those first informal operatic productions in the organ room at Glyndebourne which were soon to lead to the building of the Glyndebourne Opera House. Gradually he came to realise that he could not make a financial success of organ-building. In August 1932 he confessed to his mother:

> I have lost a lot of money in agriculture and organ work.* Agriculture is impossible except on a small scale and perhaps as a dealer. We have put a great deal of time into the organ works, and energy and brains. Our difficulty there is that we are let down by the executive staff on the organ-building side. It is they who fail and we cannot replace them as the Trade is so small. . . . All my other concerns except farming make money. The R.B.W. are now leaders in the building trade and they are making money when others are doing poorly.

★ ★ ★

"All through these years", wrote Donald Beard, "John and I were really good friends and he was most generous and kind to me in a great many ways. Glyndebourne was almost an open

* Later, after a great deal of reorganisation, modest profits were for a time made from the organ business.

house to me at week-ends." In 1929 he went for two years to Australia on behalf of the firm; he returned to find everything changed. His father had retired, and John, who had completely lost interest in organs, was now absorbed in his schemes for Opera at Glyndebourne, leaving Edwards to clear up the financial muddle at Hill, Norman and Beard:

> John said he had lost a lot of money. I could only tell him that I was not surprised and that my father and I had done our level best to try to keep things within reasonable limits. At this time he was most friendly and just the same to me as he had always been. I went frequently to Glyndebourne and was shown all the details of the new Opera House of which he was so proud. I thought at that time that at last John Christie had found something to which he could devote his whole energy.

But at the Works Donald Beard found it more and more difficult to fit in with the new régime:

> The old feeling of the friendly family business to which I was accustomed no longer existed. . . . Then, as the months went by and things became yet more difficult, I was aware that John's attitude towards me had completely changed. I was no longer invited to Glyndebourne and when, on rare occasions, I met him at the Works, he completely ignored me.
>
> I found this a quite intolerable state of affairs. To say that I was hurt to the core is putting it mildly. I never found out what had happened to bring about this sudden change in our relationship, but in the end I decided to make a clean break and wrote to John resigning my position in the firm. He never replied and I never saw or heard from him again. All the arrangements for my leaving and handing over were carried out by Edwards.

And on this sad note we must take leave of the great organ enterprise. John continued to have financial interest in his organ firms, but all other interest had died. And, curiously enough for one who had been so interested in organs, he came in time to develop an intense antipathy to organists—especially provincial organists.

★   ★   ★

In October 1924 there comes the first mention of another project—the leasing of the Tunbridge Wells Theatre. In December of that year John wrote to his mother giving her full details of its finances and of what he hoped to make out of the Theatre in due course. "I think", he told her, "that the present owner has got into the hands of sharks and has been caught." The agreement was signed, and the following spring certain necessary alterations were carried out on what he was soon calling "The Tunbridge Wells Opera House". In March he wrote:

> I have just settled the material for the curtains, carpets and seating for the Opera House and we have already begun decoration there. . . . This evening I hope we obtained permission to take down a wall to give more room for the organ and stage. I am trying to find a young genius as musical director as I hope to develop the musical side very strongly. He will have an assistant organist and I suppose three or four others permanently in the orchestra, but at times I hope considerably to increase the number by getting pupils from the Royal College. We shall probably open our career with a week of Gilbert and Sullivan and we might perhaps take as much as £2,000 in a week, of which £500 should be profit. . . .

In July the first Christie season opened, not with Gilbert and Sullivan but with *Saint Joan*, Shaw's most recent success. It was followed by a variety of popular plays such as *The Cat and the Canary* and *Spring Cleaning*. Sunday concerts, which would include staged excerpts from Wagner's operas,★ would be given in the autumn. The leading theatrical agents, he told his mother, were busy trying to secure dates. Takings were twice what they had been under the old régime, and the neighbouring cinema had been obliged to redecorate itself to avoid losing its customers. In

★ These operatic ventures, the result of John's visits to Germany in 1925 and later, will be referred to again in the next chapter.

March (1926) came the postponed Gilbert and Sullivan season,. but John does not mention whether it was a success; his letters from now on are almost entirely concerned with other matters which had come to the front in his life; but a year later he wrote to his mother:

> The theatre is doing well. . . . We have changed our pro-gramme and in Lent and in certain other bad theatre seasons we are running twice-nightly shows and catering for the cinema and middle-class public: performances well done but short and cheap.

By September he was "investigating the possibility of doing Mozart's *Entführung* as a matinée in order to collect funds for Sadler's Wells. The Old Vic Singers might help. I might get Royal Patronage. It would be a good advertisement for both theatres. We are running through the opera at Glyndebourne on Sunday 14th November as a preliminary test. We have three weeks film at the theatre beginning on 9th November with *I.N.R.I.* (the Life of Christ) and on the 16th *The Epic of Everest.* Would you care to come to these?"

1927 began well. But it would appear that John was losing interest in Tunbridge Wells; nearly eighteen months elapse before the Opera House is again mentioned in his correspondence, and thereafter there is complete silence. For some reason or other, the Tunbridge Wells venture was not one of which he was proud, and he rarely referred to it in later years; yet undoubtedly he learned a great deal from it—as did Edwards also—which was to prove invaluable when the Glyndebourne Festival Opera came to be started a few years later.

The Tunbridge Wells Opera House eventually became a cinema. In August 1967 it was acquired by Essoldo Circuits Ltd., who propose to use it for "bingo and other indoor games".

PART III

II

The Genesis of Opera

IN MAY 1923 John wrote to his mother: "I am taking in [as paying guests] two families, Warres and Mounseys, in August and September, for £500 (seven weeks). There's a good profit in it, free of tax, and it will also keep down expenses." The Warres were not to make any contribution to John's musical life; but without the Mounseys there might never have been opera at Glyndebourne.

Johnnie Mounsey, a Quaker by upbringing, was a director of Barclays Bank. He was a good amateur pianist and ran the Barclays Bank Choir. His wife, Fanny, a much more forceful person than her husband, had a passion for music; she was technically a better pianist and had a wider musical knowledge. Bach was her god—"the greatest man who ever lived", she said. They both had the artistic temperament, which John had not. There were four children: the eldest, Patrick, was eleven at the time, and all of them were intelligent and musical.

John had always liked the parents but he had not known them well. As a result of that summer visit, however, a close friendship sprang up; the two men, it was said later, became "more like brothers". Fanny Mounsey, for her part, soon saw John's potentialities and decided to take his musical development in hand. "She is very anxious to help with music at Glyndebourne," John told his mother, "and being a good musician is well able to do so."

The Mounseys often came to Glyndebourne for week-ends, and John could always find a bed at their house when he was in

London during the week. They were at Glyndebourne again for Christmas; and two months later, when Johnnie Mounsey went to Egypt on business with his wife and some friends, John was one of the party. They were away for six or seven weeks.

While he was abroad John wrote no letters, but on his return he reported to his mother that the trip had been a success: "I spent most of the time with Fanny Mounsey whom I like very much," he told her. "She and Silvia will I think be quite good friends; they are rather alike in character." He wrote at great length of the heat and the flies and the poverty and the dearness of everything; Egypt's wonderful civilisation—its architecture and its art trea-sures—is dismissed in a single sentence.

Sir George Schuster, at that time Financial Secretary to the Sudanese Government, had entertained the party at Khartoum. He says:

> My recollection of John Christie is as a lively tourist with intriguing eccentricities. He was in those days already very bald and he had an idea that to sprinkle bay rum over his head gave a very pleasing feeling in the heat. I have a vivid picture of him in my mind, sitting in my garden watching a game of tennis, and every five minutes taking out a bottle of bay rum from his pocket and giving his bare scalp a liberal sprinkling. My general feeling is that he was going through a rather confused stage at that time and had not really found himself.

That summer John heard excerpts from *Fidelio* sung at the Mounseys' London house and was much impressed. The per-formance was given by the Thornely Gibsons (professionals con-nected with the Webber-Douglas School which had its own little theatre in London for opera sung by students), Hubert Langley and Odette de Foras, under the direction of Susan Lushington. In August John went with the Mounseys to Italy, and at Christmas the whole Mounsey family, together with three maids and the children's pony, spent three weeks at Glyndebourne. The visit was such a success that soon afterwards it was agreed that the Moun-seys should share Glyndebourne with John, while John used the Mounseys' house when in London during the week. Fanny

Mounsey spent much of her time at Glyndebourne, where she helped to beautify the house and to advise on the garden; she also lent a hand when John bought a house in London—5 Hyde Park Terrace.

Fanny Mounsey threw herself energetically into the musical life of Sussex. This was centred on the Lewes Musical Festival, which had been started by Mrs Alfred Lampson soon after the War and had become an annual summer event; John joined the Committee in 1926 and Fanny Mounsey a year later. Preparations for the Festival would begin in the autumn, when choir masters and mistresses met at Glyndebourne to be coached in the Organ Room by professional conductors such as (Sir) Malcolm Sargent and Dr Armstrong Gibbs; on the occasion of Dr Harold Darke's* visit John entertained one hundred and thirty people to lunch. During the Festival itself, which was held in Lewes Town Hall, the judges and others concerned with it were put up at Glyndebourne.

An extra day was soon added to the Festival for the performance of a major choral work in which the combined competing choirs took part. The orchestra consisted of local amateurs, strengthened by the addition of a few outside professionals. On these occasions John always made one of those improbable, unpredictable speeches for which he later became famous in his own Opera House.

In August 1925 John went to Germany with the Mounseys and other friends to hear Wagner at Bayreuth and Munich. In Munich he also heard Mozart operas performed in the exquisite rococo Residenztheater—a building which was destroyed during the last War.† It must surely have been theatres such as this—theatres attached to a palace, as was the custom in the German courts—which were to inspire John one day to build his own Opera House at Glyndebourne. This trip was the first of a series of annual

* Organist. President of the Royal College of Organists, 1940–41.
† But not its contents. Cuvilliés' interior was bodily removed to safety before the War and has now been set up in a building in the Alte Residenz. On the site of the former Residenztheater a new theatre in a functional style of architecture has been erected.

musical pilgrimages that John made with the Mounseys, and which came to include Salzburg and, on one occasion, Dresden. From Munich he wrote:

We left Bayreuth yesterday after hearing a bad performance of the *Ring*. There was practically nothing good about it, in spite of wonderful opportunities. . . . The scenery is over forty years old and the lighting arrangements are hardly used, probably because the scenery looks so bad when properly illuminated. For much of the time the stage was dimly visible and when the lights were increased it looked as if made of Noah's Ark materials. However, the copious use of steam for transformation and fire effects was admirable, as also the use of real fire on the mountains. The orchestra was taken too slow. The great asset of Bayreuth is the Fichtelgebirge surroundings of the theatre in contrast to Bow Street.

I am getting ideas for Tunbridge Wells. I am hoping to show various scenes from the operas as the concluding items on the Sunday concerts, instead of having them sung in tail coats. . . . I propose to try to popularise Wagner at Tunbridge Wells by organ and orchestra arrangements at the Sunday concerts, with a view to subsequently having a week of operatic selections or even performances of whole operas. I do not think I can expect to get even any of the separate scenes ready for this winter's concerts . . .

On his return to Glyndebourne he told his mother:

We got back from Germany about a fortnight ago and enjoyed ourselves very much. In fact we might easily go back to Munich or to Vienna next year. As a result I wish to give an operatic Festival in two years' time at Tunbridge Wells. *Parsifal* and Mozart's *Die Entführung aus dem Serail*. Mozart wrote this opera when he was eighteen years old.* It is excellent and also amusing. The Residenz Theatre is quite wonderful— very very ornate and a complete success at that. . . .

★   ★   ★

The party's base in Germany was invariably Haus Hirth, in the Bavarian Alps about six miles from Garmisch.

* Mozart wrote *Die Entführung* in 1782, when he was twenty-six.

Walther and Johanna Hirth had lost their savings in the post-war inflation and were obliged, as were so many other Bavarians at that time, to take in paying guests who approached them with a personal introduction. Johanna Hirth was a sister of Emil Pretorius well known as a stage designer, and her house had become the meeting-place of music-lovers from all over the world. John and the Mounseys were in their element there, and the atmosphere of Haus Hirth was largely responsible for pre-Hitler Germany becoming John's spiritual home. In August 1927 he wrote to his mother:

> We got back from Germany last Sunday after an extremely good holiday and feel very strongly pro-German and anti-English. Bavaria is so far superior to England. München is a wonderful city: no close squares for the children of the rich; flowers everywhere; perfect roads of small granite sets or tarmac; good houses everywhere and rich and poor living in the same building; no hall porters, but automatic devices instead; clean streets; fountains; good beer, good and cheap food; efficient though rather expensive train services; good shops; cultured people; picturesque clothes; cheap and good music and opera (except in the Festspiel season) maintained out of the rates. Perfect traffic control and no policemen.

When John wrote that he was "pro-German and anti-English" he was not, of course, thinking politically. Also, like so many foreign visitors at that time, he turned a blind eye to the misery and the unemployment that were soon to make Germany an easy dupe to the oratory and machinations of Hitler. Of course he found food cheap: the rate of exchange made it absurdly so—for the foreigner. Of course he found that the Germans made him welcome: their very survival depended upon the tourist trade. Very properly and very naturally he admired German music, craftsmanship and scientific achievement, and the energy with which the defeated country was attempting to rehabilitate itself. Politics had never interested him; and poverty he never understood.

John also admired the Bavarian Alps—admired them so much that they grew to Himalayan heights in his imagination. After ascending the Kreuzeck (under 6,000 feet) by cable railway, he "looked sheer down for about 12,000 feet". He also took the cable railway up the Zugspitze, which he declared to be "about 25,000 feet and the highest mountain in Germany". The actual height of the Zugspitze is 9,722 feet.

The previous year (1926) there had been an extra visit to Germany with the Mounseys and the Thornely Gibsons. Its principal object had been to lend support to Professor Dent,* who was giving an illustrated lecture at Münster on Purcell. Dent, a good linguist, spoke in German and was received "with repeated cheers from the whole audience of about seven hundred"; John found he could understand him quite well, whereas a native was very difficult to follow.

They also saw a ballet, and attended a concert performance of two short operas by Scarlatti and Purcell, given by the English singers. Later the same evening they were entertained, together with the cast and the officials of the Opera, at a party which went on until 4 a.m. and at which John, quite unabashed, was the only guest in a lounge suit (and a loud Harris tweed at that). Next day they were shown around the Museum by its Director, who had opened it especially for them, and the same evening they returned to London.

In the summer of 1928 John went to Dresden for a week—and it would appear that he went alone. In that time he heard seven operas. "I went all over the Opera House," he wrote, "and the scenery arrangements were all operated for my benefit." Was he merely getting ideas for Tunbridge Wells, or was he perhaps already beginning seriously to consider the possibility of one day building an opera house of his own at Glyndebourne?

*   *   *

Before long the effects of these visits to Germany made themselves apparent at Glyndebourne and also in the Tunbridge Wells

---

* Edward Dent, the distinguished musicologist. After the opening of the Glyndebourne Opera House, Dent, who wanted opera for the masses, expressed his disapproval of John's "opera for the rich". "Dent knows nothing about music," said John—courageously.

Opera House. At Glyndebourne the organ began to assume secondary importance; where once it had been used principally as a solo instrument, it was now more often called upon to support a small orchestra in giving excerpts from operas.

John's thoughts naturally turned to his beloved Wagner; but Fanny Mounsey had been skilfully indoctrinating him with Mozart, and his first project was in fact to tackle *Die Entführung aus dem Serail*, better known in England as *Il Seraglio*. John's temerarious idea was to give *Die Entführung* a "new look". He proposed getting Frank Mitchell to remodel the dramatic side of the opera; Professor Dent was to translate the arias into English, and Frank Birch★ to produce. "We might evolve a very popular play out of the opera," he wrote. "The material is excellent." On 14th November 1926 (as has already been mentioned) Fanny Mounsey ran through *Die Entführung* in the Organ Room "with four or five singers as a preliminary test". These singers included Thornely and Dolly Gibson.

It was probably just as well that John's project for an "improved" version of *Die Entführung* was shelved. Immediately after, however, he decided to do a concert version at Glyndebourne of Mozart's little *Der Schauspieldirektor*, with some of his friends singing. "We want to have a few small operas in our repertoire," he wrote, "and we might even tour with them." Thus was set the pattern for much of the music-making at Glyndebourne during the next few years: performances, partly amateur and partly professional, of small operas or excerpts from larger ones. At first these were concert versions, but later they were acted in costume. At first, too, they were accompanied by the organ and a few strings; later Mr Potter, the organist, retired and a small orchestra was formed.

The audiences consisted of estate employees, tenants, house guests, and anyone living in the neighbourhood who cared to come. There was usually a collection for the benefit of Childs's troop of Boy Scouts at Ringmer. Matthew Craig, who worked with his brother at the farm, lent a hand with the seating; and on

★ Brother-in-law of Lord Gage, John's friend and neighbour, and producer of *Berkeley Square*, etc., etc.

occasions the difficulty of satisfying everyone was so great that, as
he put it, he "would sooner have tied up a hundred cows".

The three most memorable of the operatic performances were
Act II of *Figaro* and Act III, Scene 1 of *Die Meistersinger* in 1928,
and Act I of *Die Entführung* in January of the following year. In
March 1928 John told his mother: "I am playing the part of
Antonio the gardener in *Figaro* in a month's time and possibly
Beckmesser in a part of *Meistersinger*". In April he reported the
success of the *Figaro* performance:

> *Figaro* went well enough for the audience on Saturday but
> went very finely on Sunday. I personally had a great success on
> the Sunday and was judged in the Professional Class by an
> honest critic! On the strength of it I am going to be the
> "Dumm" in *Serva Padrona* (Pergolesi) later on. The stage was
> pretty and is being left up for further experiment. I am very
> sorry you were not there. The house was full for each per-
> formance. 58 cars on Saturday, 40 on Sunday, and both days
> wet. A very happy week-end. About 200 to tea on Saturday
> and 22 people staying in the house. . . .

No doubt John was only half serious when he wrote of his
triumph as Antonio; apparently, however, he was sufficiently encouraged by his performance to "agree" to taking—in other
words, to *insist* upon taking—the part of Beckmesser in *Die
Meistersinger*. This was to be his one and only major role and in it
he scored a considerable *succès d'estime*. He took infinite trouble to
prepare himself for the part, Fanny Mounsey coaching him in it
for no less than three hundred hours in all. Though he had little
voice and could not always be relied upon to sing in tune, he
triumphed over these disabilities by some very skilful acting. His
performance "brought the house down", and it was no small
tribute to his interpretation of this the most farcical role in all
opera that one of the Glyndebourne housemaids had to be carried
out in hysterics.

Thornely Gibson took the part of Sachs, and his wife that of
Eva. Mr (later Sir) Steuart Wilson was Walther, Mr William
Biggs David and Mrs Robertson Magdalene. Mr Potter was at the

organ and Mrs Lampson at the piano. There was a second performance in the autumn.

★   ★   ★

Perhaps this is a suitable moment to consider how musical John
really was.

That he had a real *love* of music is indisputable. Clive Carey, the
singer, alleged later that he spotted quite early that John had "the
bug", and he was possibly one of the very few of John's friends
who was not completely taken by surprise when the Festival
Opera was founded. But John was not a trained musician. He liked
a good tune, he had a sense of rhythm, but he knew little or nothing of harmony; some very mild strumming on the piano, a brief
flirtation with the 'cello, was as far as he ever got as a performer on
any instrument.

Edwards recalls that he came upon John one day, playing on the
grand piano which was then in the Organ Room. Seeing the surprise on Edwards's face, John stopped and said, "I gave it up,
Edwards. I found I couldn't be better than ——" and he mentioned the name of a well-known pianist. He added: "If you can't
do a thing better than it's ever been done before, then there's no
point in doing it at all. It means nothing to say, 'as well as one
possibly can'." Yet John undoubtedly had a flair which enabled
him to appreciate the difference between good and bad orchestration, or to spot a promising voice; and he was always one of the
first to notice when, at Glyndebourne, a famous singer was "off
colour".

John's interest in the organ may be compared to his interest in
his cars; he was fascinated by the elaborate mechanism and by the
performance made possible by that mechanism. The piano was
too dull an instrument to excite him; it was as boring as is a
bicycle to a racing motorist. His interest in opera was very closely
associated with the technical side of the production: with lighting
and sound effects and scenic devices. After all, he was a scientist
first and a music lover only second.

★   ★   ★

In January 1929 the first act of *Die Entführung* was given at Glyndebourne. This time there was a nineteen-piece orchestra, conducted by Arnold Goldsbrough, in which John played the cymbals. Thornely Gibson was Osmin; Dolly, Gibson, Blonde; Williams Biggs, Pedrillo; Margerie Harrison, Constanze; and Philip Warde, Belmonte. Johnnie Mounsey took the unrewarding spoken role of Pasha Selim and his son Patrick played the triangle in the orchestra.

It must not be assumed that music at Glyndebourne was now confined to operatic excerpts. For example, one autumn Harold Samuel, Myra Hess and another professional pianist played Bach's concerto for three pianos, the organ replacing the orchestra. In February 1927 John mentions that the Sunday concerts at Glyndebourne were "a growing success" and that they were soon going to do the Brahms *Liebeslieder*; of these he later wrote that they were "very finely performed—in fact I doubt if they have often been done better. I hope to do them at an extra Christie Concert at Tunbridge Wells."

There were also more amateur occasions. At Christmas 1927 came a Hauskomödie in which the Mounsey children took an active part. The programme ranged from Bach cantata to a setting of A. A. Milne's "The King asked the Queen and the Queen asked the Dairy maid" in which John, wearing a papiermâché mask, played the Cow. He had only one entry, only a single word to utter: "Moo!" It was all great fun for John and for Fanny Mounsey and the Mounsey children; but for Johnnie Mounsey, hard at work all the week in London at his bank, the pace (he confessed to a friend) was becoming intolerable.

★   ★   ★

John's holidays were not quite restricted to travel with the Mounseys. In the summer of 1927 he went salmon fishing in Norway with C. M. Wells. But fishing—even with his old friend Wells—had already begun to pall. There was, he said, "always too much water, or too little"; and sadly he wrote, "I am bored with fishing". Though John's friendship with Wells remained intimate and unclouded, Wells was no lover of music—"I dislike the noise", he used to say—and his visits to Glyndebourne had to be carefully timed to coincide with lulls in musical activity. Indeed, this spate of music-making and, still more, the constant presence of John's new circle of friends in the house, led to something of a break with his former colleagues at Eton, who could no longer announce their intention of coming to Glyndebourne, but were obliged to write first to Fanny Mounsey to find out if there was room. Life at Glyndebourne had lost something of its easy informality.

★   ★   ★

In August 1928 John and the whole Mounsey family were again at Haus Hirth, where other friends joined them. From there they went on to hear operas in Munich and Salzburg. The Hirths used to wear Bavarian costumes in the evening; John therefore now fitted out all the men of the party with *lederhosen* and Tyrolean hats, the women with *dirndls*. The wearing of native dress, much affected by foreigners, and especially by American visitors to Bavaria, in the twenties and early thirties, was at least understandable in the country of its origin; when, however, John continued to wear it in Sussex, even to dine out in, it became incongruous and slightly absurd.

Johanna Hirth recalls John's visits to Haus Hirth. Her attempts to improve his German had not been very successful, and conversation was mostly in English—or English of a sort, for in general the Germans spoke English almost as indifferently as he did German. There were often animated discussions, especially with the German conductor, Erich Kleiber, who was properly scandalised by John's proposal to tamper with *Die Entführung*.

At the end of the holiday the party returned to London. At Victoria John, as always, refused the services of a porter, and the males were obliged to lug the heavy suitcases to a taxi. When they reached their destination John gave the driver the exact fare, explaining (as was his custom) that a tip was an insult to the recipient. The driver, who was more than willing to be thus insulted, became insolent. "A vulgar fellow!" said John, turning away.

This was to prove the last of those happy parties with the Mounseys at Haus Hirth. At Whitsun 1929 the Mounseys came to Glyndebourne, and on the Tuesday Johnnie Mounsey went out for a walk alone. He did not return.

A week later his body was found in a wood near Redhill. The verdict was suicide.

A few days later John wrote to his mother:

Johnnie's death is a great tragedy and was quite unexpected. His home life was very happy and he had four charming children. He was very fond of Fanny and she in a queer way of him. I have never known an angry word between them. Johnnie was in practice a Quaker and it was impossible to think ill of him. He always turned the other cheek. I have never met so kind a man and one who was yet sensible. . . . His finances were in excellent order and he was never a wild speculator. . . . He was a cultured man. He could paint respectably. He could write, criticise and analyse music, and he had a good knowledge of literature. He had travelled considerably. He was always kind and always helping others. He had the warmest friends amongst good men and good women.

Fanny and the children have no definite plans at present, but this week they move to London and their belongings will gradually follow. The children and the rest of the Mounsey family have all taken it well. All are kindly and successful Quakers. They like to think of John happily and not with tears. His death seems to have been the result of a brainstorm resulting from the heat which affected him and from hard work in the City. . . .

Christie *v.* Oerton and Nicholson

AUGUSTUS CHRISTIE, after his strokes, had developed a split personality. Outdoors, and especially when at his club in Instow, he was usually amiable and relaxed; indoors he was more often morose and at times even violent. Thus the staff became partisan: the outdoor staff—"my men" as he called them—supported him; the indoor staff—"Ladyship's men"—supported Lady Rosamond. Many of the neighbours too, who saw him at his best, believed that he was being persecuted by his wife, and he was only too ready to enlist their sympathy. He resented his wife's attempts to take control, and would constantly countermand her orders. To try to assert his authority he coined a phrase which was often heard at Tapeley: "Me captain!"

In August 1923, while attending a local race meeting, Augustus suddenly found himself temporarily quite blind and came home very frightened. There was a fresh crisis in the summer of 1924 when he had another and serious stroke. He refused to eat and grew violent, seizing Lady Rosamond's companion by the throat. Dr Toye, the family doctor for more than twenty years, was called in; he declared that Augustus must be certified and sent to a home.

John, informed of this by his mother, decided that he had better keep away. He did not wish to become involved; as he later said, he always tried to avoid "taking sides" in the troubles that arose between his parents. On 12th June he wrote to his mother:

> Personally I think it would be better not to come down. There is nothing that I can do, and if he is to be certified it is inadvisable for me to rush in and get it done. It might appear that I was the active force in getting him certified. I am of

course supporting you, but as I never go to Tapeley I think it unwise to go there just at the moment when he is being certified. Of course it is far the best thing that this should have happened. Life on the old lines was impossible for all concerned. . . . I am of course ready to go to Tapeley at once if wanted. . . .

A magistrate and a second doctor—Dr Eager, a mental specialist from Exeter who had never met Augustus before—were called in; they certified Augustus, who was taken to a home near Bristol. But he could not settle down in his new surroundings, and continued to refuse his food. Lady Rosamond, when she learned that he was about to be forcibly fed, rushed to Bristol and was successful in persuading him to eat. She found him dirty and neglected, and when he implored her not to leave him where he was she obtained permission to take him back to Tapeley. It was a step that later she must often have regretted; by taking it she cancelled the validity of the order of certification. But, as she told Dr Eager, "I've given nearly forty years of my life taking care of him and I want to do so until the end. Then perhaps I've earned a little peace."

To John it seemed, inevitably, that his mother had mismanaged the affair—as indeed she no doubt had. It was all very inconvenient because he happened at that moment to be exceptionally busy with his organ and building works and with social engagements. From London he wrote rather peevishly:

I have had two letters from you but they tell me little of what has happened. I hope you are not sending round to your relations details of the medical home as you describe them to me; I do not think people would care to read them. I think the case has been bungled. If my Father wasn't bad enough to go to a home, why was he sent there? And if he *was* bad enough, why did he go to the wrong home? [And why, he might have added, was he given his freedom again?] I foresee considerable difficulties if my Father's condition improves appreciably. . . .

Whether John went to Tapeley is not known. On her husband's return there, Lady Rosamond successfully applied to the Court in

London, through the family solicitor, to be appointed his Receiver,* thus gaining full control of his affairs. John, when he was told, informed her that this was no job for a woman and that most certainly she would find herself in difficulties before long.

Back at Tapeley, Augustus was soon sufficiently recovered to be able to go about again and to visit his club. He had no recollection of his brief confinement in the asylum, believing that he had been having a holiday in London; however, one of the members disillusioned him, telling him where he had been and who had sent him there.

Augustus was now always accompanied by an attendant (a man named Shaxton) whom Lady Rosamond, on Dr Toye's advice, had engaged lest he should have another attack while he was out. His friends saw little change in him; they were soon saying that Lady Rosamond had had her husband certified, and herself appointed his Receiver, by a trick. They said further that because the attendant followed him at a distance (which had been arranged so as not to embarrass him) he was there as a spy. There was a campaign to get him freed from his wife's control, the ringleader of this being a Colonel Gerald Oerton, solicitor to the estate and a member of the club.

There is no doubt that Augustus now had a number of *idées fixes*—some of long standing, others more recent: his wife and son hated him ("Ladyship and Jack hate me"). His wife had without good reason deprived him of the control of his property. John did not like Tapeley and only cared for Glyndebourne. John would never marry. When he, Augustus, died, Tapeley would be sold, and that it must at all costs be preserved for a descendant of the Clevlands. His neighbours, who never saw him at home, almost without exception thought these views reasonable; very strong support came from those who annually enjoyed his shooting parties. All maintained that although he was inarticulate he was perfectly sane, that his wife was unkind to him and aggravated his condition, and that she ought not to be his Receiver.

---

* A Receiver is appointed by the Chancery Court and has absolute powers to control a person's affairs. A Power of Attorney is given voluntarily, is often more limited in scope, and can be withdrawn at any time.

This was the general opinion, and Colonel Oerton felt so strongly on the matter that he agreed to take action; he appears to have been quite unembarrassed by the fact that he was playing a double game: while still acting for Lady Rosamond in her capacity as Receiver, he was also secretly opposing her in his capacity of her husband's local solicitor. Without informing Lady Rosamond he went to London to see the Master in Lunacy. The opposition also enlisted the support of Colonel Nicholson—a cousin of Augustus, a descendant of the Clevlands and a Member of Parliament. The Master sent down an expert Visitor who heard both sides and reported that Augustus was not fit to manage his affairs. The Court ruled therefore that Lady Rosamond should continue to act as Receiver; the opposition maintained that the Visitor had been tricked.

When the shooting season came round, Augustus wanted to invite his friends as usual; but he was in no condition to organise a party. Lady Rosamond, therefore, at the suggestion of one of the opposition, rashly asked John to come down to run the shoot. This seemed to John an occasion when he might possibly be of some help; he therefore agreed. He arrived on the evening before the shoot and went straight upstairs to see his father. The meeting was disastrous; Augustus flew into a rage, stamping and shouting. John, seeing that there was nothing to be done, left early the next morning, having made what arrangements he could with the keepers.

Lady Rosamond decided after this that the shooting was simply good money wasted on "a lot of mean scoundrels who want good shooting for nothing", and must be given up. This was an unwise move, for the opposition considered it to be yet another instance of her meanness and unkindness; she was depriving her husband of one of his few remaining pleasures. Loudest in the outcry were the keepers who thus lost their jobs.

For Lady Rosamond these were dark days. John was difficult, her husband impossible. She was lonely and miserable. Her neighbours were hostile, showing "such extraordinary feeling" against her (she told Dr Toye) that she did not dare to attend any public function. She adopted "a position of silent and civil aloofness" and was "determined to see it through" ; but she confessed to a friend that she sometimes wished she were dead.

Now came a yet worse blow: she learned, no doubt from Shaxton, that her husband was paying frequent visits to Colonel Oerton's office with a view to making a new will. In due course she discovered that this will, revoking that made in 1901 which left all the Devon property to herself, had been executed, and it was fairly certain that the Tapeley and Saunton estates had now been left away from her and her son, probably to one of the Nicholsons. On 11th February 1925 John wrote to his mother:

> I think there is little doubt that my Father has made a will leaving his property from you and from me, and this will mean expense and publicity or else a compromise with the Nicholsons. Anyhow I think the whole affair will make the prospect of living at Tapeley unattractive. Personally I have always felt that Tapeley—if it ever comes to me—will be in the nature of a windfall. For this reason it is undesirable that you should conduct my Father's financial affairs in such a way as to have a surplus income, or as not to spend more on yourself and the household expenses than you spent before the war. Otherwise I think you will find that the surplus has to be invested or retained on my Father's behalf and that the savings will have been left to the Nicholsons. Besides, it will convey the impression that you are not making my Father as comfortable and as happy as you might make him. . . .

Three days later he added as a postscript to this letter:

> I went to see Rowcliffe* on Thursday. He is of the opinion that the best thing would be for my Father to leave everything away, as in that case the will would probably be torn over; but if he leaves £10,000 to £20,000 to his friends such legacies will probably be allowed. When a lunatic makes a will, it is allowed to stand if it is sensible. . . .

Meanwhile Augustus grew steadily more difficult. He took to spying on his wife through field-glasses whenever she left the

---

* Of the firm of Gregory Rowcliffe & Co, the family solicitor in London. Sir Roger Gregory of the same firm was Lady Rosamond's principal adviser and staunch friend throughout this difficult time.

house. He could not bear people standing behind him, believing that they might "get him by the throat", and in church for this reason insisted on sitting in the very back pew. He threw a pepper-pot at his wife and "howled that horrible word" at her "so that it could be heard half-a-mile away". He called the butler "Rosamond". And as he trampled a plate of scrambled eggs into the dining-room carpet he cried, "Wonder how Ladyship will like *that*!"

In view of all this, it is difficult to avoid feeling sympathy for Lady Rosamond; yet it cannot be denied that by her foolish handling of the situation she greatly aggravated it. Whenever she thwarted Augustus—and she was always thwarting him for what she considered to be his own good—he lost his temper; whenever she tried to trick him—again, of course, for his own good—he discovered the trickery and became angrier than ever. For example, Augustus ordered some wire fencing for one of the farms; Lady Rosamond considered it unnecessarily expensive, countermanded his order and bought an inferior kind. She got a "dummy' cheque-book and encouraged Augustus to write worthless cheques to keep him amused. She had bars put on his bedroom windows. She made him go to bed at 9.30 and secretly locked him in after he had fallen asleep; but he woke up, discovered what she had done and made a fearful scene. Sir Robert Armstrong-Jones, one of several Visitors sent down by the Master in Lunacy, immediately formed the opinion that Lady Rosamond should have humoured her husband and let him have more of his own way.

In August 1926 Augustus had yet another stroke, and at the same time Shaxton gave notice. He had not meant it to be accepted, he was merely angling for more pay; but when he asked to be taken back at his old wages, Lady Rosamond refused. So Shaxton, who had been "one of Ladyship's men", went over to Oerton and the enemy and wrote to Lady Dixon-Hartland, Augustus's sister, a letter which, though it contained an element of truth, was spiteful and intended to create mischief:

Dear Lady Hartland,
. . . I cannot stand the treatment he is receiving at the hands of her Ladyship any longer. In fact he will die of a broken

heart or commit suicide if things go on as they are. He is not allowed to have anyone about him he likes or anything he wants. He is becoming abjectly miserable and he has begged me to try to put him right so I have left him to try to do so. I consider he is now quite all right with an agent to manage his own affairs. He says it nearly breaks his heart to think that when he is dead his dear mother's wishes will not be fulfilled. . . .

His mother's wishes were, of course, that Tapeley should remain in the hands of a Clevland. John was as much a Clevland as anyone, but Augustus was firmly convinced that his son had no interest in or love for Tapeley and would sell it as soon as it became his.

In October (1926) Lady Rosamond secured an Order of the Court preventing Colonel Oerton from having any further dealings with her husband. John generously congratuated her on the way she had played her cards:

> I am so glad about Oerton. You have won handsomely and if you are careful you should have much less trouble in the future. But you must not worry the Master in Lunacy. Don't write to him at all and don't go to see him. I have talked to Rowcliffe about it and I think the Master is bored by your continual letters and requests. Just act as you think fit and say nothing about it. . . .

Freed from the machinations of Colonel Oerton, Augustus grew more tranquil and more reconciled to his disabilities, though his mind steadily deteriorated. With professional help (there was a new attendant, Pilkington) Lady Rosamond nursed and tended him, watching helpless as his reason gradually declined. Often he would cling to her "like a little child", and when he took to his bed he would allow no one but his wife to carry out the most sordid duties of a sick room. Though Augustus had so often behaved intolerably, she had not quite ceased to love him. She had sacrificed her life for him, and he cannot have been wholly unaware of what this had meant to her. For how great this sacrifice had been! Rather than leave her husband, she had been obliged to see her son grow up largely away from her. For nearly fifty years she had endured her husband's jealousies and periodic outbursts of temper.

Perhaps she now found her greatest happiness in her garden, which under her skilful direction had become one of the finest in Devonshire. She loved Tapeley and had done so much to beautify the house which she had always assumed would one day pass to her son; and in time to her son's son—for, unlike Augustus, she still believed that John would one day marry. But now there was every reason to think that Tapeley would be left away from the Christies. What made this the more bitter was the knowledge that, if she had not in her compassion brought Augustus back from Bristol, the second will would in all probability never have been made.

In January 1929 John wrote to his mother: "I am sorry to hear that my Father is failing. I cannot make him understand, and interviews seem only to lead to difficulties. We are now quite good friends, but when we are together we only realise the difficulty of communication." In October he wrote again: "I am sorry my Father has had another stroke and that as a result he may be more or less incapacitated. It is difficult to see how it can make matters easier. He may require much more attention, and inasmuch as he cannot escape he may become much more bored with this attention. The position seems likely to be difficult. I hope it will not worry you." Six months later, on 7th April 1930, Augustus Christie died. He was seventy-three.

John had been right: Augustus had indeed made a second will in 1925 whereby, after revoking the first, and after making a few legacies, he had left the residue of his Tapeley estate and a large sum of money to a younger son of Colonel Nicholson, a second cousin aged twenty-six and a bachelor, whom he had never seen, but who was a descendant of the Clevlands. Colonel Oerton was the only surviving executor of the will, with power to exact full legal charges. It appeared to be perfectly valid.

For Lady Rosamond and John the prospects may well have seemed black. Their only hope was to upset the will on the grounds that at the time it was made the Testator lacked "testamentary capacity". But the will had been signed in the presence of four doctors, and witnessed by two of them, both of whom were members of the Instow Club and knew Augustus well; how possibly in the face of this could they hope to establish that Augustus was not at the time competent to make a will? Lady Rosamond was, however, determined to fight; five days after the death of Augustus a writ was issued on her behalf, challenging the validity of the will.

During the months that followed there was feverish activity on both sides: witnesses were interviewed, statements taken and sworn. The feeling against Lady Rosamond grew stronger than ever, and outside her own house she had few allies in Devon other than the ever-faithful Dr Toye. Sir Roger remained optimistic: as he told Lady Rosamond, the burden of proof rested upon the parties who were propounding the 1925 will. He was preparing for "a big fight" but considered that his forces were well in order and that he was ahead of the other side.

★　★　★

The case came up before the President of the Probate Division of the High Court, Lord Merrivale, in March 1931. It lasted fifteen days, and, because the two leading Counsel employed were the most eminent men of the day in their profession, it caused something of a sensation.

For Lady Rosamond, the Plaintiff, appeared Sir John (afterwards Lord) Simon, K.C., dispassionate and calm and with a great mastery of detail; he subsequently became Lord Chancellor. Sir Patrick Hastings, K.C., appeared for Colonel Oerton. He was then reckoned to be the most eloquent member of the Bar—a witty man, something of an actor and a ruthless cross-examiner; he had been Attorney-General in the first Labour Government. Mr Nicholson was joined as second Defendant, but took no active part in the case.

It is the strange procedure of the Probate Court that cases are opened by the Defence. Sir Patrick, in his opening speech, said that it was one of the most remarkable that had ever come to his knowledge. The deceased was a gentleman known to and beloved by his neighbours in Devonshire, by his tenants and by his servants. Sir Patrick was in a position to call literally scores of them—doctors, solicitors, land-owners, tenants and servants—who would say that, so far as they could see, up to the date of his death the Testator was absolutely sane; his only trouble was that, as the result of a stroke, his speech had become impaired. Furthermore the Defendant, Colonel Oerton, had taken the precaution of having the will signed in the presence of no fewer than four doctors, three of whom knew the testator well, and witnessed by two of them; they had all satisfied themselves that he was perfectly sane and had fully understood the contents before he signed it. Yet here was the Plaintiff, who of course stood to lose much from the will, alleging that the deceased had lacked testamentary capacity. The other person who seemed to think the Testator insane was Dr Toye, who had been prepared to certify this poor old gentleman. For such a person no word that Sir Patrick might use could be too strong.

Sir Patrick did in fact call thirty-two witnesses—a formidable array—to prove his case, and was prepared to call more when Lord Merrivale intervened and said that he had heard enough. They were duly cross-examined by Sir John Simon, and Colonel Oerton in particular was subjected to some stern questioning. In his judgment at the end of the case Lord Merrivale said that, having heard their evidence, he had been satisfied that the Testator had known and approved the contents of the will.

After seven days Sir John made his opening speech and then called Lady Rosamond. It would seem that she had never been able to bring herself to tell John all that she had to endure from her husband during the last years of his life; now John learned of the occasions when Augustus had struck her, and of how she had patiently tried to reason with him:

"You know you were very bad to me yesterday—you gave me a great big bruise."

"Silly—silly"; Augustus had no recollection of it whatever.

Lady Rosamond told the court how her husband had spat at her and used filthy language; how he had torn a door off its hinges and hurled it to the ground; how he had kicked the servants and her companion. She told of his shouting and screaming, of his wandering naked down the corridors, of his obsession that his bedroom was full of sheep, of "wasps all day and mice at night". She told of his pulling up her plants in the garden, of his damaging the furniture, of his attempts to tear the pictures off the walls, of his hurling the breakfast plates on the floor and stamping the food into the carpet.

She was in the witness box for two days and underwent a long and ruthless cross-examination by Sir Patrick—a considerable ordeal for a woman of her age. Sir Patrick trapped her into admitting inaccuracies of detail. He was able to show that for much of what she alleged she could not produce corroborative evidence, and by the time he had finished with her it may well have appeared to those present in court that incidents such as she had described had been only of rare occurrence. He considered her language to have been, in its way, as intemperate as her husband's. She had described Colonel Oerton as "a greedy scoundrel", the tenants at Tapeley as "villains who are after his [Augustus's] money"; she had written to her solicitor to say that a cheque for £40 that she had found "would no doubt explain why Colonel Stafford Harding was anxious to help my husband", and so on. However, Lady Rosamond completely satisfied Lord Merrivale of her integrity, and, as he said in his judgment, he accepted her evidence on all essential points. This was really the turning-point in the case.

Moreover, Lady Rosamond had more than once scored a neat point off Sir Patrick. In one of her letters she had referred to the "vermin" who had poisoned her life in Devon. "Looking round this court," Sir Patrick said, "do you see any of these *vermin* here today?" Lady Rosamond calmly surveyed the scene and then replied, "If the cap fits, Sir Patrick, they may wear it."

There followed evidence from Miss Rhys (Dobbie's successor) and the indoor staff, from Sir Thomas (afterwards Lord) Horder and other doctors including the Court's Visitors, and from John.

John told the Court of the occasion when he had visited Tapeley to run the shoot but had been obliged to leave on the following morning. But he added that during the very last years of his father's life his visits to Tapeley had been satisfactory. His cross-examination provided the only light relief in an otherwise sombre case:

> Sir Patrick: "Do I put it really as you would wish if I say that your relations with your father were not an affectionate relationship in the ordinary sense of a normal affection between father and son?"
>
> John: "I think they were affectionate in the right surroundings; by that I mean over the fireside in the evening. He was a very shy man, which altered our relationship outside." (John then agreed with Counsel that when he came home on leave during the War, his mother had come up to see him, but not his father.)
>
> Sir Patrick: "After you had sold your interest in part of the estate to your father, did you take not much interest in the Devonshire estate at all?"
>
> John: "I have endeavoured to help my mother from time to time, but how could I take any interest? I do not see what interest I could take—I should have been immediately competing with my father."
>
> Sir Patrick: "Had your father any reason to think you were not likely to marry?"
>
> John: "Well, he was wrong if he had."
>
> Sir Patrick: "Did you at any time convey that information or suggestion to him?"
>
> John: "Yes."
>
> Sir Patrick: "What information?"
>
> John: "I conveyed the information that I *was* likely to get married."
>
> Sir Patrick (incredulous): "Likely to?"
>
> John: "Yes."
>
> Sir Patrick: "Will you tell me when?"
>
> John: "When he stayed with me—but it did not come off."
>
> Sir Patrick: "Suppose people were helping him to set aside the receivership of his wife, and he found you were not helping him, do you not think that would make him very angry with you?"

John: "I do not think the thing occurred to his mind at all. I think my father began to realise *because he was told* my mother was managing his affairs, and he would resent that because it would upset his plan of being 'captain'; and if he was told I was not helping to remove my mother from his control, I am sure he would be hostile to me. He was most demonstrably affectionate to me during the last two or three years of his life—quite demonstrably. On the last occasion when he was walking about he smiled and shook hands with me, and as I was going away he took off his hat to me."

(Laughter in Court)

Sir Patrick (ironically): "Is that what you call demonstrably affectionate?"

(more laughter)

An Usher: "Silence in Court!"

John (exasperated): "Well what do you expect, Sir Patrick? Do you expect him to have kissed me?"

Then came the closing speeches. Sir John Simon's, after a discussion of the legal aspects, was for the most part a close analysis of the evidence, but he made two observations of particular interest. He said: "My learned friend, Sir Patrick, was actually instructed to put forward a case—deeply wounding, if it was justified—that Lady Rosamond was guilty of a plot." He also said "This is a terrible example of how local gossip and suspicion may build up a false case that does not bear the slightest glimmering of resemblance to the truth."

Lord Merrivale, in his judgment, described Sir Patrick's closing speech as one of the most powerful addresses he had ever listened to at the Bar. Doubtless it would have made a great impression on a Jury, if the Defence had insisted upon having one; but Lord Merrivale was impervious to it. Lady Rosamond and Dr Toye, he said, had been "doing their best in circumstances of indescribable difficulty, and believed what they have since come here and said". He considered that "the Testator, by reason of the progressive deterioration of the brain, due to arterio-sclerosis, was wholly insane and unaccountable for his actions" when he signed the will. The disease had "deprived him of the means of knowledge, of the scope of knowledge and of the capacity for judgment which were necessary to give him testamentary capacity. With regard to his wife and son, whom the will of 1925 was intended to dispossess, he had an insane delusion that they hated him. . . ." After a long and careful summing up he pronounced: "It is impossible that I should find a verdict in favour of the Defendant: that, to my mind, is wholly out of the question. I pronounce against the alleged will of January 14th, 1925."*

★   ★   ★

"As you will see from the papers and my wire," John wrote to his mother, "we pay our costs. Otho [Nicholson] pays his, and our contribution towards Oerton's costs is limited to £5,000. Rowcliffe thinks Oerton's costs will be about £15,000 and Otho's about £2,500 so that Oerton and Otho will be about £12,500 down. However, Oerton may get all his costs out of Otho and may make a good thing out of it." But in the triumph of having won her suit, Lady Rosamond could afford to overlook the minor irritation of having to bear a part of the costs. Tapeley had been saved; Colonel Oerton had been exposed as the villain of the piece; the opposition party in Devonshire had been trounced. And as though her cup of happiness was not yet full enough, there were now also unmistakable signs that her most cherished desire was about to be fulfilled: John intended to marry.

Not the least important by-product of the case was the change that came about in the relationship between John and his mother. He had suddenly become aware of the full extent of her misery and humiliation over the years; and perhaps he had also come to forget that by her unwise treatment of her husband she had aggravated his condition. His letters to her became more cordial, even affectionate, though he continued to be exasperated by what he considered (and what probably was) her mismanagement of the estate. After Lady Rosamond had had bound for him the four volumes of the verbatim account of the law suit, he wrote to her: "Thank you very much darling Mother not only for binding but

* The medical aspect of the case is discussed in an article in the *Lancet* (4th April 1931).

also for winning our law suit. It was a great success for you in the autumn of your life. I respect you very much for it, and I am grateful."

What John felt—or came to feel—about his mother is perhaps best summed up in a letter that he wrote in 1939, four years after her death, to Mrs Kelham, the housekeeper at Tapeley:

> I was glad to get your second letter and hope that you will help to build up my mother's good name, which is so much honoured by those of us who saw what she was struggling against. Her life was really unendurable and it was only at the very end that the gates of Heaven began to open. The correspondence that was discovered shows the hideous conspiracy that grew like a snowball, actively assisted by those who had axes to grind and guilty consciences. These dragged in many others who did not know. My mother was conscious of all this but came to the conclusion that the only possible course was to ignore it and to keep on the course that she had heroically set herself.
>
> Of course she was difficult, very difficult. She was a mass of nerves. Mentally she was tired out, but she still clung to her purpose. She found so many were foes, that she asked for no friends. It became so bad that she expected all to be foes, unless they had taken steps to show they were friends. She was prepared to fight the battle alone. She was not going to fail in the last round. In the end she won magnificently. I believe she kept me out of it so that I should not incur the odium. I cannot find words to describe the pride I feel that she was my mother and the luck I have had that she did not marry Joe Chamberlain as I have heard was at one time thought possible. . . .

13

Marriage

AFTER THE death of Johnnie Mounsey a great gloom had descended upon Glyndebourne. For many months John could not even bring himself to sleep in the house, and had therefore gone to Childs's cottage in Ringmer. The Organ Room, with its bittersweet memories, stood silent and deserted. Then, to take his mind off things, he went alone to Germany, "sampling opera houses and ready to return at short notice" if business called him. But at last he pulled himself together and went back to Glyndebourne. Little did he then guess the great happiness that was soon to transform his life.

By the autumn of 1930 he was so far recovered as to contemplate a revival of the excerpt from *Die Meistersinger* at Christmas; he therefore wrote to Thornely and Dolly Gibson to ask them if they would be prepared to sing Sachs and Eva again. But the Gibsons replied that they could not leave their family over the Christmas holidays. So John decided to repeat the first Act of *Die Entführung* instead. It was hoped that it might not be impossible to find a singer to replace Thornely Gibson as Osmin, but John was quite at a loss for another Blonde. He implored Mrs Gibson to change her mind, but she was adamant.

Then Johnstone Douglas, co-founder with Amherts Webber of the Webber–Douglas opera school, hearing of John's predicament, recommended an old pupil of his, Audrey Mildmay, who was now a member of the Carl Rosa Opera Company. John wrote to her, and it was agreed that she should sing Blonde for a fee of five guineas, together with free board and lodging at Glyndebourne. A tenor colleague from the Carl Rosa came with

her; but the remainder of the cast was amateur, and the performance, a hilarious affair, had little of the professional about it.
Indeed it would scarcely have deserved mention had it not been
for the fact that within six months Audrey Mildmay had become
Mrs John Christie.

★ ★ ★

Audrey Mildmay had been born at Herstmonceux, not so very
far from Glyndebourne, on 19th December 1900. Her father, the
Rev (later Sir) Aubrey Mildmay (Bt), had emigrated to British
Columbia to accept a living at Penticton, Vancouver. There
Audrey had been brought up; and there she had studied the piano
until a teacher of singing discovered the greater potentialities of
her voice. She gave her first public recital at the age of eighteen,
and six years later came to England to work seriously with
Johnstone Douglas.

Next came a long tour of Canada and the United States as Polly
in *The Beggar's Opera*, after which she returned to England and in
due course joined the Carl Rosa Company at a salary of £2 10s. a
week. With this gallant company, which almost single-handed
had kept the torch of repertory opera burning in England, Audrey
toured the country. In sixteen months she had sung as many
different roles, including Musetta, Gretel, Micaëla, Zerlina, the
Doll in *The Tales of Hoffmann*, Lola in *Cavalleria Rusticana* and
Nedda in *Pagliacci*.

It is alleged that before Audrey left Glyndebourne after singing
in *Die Entführung*, John showed her over the house. Opening the
door of the bedroom called "Broyle" (all the bedrooms at
Glyndebourne have names associated with the Christie family
and estates), he said abruptly: "This is where we will sleep when
we are married." In its context the proposal did not appear to be
one to be taken seriously, and Audrey brushed it aside as a joke;
she was not long in finding out her mistake. Possibly this is a true
story. But one thing is certain: this 47-year-old bachelor had
fallen in love with a girl seventeen years his junior, whom he had
known only for a few weeks at the most.

Back at Dogmersfield, near Basingstoke, where she was living with her uncle, Audrey wrote to John (29th December):

Just a line to say once more how enormously I enjoyed the most amusing Christmas I've ever spent. It was such luck for me that J.D. suggested it and you asked me—I simply loved it. With so very many thanks and also ditto for my most excellent "suit-case" which will last for simply years and will always remind me of Glyndebourne and its charming host. . . .

John replied by return, sending her her fee—or rather double the agreed fee—for singing; the suit-case had presumably been thrown in for good measure:

Dear Audrey,
    I enclose a cheque for ten guineas and after that I don't know how to go on. You are quite delightful and you made Christmas very happy. . . . Audrey, you are delightful and restful together, which is rare. . . .

Perhaps he considered this in the nature of a business letter, for the same day he wrote again in still more affectionate terms:

My darling Audrey,
    What are you doing this week-end? Can you find an excuse for coming back to Glyndebourne . . . ?

However, Audrey could not—or would not—accept the invitation. Charmed though she was by John and his now almost daily letters—"yesterday's I think is one of the very nicest letters I've ever had in my life", she wrote on 6th January—she knew that she needed time for reflection; and she added, "You are such a darling, John, that I don't want you to fall in love with me—please."

But John *had* fallen in love, and he proceeded to storm Audrey as a military commander might storm a fortress. "I have never met anyone like you," he wrote; and again, "you are the most perfect creature". There was a dinner party in London followed by a box at the Strand Theatre, and further invitations to Glyndebourne which Audrey was obliged to refuse because the Carl Rosa Company was just about to go on tour and she was endlessly busy with rehearsals.

Now John began to shower her with gifts—with "scrumtiously soft" Charbonnel chocolates, with a blue travelling rug ("an absolute godsend"), with a hired car—another "godsend"—to take her to the matinée in Dublin. To Sheffield, where in February she was singing in *The Bohemian Girl*, came pheasants from Fortnum's, flowers constantly, a watch, a game pie and innumerable letters. On 11th February he wrote to her:

> Darling, I love you terrifically. . . . I dare say you won't marry me! But building castles in the air I should like to marry you as early as you like! Why not get married at Bonn, fly there in the morning, i.e. to Köln, tram to Bonn, marry, stay there for a day or so on the banks of the Rhine and drift about in Germany? It would be like a honeymoon first, i.e. flying off together before marriage, and we should be free of all fuss. Should I have to be inspected by your mother first, or could I be taken on recommendation? Darling, I am not trying to rush you. . . .

But Audrey knew that she *was* being rushed; she wanted to be sure. Was it really love that John felt, or was it an infatuation that would pass? As for John, he had no doubt whatever: he saw now that his abortive little love affair in Scotland had been nothing; he knew that for the first time in his life he was *really* in love. A middle-aged bachelor in love for the first time? It was extraordinary, but it was true. He hastened to Revillon's, chose some magnificent furs, and had them despatched immediately to Sheffield. The box was delivered at the theatre where Audrey, imagining that it contained flowers, unluckily allowed it to be publicly unpacked and so revealed to the whole cast "a fur coat and fox fur?!!!!!!":

> My name is MUD [she wrote]. You say you don't want to compromise me—and I *am* compromised! Darling John, it's simply too sweet and generous of you and, much as I would like to accept, it *is* against the rules. If I had made up my mind, John, that I would marry you, it would be different, I suppose— but please, my dear, do realise that I can't really accept such a large present from you under the present conditions. I am very

fond of you and love your unprecedented generosity, but I am so afraid of letting you sweep me off my feet, before I've made up my mind. There are so many unhappy marriages all around one, John—and there are so many years after the delicious honeymoon you outline!! And I still feel you have no idea how much I want to do with my job. . . .

John fought hard to make Audrey keep the furs. Finally a compromise was reached: she agreed to accept the little fox fur and return the fur coat. But from Sheffield there soon came bad news: the tour was being a financial failure. For the last two weeks the cast had been on half salaries, and on 15th February, though there were bookings in the provinces for nine more weeks, they were given a fortnight's notice. John hurried to Sheffield to the rescue, and to attempt, though without any success, to be allowed to pay a cheque into her account; she did, however, agree that if she were ever in real difficulties she would ask him for a temporary loan.

From Sheffield the Company went briefly to Northampton, where *Die Götterdämmerung*, of which John had attended an indifferent rehearsal in Sheffield, was successfully performed; then, abandoning the rest of the provincial tour, it returned to London for a short season at the Lyceum. There Audrey sang Nedda in *Pagliacci* and Micaëla in *Carmen*, and during March was also twice to be seen with John in court, where Lady Rosamond's law suit had just begun. After the closing of the Lyceum season Audrey resumed her operatic coaching with Mrs Violet Bridgewater, and John immediately conceived the idea of also taking lessons from Mrs Bridgewater.

It was probably some time early in April that Audrey finally capitulated and agreed to marry John, for we know that the date of the wedding remained for a while in doubt because of the illness of her uncle, with whom she had been living. Towards the end of April her uncle died, and June was proposed; but Audrey at first wanted to wait until August in order to be "quite sure". Finally, however, 4th June was agreed upon—an appropriate day for an Old Etonian. Audrey also hoped that this would help John to remember the anniversary of their wedding; but in the event,

9 John Christie as
Beckmesser, 1928

10   Audrey Mildmay about the time of her marriage

though he was never to forget to associate June the Fourth with Eton, he always forgot its connection with his marriage.

That spring John took Audrey three times to hear *Der Rosenkavalier* at Covent Garden: on 27th April, 1st May and 7th May. It was at one of these performances that, at that magical moment when Oktavian hands Sophie the silver rose, John took Audrey's hand and into it pressed a beautiful antique diamond brooch, in the shape of a rose, as a pledge of his affection.*

Probably John and Audrey had for a time kept the secret of their engagement to themselves, and possibly Georgina and Childs were the first to be told of it. Audrey was staying at Glyndebourne when John plucked up the courage to break the news to Childs. It took Childs a moment to recover from the shock; then, turning to Audrey, he said: "Well, Miss Mildmay, if you're as happy as I am after twenty-three years with the Captain, you won't have much to grumble at." But it was some time before he finally succumbed—as did all who came to know her—to Audrey's charm. Lady Chichester was one of the first of John's friends to be let into the secret; "I am engaged", he informed her, "to a *moderate* soprano."

The wedding took place at Queen Camel, a village in Somerset with which the Mildmay family had been associated for many generations. Childs was best man, the obedience clause was omitted and wedding presents had been forbidden by John. To a cousin who was not able to be present, Lady Rosamond wrote: "I shall never forget the look of brilliant happiness of Jack and Audrey as they left the church." After Childs had proposed the health of the bride and bridegroom, Audrey asked him, "How could you allow John to get married?" Childs replied, "I had to get one back on him, Madam."

★   ★   ★

It was of course obvious that the honeymoon would be spent

* A number of stories associated with John's engagement, some untrue and others inaccurate, are in wide circulation, and I have tried to sift fact from fiction. It always amused John to perpetuate, and perhaps even to invent, Glyndebourne myths.

in Germany, and that its principal ingredient would be opera; in the event, they were to spend quite a large part of it in hospital, and Audrey was later to say that it might better have been described as a "funnymoon". For she had not been well when she left England. Not at all well: she was suffering from tonsillitis, rheumatism, anaemia, a hammer-toe and what she believed to be colitis (though John first diagnosed over-eating); but she put a brave face on it and was determined not to let her troubles spoil John's pleasure at Haus Hirth and in the operas in Munich. John wrote on 19th June from Haus Hirth:

> We have heard the first three of the *Ring, Schwanda der Dudelsackpfeiffer, Fidelio* and the first performance of Mozart's *Idomeneo* in München since 1780.* It was an early Mozart, some good arias and good spectacles but not interesting. On Wednesday we return to hear *Meistersinger* and on Thursday we fly to Dresden for the last week of their opera season. Thence to Berlin for a few days opera and then home.
>
> Audrey has been rather ill with colitis and I hope to arrange for her to see Johanna's† doctor. . . .

Two days later Audrey told Lady Rosamond:

> I do feel very ashamed of not having written sooner—but John has provided such endless amusements that there has never been a moment for letter-writing. . . . Germany, as displayed by John, is absolutely delightful—I simply love it—despite the fact that I started by disgracing myself and being ill! Poor John —it was too maddening for him! On the other hand it gave him a chance to show what a super-nurse he is.
>
> We had an orgy of opera in Munich, which I simply adored, and came on here last Thursday. The Hirths talk of you constantly and are very anxious that you should come here in August—you must! It is a delicious place. . . .

But Audrey was more ill than either of them realised. On 5th July John reported to his mother:

> We saw Lampé, Johanna's doctor, who made a most thorough

---

* *Idomeneo* was written in 1781 and first performed in Munich in the same year.
† Frau Hirth.

examination of Audrey. . . . He had no doubt about appendicitis. There is also tonsil trouble. . . . Audrey came in the same evening (last Thursday week) to the clinic, and they operated on Saturday evening. She had a bad night and an uncomfortable Sunday. On Monday she stood up—the object apparently being to prevent congestion of the lungs which often accompanies this operation. Since then she has been getting better and better and is now lying on a sofa. I expect she will be here for another fortnight. . . . A tonsil specialist sees her next week. . . .

We should be glad if you would come out here next week . . . and please bring Miss Rhys. In any case I intended to persuade you to come out; you cannot expect many more years when you will feel inclined to come out, and in this year Audrey is an additional excuse.

Lady Rosamond and Miss Rhys did not, however, go to Munich. Audrey recovered—but very slowly—from her operation, and when she was well enough Lampé provided the right doctors to drain her tonsils and deal with her other troubles. John, having had occasion to observe Lampé's methods, seized the occasion to deliver a little homily to his mother on the theme of organisation:

Lampé, who took out our appendices, is a marvellous doctor. He is the authority and the specialists work under him. . . . It would seem that our affairs are being conducted by Lampé in the same way as I conduct my own business affairs. Edwards and I are central control, and we employ the best experts as consultants and for executive work, but always under continuous control. . . .

John wrote, "*our* appendices". For his turn had now come to join Audrey in the clinic:

My own case is very simple. I started a thinning cure and a *Box-Sportmann* was hired to give me *Bewegungen und Massage*. This he did with terrific energy which revealed a tender appendix. I then joined Audrey in the clinic for examination and consultation. An operation was not necessary,* but I took Lampé's advice. I was operated on at 8.30 in the morning. The

* He is reported to have said, "I really had my appendix out to keep Audrey company."

operation was over at 9.30 and I became conscious at 11, talking German and saying "Ich lebe noch"* and singing *Parsifal*.

I was quite well the rest of the day but I had a dreadful night —no pain but awful discomfort on a *Gummituch* [rubber sheet] and with a perfectly idiotic nurse. . . . She took away everything I wanted, kept doing everything I did not want, and finally in the morning when she proposed to wash my hands and face (which I had been washing all night with ice-water) dropped a full-sized basin full of water and weighing about thirty pounds on my wound. I cursed her head off, but otherwise no harm done. . . . I hope and expect to go to the Opera next Wednesday—the $7\frac{1}{2}$th day. . . .

John made a speedy recovery and they were both able to hear further operas in Munich before flying back to England on 4th August.

★   ★   ★

While John was still in the clinic he had written twice to his mother at great length on the subject of the Devonshire estate. He was "very upset" by her letters to him. "Do not think me undutiful if I express myself strongly. . . . Audrey is as indignant as I am. . . ." And so on.

John's views on the matter are made clear in a letter that he had written to his mother earlier in the year. The Devonshire estate, he said, had been mismanaged by his father for years, and even after she had gained nominal control of it her hands had been tied by Augustus's behaviour and the interference of neighbours. He urged an immediate investigation by his accountants, Gardiner, Hunter & Co., and in particular an enquiry into the work done by Bowden, the estate agent; he had no confidence in Bowden.

This "cleansing of the Augean stables" would not be a "pleasant or ladylike" job, he told her; he would therefore be willing to incur the inevitable odium himself. He would suggest that she

---

* Perhaps John was thinking of "So leb' ich noch!", the opening words of Nureddin's aria in Cornelius's *Der Barbier von Bagdad*. The Munich production of it at that time, with Bender and Patzak, was memorable. (The opera would, incidentally, be an excellent one for Glyndebourne.) There is a somewhat similar ejaculation in Strauss's *Ariadne auf Naxos*.

authorised him to act for her, and that in due course a business board should be constituted with himself, his mother and Edwards as Directors, and Gardiner, Hunter & Co as accountants. "In making these suggestions I am not in any way endeavouring to remove from you the control of the Estate. . . . My only object is to help if I can."

Such were his views, but it seems that he simply could not get his mother to act. Whether she really objected to his proposals, or whether she was merely dilatory, it is impossible, in the absence of her side of the correspondence, to tell with any certainty; but it is clear that he could not shake her faith in Bowden.

There is little doubt that John was unjust to Bowden. Acting upon Bowden's advice soon after his appointment, Lady Rosamond had agreed to the development of the two Devon estates. After a survey had been made, a new golf club house was built at Saunton in 1929, alterations made to the links, and certain building sites sold. The rebuilding of the Saunton Sands Hotel had also come under consideration, and Bowden, rightly as it was subsequently shown, had recommended that it should not be made to contain more than fifty bedrooms.* Bowden very properly claimed that all this work was outside his normal duties as agent and deserved separate payment; after the death of Augustus he therefore sent in an account for an additional £2,000, covering his special services over a period of five years. John considered the sum excessive (which possibly it was), and that in any case the bill should have been submitted earlier, when it could have been checked in detail.

Lady Rosamond, very conscious of Bowden's loyalty to her and of the great help he had been during difficult days, was greatly distressed by John's hostility towards him. Bowden fought hard and was eventually paid in full; but in 1932 he had to go, and the

* It was in fact rebuilt in 1934 by the Ringmer Building Works in a "modernistic" style based on a hotel John had once stayed in on the Rhine. White, ugly and too large, it came in for a good deal of criticism locally; but most of the hundred and more bedrooms command a superb view of the bay. John used to say that at one time the Saunton Sands Hotel was making a profit of £25,000 a year; in fact it usually made a heavy annual loss, and was finally sold in 1964. A second golf course was added in 1937; but this was wrecked by the Army during the War and has not been reinstated.

management of the estate was then taken over by Lady Rosamond, who turned it into a trust with Sir Roger Gregory and
John acting jointly with her as trustees.

Meanwhile, as the months of 1931 passed in what to John
seemed futile inaction, his irritation grew. He could never for a
moment—not even on his honeymoon—put Tapeley out of his
mind. In the end Audrey, who had tried hard not to become involved, could bear it no longer. On 30th July she wrote to Lady
Rosamond from Munich, loyally supporting her husband:

> My dear "New Mamma",
>   I want very much to keep clear of discussions over Tapeley,
> as I said at Queen Camel, otherwise it will be so difficult for all
> three of us; but this once I'm going to break the rule because I
> don't think you or anyone can realise how the present situa-
> tion is upsetting John. During the whole of our honeymoon he
> has been obsessed with Tapeley and ideas of what is best for the
> future of the estate. What really prompts me to write is John's
> remark this morning that "Tapeley brings nothing but unhappi-
> ness and it would be far better to get rid of it." I feel sure that
> this is wrong and that you would hate Tapeley to be sold; and
> I feel that unless John is allowed to take an interest in the affairs
> of Tapeley *now*, in the future he never will. He is so tremen-
> dously keen to do now what he feels is best for the present and
> the future with the co-operation of the other Trustees, and I
> suppose it is only natural that he feels hurt that . . . you pin your
> faith on Bowden, who at every turn John, with keen insight,
> has shown to have acted stupidly.
>   Please, my dear "N.M." don't misunderstand my writing all
> this. I am naturally deeply interested in Tapeley (one can't come
> into contact with John's hot enthusiasm and not be infected).
> This is my excuse. . . .

No doubt the matter was important, but the details of the dispute make tedious reading today. It poisoned the lives of all involved in it. In October, after John and Audrey had returned to
England, things had reached such a pitch that John could write to
his mother:

> Damn Tapeley and all its affairs! Audrey and I both hate the

name. She has had nothing else from the date before we married. She cannot understand why you should fight me over the investigation and over the local office. . . . I would not agree to Audrey coming to Tapeley. The futility of this opposition to my demands has made me so irritable and unhappy and is affecting Audrey. I go to bed irritated; I wake up irritated. I curse Tapeley. I may go abroad alone. I don't think it is fair on Audrey that my mind should become obsessed by this Tapeley folly to the exclusion of all else. . . .

John's hatred of Tapeley was no doubt in part due to an attitude that he had forced himself to adopt when it looked as though it might never become his.

★   ★   ★

It has been said that when John presented Audrey with her diamond brooch at Covent Garden he also promised to build her an opera house at Glyndebourne. No doubt, ever since the day of his engagement, he had foreseen Glyndebourne as a setting for further operatic performances in which Audrey would play a prominent part, but it was not until his return from his honeymoon that the decision was taken to build a small theatre. He immediately rang up Edwards: "We are going on with Opera, Edwards. I wanted you to know. . . . This is the thing which I shall do. . . ." Edwards remembered that John had said to him at the time of his appointment, eleven years earlier: "I don't know *what* I am going to do, but I shall find out." Now the long quest was over.

The first project, which began to take shape in the autumn of 1931, was on a very modest scale: a small theatre to seat about 150 people; presumably John was not yet thinking in terms of fully professional performances with paying audiences. Plans were drawn up and a site cleared.

To Audrey it gradually became apparent that this compromise theatre was a mistake. It was too much for amateur productions; it was too little for the real thing. One evening at dinner, when the stage-designer Hamish Wilson was a house guest and the conversation had—inevitably—turned to the new theatre, Audrey said suddenly: "If you're going to spend all that money, John, for

God's sake do the thing properly!" At that moment the Glynde-bourne Festival Opera, as we know it today, was conceived. No longer was it to be a small and semi-amateur affair; it was to be an English Bayreuth (as some said) or an English Salzburg where pro-fessional performances of the highest quality would be given. The trenches were filled in and, as John was later to say, "in haste rather than in knowledge" a new building, to hold 311 people, was designed and begun almost at once on a new site.

John later explained the particular reason for this haste: "One Saturday afternoon I switched on the wireless and heard that we'd been knocked off the Gold Standard by the Labour Government. We must be quick then—we must build our opera house at once, or we shan't have any pounds left. So we started in a great hurry...." He is not quite accurate here; it was the recently formed National Government, not the Labour Government, which took this drastic step.

The new theatre occupied much of John's attention during the opening months of 1932. Though Hamish Wilson and Bear Warre were at hand with advice and rough sketches, John was largely his own architect; this was a considerable task for one who had had no professional training, and his design was surprisingly successful. For building materials he made use of what in Sussex is known as "plum pudding"—a combination of sandstone (taken from a house that was being demolished by the Ringmer Building Works) and brick. He knew what he wanted, though he could not always know how it could best be carried out; to the builders, therefore, he would pose the problem and leave them to find the solution.

John spent many happy hours on the building site. He was incessantly to be seen swarming up ladders or tiptoeing along perilous girders, often dragging some reluctant, dizzy visitor by the hand and assuring him that there was no danger. By January the stage was already "rising quickly". In March the tilers arrived and the concrete floor was laid. There still remained the installa-tion of the electric light and the heating, and the apparatus for the stage. "I am pleased with the general appearance and lay-out," he told his mother. "It may be advertised with me as architect! It would be funny if as a result I were asked to architect something else!"

* * *

In June John's beloved pug, George, died. He told his mother:

George died on Tuesday about teatime. He was in the middle of a bad turn of ulcers and had become very weak. He tottered occasionally and fell. I took him out about a quarter to seven in the morning and then left him to sleep in his portmanteau next the radiator in our bathroom. He took it into his head to go downstairs and it seems that his fronters [i.e. front paws] must have stumbled and he slid from top to bottom, and broke his jaw. All day he was dazed and weak but in no pain at all. His jaw did not hurt him nor was it sensitive. At 4.30 he was given a dose of stimulant by the vet; he obviously could not face an operation. Half an hour later he was given chloroform by me and slept away peacefully.

We buried him—Audrey, Childs and I—next night by moonlight in the head of the ravine in the downs, with his nose towards Glyndebourne, in an oak coffin we had lined, his body in a pillowcase and his blanket and flowers. He will have a flat tombstone 5′ × 3′ with moulded edge, mounted on a plinth and inscribed: "George the Pug of Glyndebourne, b.—, d. 6 vi. 32." There is no reason why the ground should ever be disturbed. The tomb will be surrounded by iron railings. . . .

* * *

Audrey had been having recurring trouble with her tonsils and in April (1932), on the unanimous advice of five doctors, she and John went to Tapeley where, but for an altercation with his mother on the subject of wine, the visit passed off well. At the end of June, after her tonsils had been removed, she went alone to the Adriatic to complete her recuperation, visiting Venice with whose "domes and spires [sic]" she fell deeply in love. Then in August John met her in Munich for the usual round of opera.

Among these was one that John had not heard before: Pfitzner's *Das Herz*. He thought the Munich production unimaginative, but that the opera lent itself wonderfully to dramatic stage effects. "I have worked out a marvellous *Inszenierung* for *Das Herz* at Glyndebourne," he told his mother, "but we will examine the music in Wien. It is full of magic, a demon, bloody hearts floating about, steam, astral bodies, and the earth opening." He added: "Audrey says repeatedly that she is desperately happy. We are having a good holiday and are learning some German. But Audrey must be alone to get started again at her work." For it had always been understood that marriage was not to be allowed to interfere with Audrey's career as a singer.

From Munich they drove to Salzburg and on to Vienna; then John returned to England, leaving Audrey to carry on with her studies until December. Before leaving Vienna he wrote to his mother:

> There is not much news. I don't like Wien but the opera is superb. Audrey was in tears at the end of the first act of *Walküre*. We had never in England or in Germany heard such an orchestra. We have learned a good deal for use at Glyndebourne and perhaps elsewhere. I plan scenery for all the operas [illegible] to be used at Glyndebourne and so in this way learn what stock to have which can be adapted in general use. When I return I shall at once get the lighting and the mechanism finished off. I have a better idea now of what is wanted. . . . Their permanent opera orchestra is a hundred and twenty-five. Strauss's *Ariadne auf Naxos* was suitable for Glyndebourne.* It had only sixteen strings, two harps, harmonium, piano, tympani, cymbals and wind. It has a very good part for Audrey and we could easily get the rest of the cast, but it is probably difficult to make it come off. . . .

John disliked Vienna for being "noisy and expensive"; but after he had left, Audrey discovered a pension where she could live more cheaply. She hoped to improve her German during meals; she soon found, however, that—as so often happens in continental pensions—everyone preferred to talk English. She worked hard at her singing, and though she often felt lonely and missed John very much, she had to admit that she could do "ten times as much

---

* Both versions of the opera have been given at Glyndebourne since the War (first version, 1950 and later; second version, 1953 and later).

work" in his absence. She studied Lieder and several new operatic roles, first with Lierhammer and then with a young Hungarian, Janos ("Jani") Strasser.

At first a steady stream of deeply affectionate letters flowed between Glyndebourne and Vienna. Again and again he told her how much he loved her, how much he missed her; but how he wanted her to be a great singer and that nothing must be allowed to stand in the way of her career. He also described in every detail the progress of the Opera House. She was told about switchboard controls and multiple pulleys; about steam boilers, cycloramas and air-conditioning plants. She learned the very hour when the understage lavatory basins were fitted. Then—for he was terribly busy—the daily letters became twice weekly, soon once a week, and finally, at the beginning of November, the time came when she had waited in vain for news for more than a fortnight. He was, of course, deeply penitent when she reproached him:

> I am sorry. I have just telephoned to you the second time. I understand. I have been very stupid not writing. I didn't think of your looking for my letters when I was telephoning to you. I fully understand how disappointing to you it has been and I am very very sorry. I realise now that it must make you unhappy and upset your work. I hadn't thought of that. . . .

Indeed, he wanted to leave for Vienna at once, but she begged him not to; she simply had to get on with her work and she could not risk distraction. At last mid-December came, and John went out, as agreed, to join her and bring her home for Christmas. He arrived tired, cold and with a touch of lumbago; but all this was forgotten in the happiness of their reunion.

John was soon to be found attending one of Audrey's lessons. Strasser recalls the arrival of a burly figure whose startling tweed suit, overcoat and cap, and stout country walking-stick caused something of a stir. There was talk of what operas might be suitable for the small Glyndebourne stage. Audrey had already been studying Susanna and it was now agreed that she should also re-study the part of Zerlina in *Don Giovanni*, which she had sung (in English) when she was with the Carl Rosa.

Impulsive always, John tried, on their very last evening in Vienna, to carry Strasser back with him to England. He was amazed when Strasser announced that it was impossible for him to uproot himself at a few hours' notice. It was agreed, however, that he should come later; but when January had passed in silence, Strasser presumed that the project had been abandoned. Then, in February, Strasser heard John's voice on the telephone: What had happened? Why had he never come? They had been expecting him for weeks. This time Jani Strasser and his wife Irene did agree to come to Glyndebourne, where they were to remain for five months. So began Strasser's invaluable association with Glyndebourne—an association which continues to this day.

*   *   *

Meanwhile Lady Rosamond had arrived at Glyndebourne to spend Christmas with John and Audrey. Audrey had soon established excellent relations with her; and this, incidentally, had been a great help towards John's reconciliation with his mother. The two women had corresponded at length about their gardens, and there was a constant exchange of plants and cuttings. Once, it is true, Lady Rosamond had written sharply about Audrey's extravagance over dahlias; but the matter was soon cleared up: Lady Rosamund had understood "pounds" where "shillings" had been intended. John and his mother, too, were now completely reconciled. A year or two earlier he could never have written, "Best love, my darling Mother. Take things easily."

In February (1933) Audrey was singing at Glyndebourne in a concert with Arnold Goldsbrough, and also Micaëla and Musetta in performances of *Carmen* and *La Bohème* at Brighton. On the 23rd she wrote to Lady Rosamond: "I don't want to raise your— or my—hopes too soon, but I think that next autumn you may have a grandchild." The news was also reported in due course to Lady Rosamond by the faithful Georgina:

My Lady,
    I am writing to tell you the exciting news only I knows it as it is not to be public just yet a baby is expected so Glyndebourne

will be quite complete then and I shall die happy as it is always what I have wanted to see and I pray I shall do my duty for the fourth generation of the family and so pleased I am to say Mrs Christie is so well and happy and the Captain and her takes there daily walks so happy together Im sure my Lady will be delighted and she sang lovely at the concert. I am enclosing to you the account of it, the opera house is still improving looks more like a finishing touch to it now, and the garden is looking so nice and tidy and when we are extra busy we have Mrs Canning to help the cook it all answers very nicely we have had such a lot of rain here and so cold all the bulbs are coming out so it looks like spring time trusting My Lady and all are quite well as it leaves us at Glyndebourne

I am my Lady
yours faithfully
Georgina Daniels

Lady Rosamond was of course delighted. After her long and tragic life, happiness had indeed come to her in her old age. She had won the affection of her son; she had a daughter-in-law to whom she was devoted and who returned her affection; and now she was about to become a grandmother. She wrote at once to Audrey that the news "took her breath away with pleasure", offered a heap of advice on suitable employments for a prospective mother, and concluded with an enquiry as to whether steel or concrete ventilators were better for greenhouses.

It was no doubt to celebrate the good news that John now made his wife a very handsome present. He wrote to his mother on 15th May:

I bought the Empress Josephine's diamonds last week for £910 at Sotheby's, having valued them myself at £900. Tiara, necklace and brooch; moderate-sized stones but beautiful settings. They haven't yet been stolen; perhaps they won't. I left them on my seat in the railway carriage when I went to get a paper and they were still there when I came back.* Audrey is pleased with them and I think you will like them. The tiara makes a number of ornaments. It is exactly the right shape for

---

* John always stoutly maintained that if one left something valuable done up in brown paper in a railway carriage, nobody would think it worth stealing.

Audrey, but she must become a famous singer before she wears it. . . .

Audrey, in her turn, wrote ecstatically to her mother-in-law about the "tiarra (is that how it's spelled?) necklace and broach"; beyond all doubt the marriage was being a success. On 19th October the child was born and named Rosamond after its grandmother. Six months later Lady Rosamond was to be found tending it at Tapeley, witnessing its "joyful bath" and joining the whole household in adoration.

★   ★   ★

John also kept his mother informed—as he had previously kept Audrey informed—of every detail of the progress of the Opera House, and also of a "musical summer school" that he and Audrey held at Glyndebourne in July. In the Opera House nothing was too insignificant for his personal supervision, nothing too trivial to be reported to Tapeley. He assumes that she will be interested to learn that the auditorium will be lit by sixteen side-brackets each consisting of three iron rods of $\frac{1}{2}$ inch iron tapped at one end to screw into castings (whose shape he draws) holding wax candles bored to take electric light wiring. This wiring, he explains, will be attached to the outside of the iron, but will pass through the wax of the candle. Then an egg of iron will be heated and beaten out flat, and the three iron arms will be welded on to the irregular disk so formed. Another drawing follows, then an exact calculation of the cost per hour of lighting the auditorium. Presumably these written descriptions helped him to clear his own mind, therefore when Audrey was with him he used his mother as a clearing-house for his thoughts.

It is not possible to determine at exactly what moment John decided that his Opera House would be ready to open in the early summer of 1934. In May 1933 he was talking of inviting "Sir Thomas Beecham and his orchestra to undertake four performances at our opening next year. The orchestra would, I suppose, be about seventy." John optimistically believed that his orchestra pit was capable of accommodating a hundred players; he had no idea of the room many instrumentalists need, and it is doubtful whether an orchestra of seventy could ever have been squeezed in. In fact he still thought that, if necessary, perfectly adequate performances could be given with an organ supported by a handful of string-players. In the event, it was a 33-piece orchestra which played during the first Glyndebourne season.

Meanwhile, all through 1933 work continued on the fabric and its equipment. In May John bought a second-hand "cloud apparatus", sensationally reduced from £700 to £95, and ordered the seats for the auditorium. Soon a barn was built to serve as a restaurant, and negotiations begun with the Southern Railway about the running of an "Opera Special" from Victoria to Lewes. At the same time the stage manager was working on model sets for *Don Giovanni*, *Die Walküre* and *Die Meistersinger*; the first-named opera was not in fact put on at Glyndebourne until 1936, the others of course never.

The stage manager mentioned by John was Hamish Wilson, who had been designing sets and costumes, first for the British National Opera Company and subsequently for the Carl Rosa. It was through Audrey that he came to Glyndebourne, where his wide experience of the theatre was invaluable at this critical stage. In particular he advised upon lighting, which John was determined to make the most up-to-date in Europe. With his passion for detail and for gadgets of all kinds John soon mastered the problem and the way in which it could be solved. This involved purchases from Vienna and the manufacture, in his own workshops, of such equipment as was not available on the market.

By the end of 1933, though much still remained to be done to it internally, the Opera House stood splendid and four-square, dominating though not unconsonant with the Manor. John looked at it and saw that it was good. He was never to doubt its perfection: one spring morning, nearly thirty years later and not long before his death, as he walked with Edwards across the meadow from the walnut tree to the Opera House, he stopped and after a moment's silence said, "It is the most beautiful building in the world".

14

The First Season*

FANNY MOUNSEY had widened John's musical horizon, and in particular had made a Mozartian of him; but he still clung resolutely to the weighty Teutonic operas of Wagner. Bavaria, rather than Austria, remained his spiritual home, and he raised no objection when people spoke of Glyndebourne as designed to become "the English Bayreuth". The summer of 1933 saw the apogee of his Bavarian phase, when every visitor to Glyndebourne was expected to wear *lederhosen* or *dirndl*.

Though the musical world and John's immediate neighbours in Sussex had long been watching with interest and amused curiosity the progress of the Opera House, the general public was first made aware of the venture by a note in the London *Evening News* on 29th June 1933. Its readers were informed that a "beautiful miniature opera house", designed to be the "permanent home of international opera in England", would open its doors the following year, either with *Don Giovanni* or *Die Walküre*. Captain Christie, they were told, intended also to produce *The Ring* and *Parsifal*, probably at Easter.

John provided the reporter of the *Evening News* with further information. "We have asked Sir Thomas Beecham and his orchestra to come down here but that is not settled yet. We shall secure the services of two [*sic*] first-class singers from this country and from the Continent. My wife will take part." He told of the

---

* As I have stated in the Preface, for my account of Opera at Glyndebourne I am deeply indebted to Mr Spike Hughes's *Glyndebourne*. I shall describe the first phase in some detail, the later seasons only very summarily.

11 Audrey Christie at
Glyndebourne in the thirties

11 Audrey Mildmay as Zerlina

12 John Christie by
Kenneth Green, 1937

12 Childs by Kenneth Green,
1937

splendours of his system of stage lighting, and added that it was intended to give English composers "every chance".

The public was entertained by what it read, but it had faint confidence in the success of this quaint experiment. It mistrusted an artistic venture run by a rich man—and apparently a military man at that—to put his wife on the road to stardom. It very properly wondered how *The Ring*, with the vast orchestra that it demanded, could conceivably be given in a "miniature" opera house. As for English composers, it did not want to give them any further encouragement whatever. Had it known that Sir Thomas Beecham had not even troubled to answer John's letters it would have been even more sceptical.

The public also began to wonder whether it really wanted more performances of *The Ring*, even if it were possible to stage them. Not only did Covent Garden provide as much Wagner as was needed, but also, as the Nazi menace became each day more apparent, there was a swing towards things Austrian. When, in October, the *Daily Express* decided to revive the subject of Glyndebourne, emphasis was laid upon John's hope of getting the Vienna Opera Orchestra to his new Opera House. It was now announced that the season would open the following June with *Don Giovanni*; nothing was said about *Die Walküre*.

In November John wrote an article for the *Monthly Musical Record*. In it he stressed the efficiency of his stage equipment, the excellence of German and Austrian singers, and the beauty of the setting of Glyndebourne. Part of the public, he said, despised opera because it was only familiar with second-rate productions in this country; "the enthusiast, owing to the low English standard, goes abroad". He proceeded to announce his policy.

There were, he said, two possible alternatives. On the one hand Glyndebourne might provide "superb performances" which the public would treat with the respect they deserved and not attempt to "sandwich between business interviews and a society party"— a difficult feat in any case, Glyndebourne being so remote. Or it might provide educational performances at an ordinary level of competence.

He inclined towards the former, with "a marvellous holiday

12

'Festspiel' atmosphere" and no expense spared. For music-lovers who could not afford what would inevitably have to be high-priced seats, there might be a later and simpler season. There would also be Shakespeare festivals and concerts. He added, "At all performances the feeling of general happiness and benevolence should be conspicuous. The scenery and lighting, being designed anew for every opera, should be superb. There are no vested interests, no traditions in the way."

The *Daily Telegraph*, a few days after the publication of John's article, sent its new musical editor, Richard Capell, to interview John. In a long feature article reference was again made to *Die Walküre* joining *Don Giovanni* in the first season. Capell concluded: "The Glyndebourne Theatre will be inaugurated early in the New Year by a private performance of the third act of *Die Walküre* for Mr Christie's friends and tenants." This performance was never to take place. The following January, with less than five months to go before the opening night of the season, something occurred which was to give a new look to, and a new hope for, the whole policy of opera at Glyndebourne. This was the arrival on the scene of Herr Fritz Busch.

Fritz Busch, formerly *Generalmusikdirektor* of the Dresden Opera House, was at this time barely even a name in England where, if he was mentioned at all, it was merely as the elder brother of the famous violinist Adolf Busch. Though not a Jew, he had come to find Nazi interference in his work increasingly intolerable; in May 1933, therefore, he had left Dresden for good and was now dividing his time between Copenhagen and Buenos Aires.

The merest chance was to bring Fritz Busch to Glyndebourne. In November 1933 Adolf Busch had been giving an afternoon recital in Eastbourne. He and Frances Dakyns, the devoted and energetic factotum of the Busch String Quartet, had intended to drive back to London after the concert; but the evening turned foggy and they gladly accepted the offer, made through a mutual friend, of hospitality for the night. After dinner their hostess, Mrs Rosamond Stutchbury, mentioned Glyndebourne and the projected performance of *Don Giovanni*, adding that John had as yet not even found a conductor. Adolf Busch immediately thought of his brother, and Frances Dakyns leapt at the idea. Next morning, therefore, Rosamond Stutchbury drove her guests over to Glyndebourne, where Frances Dakyns soon persuaded John that Fritz Busch (of whom he had never heard) could be the answer to all his problems. At John's request she wrote at once to Busch in Copenhagen, saying that there was to be "a fortnight's Mozart festival" in June, and that if Busch would agree to "conduct and take things over, it would be the beginning of opera in England".

That there was now talk of a Mozart festival, rather than a hotchpotch of Mozart and Wagner, was largely the result of a mild conspiracy on the part of Hamish Wilson and Audrey. Fritz Busch, with his enthusiasm for Mozart and his eagerness to find, in exile, a fruitful outlet for his talents, must have been tempted at least to look further into this proposal. But commitments in South America obliged him to refuse. Then, quite unexpectedly, the Buenos Aires season was curtailed and he wrote to Frances Dakyns to say that "the beautiful opera project" might after all be a possibility. He later confessed that he was ready now to agree to directing the first Glyndebourne season because he believed there would never be a second.

Early in January, before John and Busch had even met, it was arranged that the latter should take charge of a fortnight's Mozart festival at the end of May or the beginning of June; it was further agreed that the operas to be given should be *Figaro* and *Così fan tutte* not *Don Giovanni* and *Die Entführung*. Shortly afterwards the two men met in Amsterdam to discuss details. John still believed that the "superb performances" that he envisaged could be achieved with a string quartet—it would, of course, be the Busch Quartet—and an organ to fill in the wind. Busch soon persuaded him that this was quite out of the question, and the idea was dropped once and for all. He echoed what Audrey had said earlier: it must be the best, or nothing.

Now that Busch had been put in charge, his first task was to find a producer. ("And what", John had innocently asked, "*is* a producer?") Reinhardt was approached and was at first enthusiastic; then, when finance came to be considered, he grew shy and finally backed out. In the end it was agreed that Carl* Ebert, a Reinhardt disciple, should be approached.

Ebert had been *Generalintendant* at the Hessische Landestheater at Darmstadt and subsequently at the Berlin Städtische Oper until, like Busch, he had chosen to leave Nazi Germany. When he received John's letter he reacted much as Beecham had done; he dismissed the whole thing as a joke and did not even reply. A second letter also remaining unanswered, John resorted to the telegram. It now seems to have occurred to Ebert that this might after all be an agreeable and economical way of paying his first visit to England; and perhaps he had also begun to appreciate that a project which had the support of Fritz Busch ought hardly to be dismissed out of hand. He arrived at Glyndebourne in February.

He arrived to find a theatre already built—a theatre which suffered from several grave faults. There was, for instance, no way of flying the scenery; and there were no proper storage facilities. He felt that his instinct had been right after all; that the undertaking was foredoomed to failure. But when he began to point out the defects to John he was interrupted and immediately involved in a discussion of no more than academic interest about the best positioning of the bells for a performance of *Parsifal*. He had never before come across anyone the least like this extraordinary Englishman.

John gave him a week to look around and confer with Busch; then the three men met in conference. Ebert had been making a rough estimate of the probable cost of the festival; he produced his budget and assured John that no private individual could possibly afford to run an opera house of his own. The figure quoted obviously came as a surprise to John, but he silenced Ebert with a "That's none of your business"; he was, he said, merely asking Ebert whether or not he would accept the post of producer. Ebert was now being made aware of what he always called John's "marvellous stubbornness"—the stubbornness which alone made possible the realisation of this fantastic and seemingly hopeless venture.

Then Busch and Ebert came to the crux of the matter. "If I am to

* Christened Charles, but almost always known as Carl.

accept your offer," said Ebert, "there is one condition upon which Fritz and I must insist—and I cannot believe that you will accept it."

"You mean", said John, "that you are both so expensive?"

Ebert hastened to explain that this had nothing to do with it. They were both exiles. They wanted, not money, but opportunity. What they demanded was the final decision on all musical and artistic matters: "If we have differences of opinion about the choice of singers, the operas to be given, the rehearsals that are necessary, and so on, we will discuss everything with you; but it is *we* who must have the last word."

John immediately agreed to their terms. He realised that these were technical matters and that he was not qualified to override the considered opinion of experts. In the event there was—inevitably—occasional friction; but John kept to his side of the bargain.

★   ★   ★

Now began the serious business of preparing for a Festival that lay only three months ahead.

In addition to Busch and Ebert, the musical team consisted of Hans Oppenheim from the Städtische Oper in Breslau, Alberto Erede from the Italian Opera den Haag, and Jani Strasser. Hans Peter Busch, Fritz Busch's son, was assistant producer. Under Hamish Wilson, Scenery Designer and Stage Manager, was the invaluable "Jock" Gough, whom John had discovered at the Tunbridge Wells Opera House, and the strength of the Ringmer Building Works. Alfred Nightingale, as General Manager, dealt with the English contracts.

The engagement of singers had already been entrusted to Rudolf Bing, an Austrian of Jewish extraction who had worked under Ebert both at Darmstadt and in Berlin; at the end of the 1935 season he was to be appointed General Manager of Glyndebourne, joining John, Ebert and Busch to constitute what John was pleased to call the Quattuorviri who ran the Festival—but a team which could not really be considered complete without the inclusion of Audrey. The Musicians' Union had made it impossible for the Busch Quartet to lead the string section of the orchestra; players drawn principally from the London Symphony Orchestra, and with George Stratton as leader, were therefore eventually engaged.

Of the audition of Audrey (who had just returned from three weeks in Vienna), Busch had written, in a report not intended for John to see, that after a disappointing start, due partly to nervousness and partly to a certain weakness after her recent confinement, she revealed "a delightful voice, well-trained and full of artistry. Sang Susanna, Italian good, and she has a great sense of style. Even better at expressing lyrical emotion than gay good spirits. Strongly recommended. If properly used, her talent would have success in Dresden and Berlin. Request, on my recommendation, that she be given the part of Susanna. Undoubtedly a good actress, and a serious worker. After tea she sang with great taste half-a-dozen songs to what she called my 'very expressive accompaniment'." Busch added that, in the ordinary way, he would have engaged her at once for Dresden.

In March, to test the acoustics of the new building, three one-act operas were given informally to an audience of friends, as a result of which certain alterations were made to the orchestra pit. All those associated with the Glyndebourne venture had by this time become accustomed to incessant changes of every kind. John now decided that a second season in September—consisting of *Don Giovanni*, *Die Entführung* and one or two English operas—would not after all take place; but he informed Francis Toye, the music critic of the *Morning Post*, that he hoped to do *Die Walküre*, *Siegfried*, *Der Rosenkavalier* and *Hänsel und Gretel* in the summer of 1935. He added that his real ambition was one day to stage *Die Meistersinger* with a chorus of 200.

Toye told his readers that he considered the choice of operas rash. He would have preferred to hear Verdi's *Falstaff* or Purcell's *Fairy Queen* in such typically English surroundings; he liked them better and considered them more suitable. But "if Mr Christie's tastes are what they are, no one in the world has earned a better right to indulge them. Practical wisdom he can and will obtain with experience. He already possesses things that cannot be taught: imagination, enthusiasm, unflagging energy and unbounded optimism. Such qualities have enabled men to win unexpected triumphs over seemingly insuperable objects. . . ."

Of the operas mentioned by John, only *Der Rosenkavalier* and *Falstaff* have, at the time of writing, ever been performed at Glyndebourne—and even these not until more than twenty years later. But John still entertained the hope of giving *Parsifal* over Easter 1935, and applied at the Lewes Petty Sessions for permission to hold performances on Good Friday and Easter Sunday. The former alone was granted, and at the same time a general theatre licence and a licence to sell drinks.

★　★　★

In April the names of the singers engaged for *Figaro* and *Così fan tutte* were published in the press, though certain alterations in the casts were made subsequently. Finally the British team included Heddle Nash, Roy Henderson, Constance Willis, Audrey Mildmay and Ina Souez—an American by birth who was British by marriage. From Germany came Willi Domgraf-Fassbaender and Lucie Manén; from Austria, Luise Helletsgruber; from Czechoslovakia, Irene Eisinger; from Finland, Aulikki Rauta-waara, and from Italy, Vincenzo Bettoni. It was Glyndebourne's firm policy to get the best singers for the parts, not the biggest names, and most of these foreigners were relatively little known in England at the time.

The press, now fully on the alert, was soon busy describing the beauties of Glyndebourne and building up the Christie "image". Wild guesses were made of the deficit that John was prepared to incur to realise the first season of his "Manor House Opera", and the sharp eyes of reporters were quick to pounce upon eccentricities such as the ancient tennis shoes which he was apt to wear with evening dress. They were provided with a prospectus giving them, in cosy and antiquated English, the basic theme upon which to compose variations suited to the various tastes of their readers:

At the ancient Tudor Manor House of Glyndebourne, situated in a beautiful wooded stretch of the Sussex Downs near Lewes, has been erected an Opera House fully equipped for the worthy presentation of Opera, and designed on the most modern lines for the comfortable accommodation of the audience.

There followed some practical information: the price of stalls —£2 for first nights and £2 and £1 10s. subsequently—which Audrey considered "quite mad"; details of trains and parking facilities (including "an excellent landing ground for aeroplanes 100 yards from the Opera House"); information about the provision of meals with adequate notice given, and of permission to "apporter son manger"—and even the family butler—to the restaurant; and the advice that evening dress was "recommended". The Organ Room, now rechristened the Foyer, was to serve as "an ideal meeting place for discussion during the intervals, or a comfortable and restful resort for patrons of the Festivals who are staying in the neighbourhood for a few days." Reverting to a pastoral mood, the manifesto continued:

The Opera House is surrounded with beautiful lawns and gardens which will be at the disposal of the public. Within a quarter-of-an-hour's stroll of the house is a chain of woodland pools following the course of a Downland stream, leading to coppices carpeted with wild flowers. The grounds are encircled by gracious hills and in whichever direction one looks the eye is met by views of unspoiled natural loveliness.

Then, in the manner of a nineteenth-century Baedeker, came a description of the Opera House itself—"a rectangular building designed in simple Tudor style and built of materials already mellowed by time" which would not clash with the older architecture of the Manor. The 300 "roomy and comfortable" stalls all commanded an uninterrupted view of the stage; a number of them had been made extra-wide for the benefit of invalids and the stout, and in a stage box four seats had been set aside for the free use of the blind. "There are also comfortable retiring rooms for ladies and gentlemen."

Finally, after an assurance of the impeccable credentials of Fritz Busch, and of the invisibility of the orchestra, the prospectus concluded with a survey of the stage and its equipment, which was "second to none in this country".

Meanwhile rehearsals were in full swing, and last-minute improvements were being made to the stage, the dressing-rooms and the auditorium. Only John, with his fantastic attention to detail, would have remembered to make the doors of the artists' ladies lavatory wide enough to allow the passage of a crinoline; only John, with his fine whimsicality, would have thought of labelling the lavatories for the audience "Damen" and "Herren" (though "Signore" and "Signori" might have been more appropriate for those attending opera sung in Italian).* And only John, with his deep devotion to dogs, would have contemplated (though he never carried out) the erection of kennels and the provision of meals for the dogs of visitors to the Opera.

He was far too busy during April and May to write at any length to his mother; such letters as he did write were mostly concerned with repeated requests for a chandelier, needed for *Figaro*, which Lady Rosamond perpetually postponed despatching from Tapeley. On 11th May he informed her that at long last it had arrived, and added, "All is going very well except that we have untold troubles with one of the German singers—or particularly with his wife—also with an Austrian singer, both of whom are superb artists." He was making his first close acquaintance with the artistic temperament.

★   ★   ★

At last the great day—28th May—arrived, and in mid-afternoon the smartest of London's "first-nighters" could be seen, in full evening dress (with several notable exceptions) setting out from Victoria on their adventurous pilgrimage to hear *Figaro* in darkest Sussex. Many of them were genuine music-lovers; but there was (and there has continued to be) a generous sprinkling of what Sir Osbert Sitwell has savagely described as "numskulls, nitwits and morons addicted to the mode [of opera-going], even if they did not care in the least for music", without whom opera has never been able to exist in England. There is no reason why the rich and the smart should *not* be musical; but equally there is no reason why

---

* Somewhat similarly, on the front door of Glyndebourne there is (with reference to the pugs) an enamelled plaque with a bulldog, labelled BISSIGER HUND.

they should be. It would be interesting to know what percentage of those who frequent Glyndebourne and Covent Garden ever find their way to unfashionable Sadler's Wells.

As a whole, the musical part of the audience came to *Figaro* (and to *Così fan tutte* also) in a spirit of open-minded curiosity, ready to praise or to condemn; they stayed to praise. First, there was the impact of hearing what was in those days a rarity: the performance of Mozart's "Italian" operas in their original language. Second, there was the novelty of the primadonna who was fit to be "seen as well as heard"; the long tradition of the elephantine diva with the golden voice was being broken. True there had been attractive opera singers in the past, such as Lily Pons and Grace Moore, but these had all too soon found Hollywood more lucrative than Covent Garden; it requires the vast distances of Covent Garden to render some of its heroines even tolerable to the eye, and Glyndebourne was too intimate a setting. A delightful and unrehearsed touch which "made" the last act of *Figaro* was the sudden entry of a number of bats into Hamish Wilson's fine moonlit garden.

But far more important than these considerations was that perfection of ensemble which was often impossible of achievement at Covent Garden, where rehearsals had sometimes to be skimpy and where soloists were gathered from afar at the last moment.* There were no less than twenty-four full three-hour rehearsals for *Figaro*, and of course innumerable rehearsals with the soloists. To this was to be added the genius of Carl Ebert, the greatest producer of his time, and of Fritz Busch, who "had endeared himself to the players from the moment when, on raising his baton to rehearse the overture to *Figaro* for the first time, he had dropped his arm and said 'Already is too loud!'"

The critics, like the public, were unanimously impressed, though naturally there were points of disagreement with the performance. Not a few disapproved of Busch's use of the piano instead of the harpsichord to accompany the recitatives,† and of his refusal to allow the time-honoured adoption of the unwritten *appoggiatura*.

* But see p. 248.
† John, perhaps recalling the harpsichord recitals given by Violet Gordon Woodhouse at Eton (see p. 40), also regretted the use of a piano.

In spite, too, of the programme's assurance that the acoustics of
the opera house were supremely good, what had proved satisfactory for the small-scale test performances in March turned out to be
inadequate for the concerted numbers and the trumpets and per-
cussion of *Figaro*. As Ernest Newman wrote, through no fault of
the artists some of the singing degenerated into "sheer noise". But,
taken all in all, John was justified in writing to his mother (on 5th
June):

> We have had marvellous notices. The *New Statesman* for
> Saturday June 2nd gave me, personally, a marvellous notice.
> Both *The Times* and the *Telegraph* of Monday and Tuesday last
> week were again most complimentary. . . . This has been a great
> achievement because the leading papers have put Salzburg,
> hitherto the leading Opera Festival of the world, second to ours,
> and our *Così fan tutte* is described as "the finest of our time". The
> *Telegraph* says that they would like their readers to know that
> "in our opinion such a *Così fan tutte* has not before been seen in
> our time. On this particular score Salzburg is not placed."

Così fan tutte was given its first Glyndebourne performance on
29th May, the second night of the season. It was at once a triumph
and a disaster. It was a triumph because of the splendid singing of
Ina Souez and Luise Helletsgruber, and what *The Times* critic described as "the exquisite orchestral playing" and "brilliant production"; it was a disaster because of the smallness of the audience,
John subsequently always alleging that only seven people travelled
by the special train from Victoria.* There was general belief that
the opera, which was then little known in England, was "dull and
sub-standard". Many of those who had braced themselves for the
expedition to *Figaro* felt disinclined to repeat such an adventure so
soon. But for those who did, then and later, come to hear *Così fan
tutte*, the rewards were great; as the season continued, it began to
attract almost as big audiences as did the more popular *Figaro*.

Such were the musical pleasures of Glyndebourne; they were
enhanced by the wholly surprising beauty of the gardens and their
setting, by the country-house atmosphere, and by the excellence of

---

* It seems probable that, owing to misdirection by a railway official at Victoria,
a number of the opera-goers travelled to Lewes by the ordinary train.

the fare provided by the restaurant in the interval. Already the wines offered—ranging from a Deidesheimer 1921 at two pounds a bottle to a relatively humble Schloss Reinhartshausener 1920 at a mere six shillings—were of a kind to compensate the tone-deaf, and what Ebert always called "die Snobs", for their fortitude in making such a pilgrimage to endure so much music.

A revue-lyric* by Herbert Farjeon, "Glyndebourne, Glorious Glyndebourne", though written at a later date, gives a fair picture of the experiences of a visitor to the Festival Opera House. The first stanza runs:

> At five o'clock, in evening dress,
> We catch the afternoon express,
> Conspicuous among the press,
>   And feeling slightly funny;
> In snowy shirts and showy gowns
> We speed through villages and towns,
> Until at last we reach the Downs
>   Where music flows like money.

It was a Glyndebourne where "dear Mozart" is ultra-smart and even more expensive; where "with tum-ti-tees and tum-ti-tas we tread the paving crazy, or loiter under pergolas discussing Pergolesi"; and above all, a Glyndebourne which "MUST be good, we've come so FAR, at so much inconvenience!"

The audience (it was said) had averaged about one hundred throughout the fortnight, and that the season ended with a deficit of £7,000 came of course as no surprise to anyone—least of all to John. This was then an enormous sum, and few people imagined that the "experiment" would be repeated, or at all events that it would be repeated on that scale. But there were plenty of signs to encourage optimism. The Press was unanimous in agreeing that this was a venture to be taken seriously and one which would grow in stature year by year, and John received from the critics much advice on the subject of operas suitable to the Glyndebourne stage.

---

* From *The Little Revue*, quoted here by kind permission of Ascherberg, Hopwood & Crew, Ltd.

Some of the operas they proposed were in fact produced there subsequently.

★   ★   ★

There was little relaxation after the last curtain fell on 10th June, though in July John escaped for a short fishing holiday in Norway. First came recordings of *Figaro* for H.M.V. Then there was the next season to shape. It was agreed that in 1935 two further operas by Mozart—his "German" *Die Zauberflöte* and *Die Entführung*—should be added to the two previously given, and the total number of performances increased from twelve to twenty-five.

Next there was the question—and it was one which was to recur at the end of every subsequent season—of alterations and improvements to the Opera House and its dependencies. John had at first stubbornly resisted the felling of an ilex tree close to the Opera House, but at last he yielded; this destruction made space for a much-needed scenery dock. The very primitive conditions endured by the artists were ameliorated by the construction of twenty-four dressing-rooms and a green-room, connected to the stage by a temporary corridor. Finally came a second dining-room, a kitchen, and a chauffeurs' room. All these operations were of course carried out by the Ringmer Building Works.

Audrey had acquitted herself splendidly, both as artist and hostess, during the first season. Only she would have had the happy idea of putting a half-bottle of champagne for each artist on his dressing-table on his first night—a gift far more welcome than the conventional flowers. She played her part too in the various activities of the succeeding autumn and winter; but her principal role in the latter part of 1934 was the production of a son and heir, for New Year's Eve saw the birth of George William Langham Christie, today Chairman of Glyndebourne. Four days later the proud father wrote to his mother, "I have rarely seen Audrey looking so well, but she intends to stay in bed for three weeks. I hope now she will sing Pamina as well as Susanna." And three months later he reported:

> Audrey and both babies are well. Rosamond is very charming, and very friendly until thwarted. Thwarting takes place

about once a minute, and then there is a row. She is most determined. George is said to be doing quite decently. At present it has red hair. It quite often moves its face and is said to be smiling. . . .

For Lady Rosamond the birth of her grandson was to be her last and crowning happiness.* The following November she died at Tapeley. "When she died," wrote one who knew her well in the last years of her life, "I saw him [John] weep as a child might. Head on his arms against a wall, deep sobbing. Not the normal emotional distress for the loss of an elderly parent." On his mother's grave in Westleigh† churchyard he had the following words inscribed:

> AN HEROIC WOMAN POSSESSED
> OF INTEGRITY, COURAGE, DIGNITY
> AND KINDNESS, TESTED AND
> PROVED BY INCESSANT DIFFICULTIES

---

* Curiously enough, to John also came, in the last year of his life, the joy of the birth of his first grandson.
† Tapeley Park is in the parish of Westleigh.

15

The Mid Thirties

TAKEN ALL in all, the engagement of singers for the 1934 season had gone remarkably smoothly; but in 1935 Glyndebourne was to have a taste of what Spike Hughes has called "the endemic bloody-mindedness found behind the scenes of the rest of the world's opera houses." He has discussed in detail the various troubles that occurred; here they can only be dealt with very briefly.

First came the general problem of salaries. After the undeniable success of the opening season, a number of the singers demanded a stiff rise of pay: one singer wanted his salary quadrupled though he was only to do about one-and-a-half times as much work as in 1934.

Then there was great confusion over the part of Pamina in *Die Zauberflöte*, from which Audrey finally stepped down to make way for the Finnish soprano, Aulikki Rautawaara, whose contract had already been signed at a time when it was believed that Audrey would not be well enough to sing. Several singers whose return to Glyndebourne had been taken for granted, had waited in vain for their contracts and had finally taken other engagements; and the same applied to about one-third of the orchestral players. This was largely the result of John's unshakable and pathetic belief that no singer or orchestral player in the world would refuse the privilege of working at Glyndebourne.

But the major crisis occurred over Ina Souez, who had orally agreed at the end of the 1934 season to sing Fiordiligi again in 1935. After delays, both on Glyndebourne's part and on hers, over the signing of the contract, she demanded more money and finally committed herself to singing Micaëla at Covent Garden.

Busch, on holiday in Sorrento, was indignant when he heard this, poured scorn on the bungling amateurs who dealt with contracts at Glyndebourne, and announced that he would resign if Souez were not available for *Così*. "This IS possible", he wrote. "That my last word."

John had never lost (and was never in the future willingly to lose) any opportunity of abusing or decrying Covent Garden; it was a subject upon which he was impervious to reason. This made a personal appeal to Beecham impossible. But eventually the matter was sorted out, and Covent Garden generously accepted that Glyndebourne had first claim on Ina Souez when performances of *Carmen* and *Così fan tutte* clashed.

But Fritz Busch had spoken truly when he said: "The idyll of 1934 was once upon a time. It will not come again."

★   ★   ★

Spring was backward in 1935, and Mr Harvey, the head gardener, was hard put to it to get his bedding out in time for May 27th, when the season opened, to a half-empty house, with *The Magic Flute*.

Those who were present agreed that it was a fine—in particular, a "complete"—performance, and a personal triumph for Aulikki Rautawaara (Pamina) and Irene Eisinger (Papagena). Domgraf-Fassbaender (Papageno) and Walther Ludwig (Tamino) misjudged the acoustics and sang too loud. The Czech soprano, Mila Kočová, was a failure as the Queen of the Night and was soon replaced by Noel Eadie.

One lapse of taste in an otherwise splendid production did not escape comment. In Mozart's day it had been the custom for Papageno to extemporise topical gags, and Ebert rashly gave Fassbaender *carte blanche* to do likewise. We have the assurance of the music critic of the *Daily Mirror* that the audience was "astonished" to hear Papageno say: "Why do you stare like that? You make my tummy feel gooey." This "set the audience laughing" and so (wrote Spike Hughes) "confirmed once more that things too silly to raise a smile anywhere else will always make an opera-house audience almost hysterical".

After the performance there was a party in the new Green Room. Fritz Busch's speech on this occasion is recalled for two felicitous observations. "I used", he said, "to divide the human race into three species: men, women and singers. Now I have found a fourth species: British singers." Sympathising with the understudies who never at Glyndebourne seemed to get a chance to play the star parts they had laboriously learned, he remarked: "No stars are ever away at Glyndebourne, because even work is more attractive than the night life of Lewes."

Three evenings later came a revival of *Così fan tutte* in which Ina Souez surpassed, if that were possible, her triumph of the previous year. The revival of *Figaro* followed, and finally, on 19th June, *Die Entführung*, with Ivar Andresen as Osmin and Irene Eisenger as Blonde. Those familiar with the esteem in which Childs, the Glyndebourne butler, was held were probably not surprised to see him in the silent role of "der Stumme" (the Mute)—a hilarious performance based on his recollections of the time when he had worked for a deaf-and-dumb employer. The opera was an immediate hit with the audience.

Glyndebourne had now undoubtedly established itself; but the 1935 season ended with a deficit of £10,000. This was proportionately less than the previous year's £7,000 deficit for a much shorter season. John, with his usual optimism, was confident that it was only a matter of time before Glyndebourne paid its way. He stepped up the publicity; a subscription scheme and "seat tokens" were organised, and sandwichmen hired to parade up and down outside Queen's Hall before and after concerts.

In 1935, too, the first Glyndebourner ate the first sandwich in the car park. Thus bravely was inaugurated the picnicking which was later to become so agreeable a feature of the opera season when the weather decided to collaborate, but "a misery of long dresses and tiaras in rain and high winds" (as one visitor described it) when it did not.

⋆　　⋆　　⋆

So far nothing had come of John's avowed intention of giving the British composer a chance. But in March 1936, when addres-

13

sing the Sussex Women Musicians' Club (whose guest he was at
the Old Ship in Brighton), he said: "If any English composer is
prepared to write an opera which the staff of Glyndebourne considered really good, we shall be prepared to put it on." He followed the subject up in a letter which appeared in the principal
daily papers. "The opera", he said, "must be suitable for our
stage and our acoustics and the composer should make himself
acquainted with these matters beforehand"; and he proceeded to
attribute the previous "inevitable failure" of British operas to
the "scratch conditions" under which they had been produced.

The substance of the letter, and its condescending tone, were
perfectly calculated to annoy the whole British musical world.
Covent Garden was indignant at the suggestion that Beecham's
highly successful promotion of operas by Ethel Smyth, Stanford
and Delius had been failures put on under "scratch conditions";
so far as is known, John had never heard any of them. Sumner
Austin, chief producer at Sadler's Wells, wondered why it needed
John's team of Germans to decide whether an English opera would
be suitable and thus "worthy to receive its due reward upon the
miniature but gilded boards" of Glyndebourne. Julius Harrison
of the Hastings Municipal Orchestra, who not long before had
been patronisingly urged by John to visit Glyndebourne and so
"keep in touch with what could be done", struck the same note
in a letter to the Press which concluded:

> The organisation of Glyndebourne is essentially German. Mr
> Christie models his whole scheme on Munich and Salzburg
> and glories in it. None of us mind that, and if Mr Christie can
> establish a musical pilgrimage to his beautiful little Sussex opera
> house it is all to the good. But if he imagines that British com-
> posers are going to rush in to submit their operas to his very
> un-British musical staff he is in for disillusionment. . .

A distinguished but anonymous British composer, in an interview with a *Daily Mail* columnist, made what was obviously a
very sensible suggestion. If the stage and the acoustics at Glyndebourne were unique, he said, then any opera specially written for
Glyndebourne would presumably be unsuitable for production
elsewhere; and what composer would want to give so much time

and creative energy to such a work—a work which might indeed even be rejected altogether? Moreover, since Glyndebourne was so well suited to Mozart, the new British opera would have to conform to the methods of Mozart—a difficult composer with whom to compete. Then he came to the point: "If Mr Christie is really keen to add a British opera to his repertoire, the obvious thing would be to commission an opera from one of our composers who have been proved to have a flair necessary to good stage music."

But no such opera was forthcoming; and though it was subsequently alleged by John that a large number of operatic scores were in fact submitted, no British composer of any distinction seems to have been prepared to come forward with an uncommissioned work. Of what has variously been described as John's "offer", "challenge" or "insult" to his compatriots, nothing more was heard, and there was to be no British opera at Glyndebourne until the staging there in 1946 of the world première of Benjamin Britten's *The Rape of Lucretia.*★

★   ★   ★

One further Mozart opera was added for the 1936 season—*Don Giovanni*; this completed the pentad of the composer's most famous operas, to which *Idomeneo* was to be added in 1951 and the little *Schauspieldirektor* six years later.

Various additions and subtractions were made to the Glyndebourne team. Charles B. Cochran had abducted Irene Eisinger to sing in his Adelphi review, *Follow the Sun*; she was replaced as Papagena by Lili Heinemann, as Despina by Tatiana Menotti, and as Blonde by the no less admirable Irma Beilke. Fassbaender had a serious illness; Don Giovanni was therefore sung by John Brownlee, while Mario Stabile and Roy Henderson took over Figaro and Guglielmo respectively.

The season opened on 29th May with the new production, *Don Giovanni*, in which Audrey was enchanting as Zerlina. But the

★ At the 1969 Festival, however, will be heard a new English opera commissioned by Glyndebourne. This is *The Rising of the Moon* by the young English composer Nicholas Maw, with a libretto by Beverley Cross and designs by Osbert Lancaster.

greatest triumph was reserved for the Leporello of Salvatore Baccaloni, who gave a performance "reeking of garlic and olive oil" and whose recitatives had a briskness and fluency which his non-Italian colleagues could not hope to emulate. Once again Ebert, who had not yet "got the wave-length" of the English upper-class opera-goer, came in for criticism for a lapse of taste as unfortunate as his permission to introduce gags into the part of Papageno. During the banqueting scene in the last act, the stage was suddenly invaded by three half-naked courtesans, more suited to a variety show than to grand opera, and to a German rather than an English audience. But in other respects the production was excellent and taken all in all, *Don Giovanni* provided a first night that compared very favourably with those of 1934 and 1935.

Ever since the opening of Glyndebourne in 1934 the B.B.C. had been clamouring for permission to broadcast some of its performances. John had refused, on the grounds that the Corporation made him an inadequate offer; but in 1936 he changed his policy and said that it might broadcast for nothing. This was apparently against the B.B.C.'s principles and money changed hands when the first act of *Don Giovanni*, and acts of *Figaro* and *The Magic Flute*, preceded by pastoral sounds to set the Glyndebourne scene, were served to the greater British public. These broadcasts became a regular annual event.

Several performances of the 1936 *Magic Flute* were conducted by Busch's assistant, Hans Oppenheim; John had wanted this, and Busch, with a repertoire of five operas now on his hands, had not been sorry to agree. Unfortunately Oppenheim's *Magic Flute* was not a success, and after two or three performances Busch took over again. But *Figaro* was better than ever, with Stabile superb in the title role and Audrey now a far more mature Susanna. She had been singing the part at Sadler's Wells in February, and the experience she had gained there, together no doubt with the stimulus of playing opposite Stabile, had given her a new confidence. It is much to be regretted that the records of the Glyndebourne *Figaro* were not made with the 1936 cast.

Only four performances were given of *Così fan tutte*, in which

Ina Souez was again magnificent. But *Die Entführung* disappointed, and the *Observer* went so far as to say that it came "in some respects as near to being genuinely bad as Glyndebourne has got so far".

The deficit for the 1936 season fell to £4,000, the large sale of wines in the restaurant (no less than 2,500 bottles) greatly contributing to this improvement. For the first time the wine list had that year been embellished with those Greek quotations which John always attributed to his friend C. M. Wells, but which were in fact largely supplied by his father-in-law, Aubrey Mildmay, who had come to live at Ringmer.* Soon wine became such a feature of Glyndebourne that a vast new cellar had to be constructed.

In November Audrey made a successful concert tour in Austria, Hungary and Germany, returning to Glyndebourne in time for Christmas. That she had agreed to go to Germany did, however, anger those at Glyndebourne who had suffered at the hands of the Nazis and who put politics before music.

★ ★ ★

Once again, after the end of the season, various structural alterations were put in hand. The size of the auditorium was increased to accommodate nearly 450 people, forty seats being kept for students at the much reduced price of ten shillings. The new Wallop Dining Halls came into service. More dressing-rooms were provided—not this time for the singers, but for the use of guests who had not found time or place to change beforehand; and the stage itself was improved by the construction of a proper cyclorama to replace the makeshift affair used previously. John was of course constantly on the spot while this work was going on.

So far as the programme for the next season was concerned, there was a growing feeling in certain quarters that the time had

* At a later date these were for a brief time replaced by tags provided by M. André Simon—e.g. "A princely wine in Gorgeous Court dress, a credit to the host, an honour to his guests." After 1956 the pretentious practice of annotating the wine lists was discontinued.

come to add to Mozart's five operas at all events one work by
another composer. Busch felt strongly on the subject and wrote
to John suggesting the possibility of Verdi's *Falstaff* or, if Coronation Year and John's frequent "promises and speeches and words
to the papers" made a British work advisable, then perhaps *The
Bride of Dionysus* by Sir Donald Tovey or *Sir John in Love* by
Vaughan Williams. Busch was only feeling his way. *Falstaff*
might, he admitted, be too big an undertaking; Tovey's opera
was little appreciated by his own countrymen, and the drawback
to *Sir John in Love* was the poor invention of the music. There
was soon to be a still greater drawback to *Sir John*: Vaughan
Williams, a stern critic of Glyndebourne, refused permission for
it to be staged there.*

As a last possibility Busch proposed the second, French, version
of Gluck's *Orphée et Euridice*, which had an excellent part for
Audrey; John, always prejudiced against French† music, flatly
rejected it and countered with *Don Pasquale* or *La traviata*, both
also with fine roles for Audrey.

Busch wanted, too, to drop *Die Entführung*, the failure of the
1936 season, unless he could assemble a really good cast; but he
finally agreed, at John's urgent request, to retain it if it was
humanly possible. However, he refused John's suggestion to pre-
cede it, as a curtain-raiser, with Pergolesi's *La serva padrona*. In the
end the 1937 season proved to be "the mixture as before": the
same five Mozart operas that had been given the previous year.
John, Busch and Ebert may have been disappointed, but Bing at
least was delighted.

In the spring of 1937 came again the now familiar troubles over
singers and contracts. John, in his eagerness to have as many
British singers as possible for Coronation Year, found himself
constantly opposed to the management in whom he had vested
the final decision on all musical matters. It was, wrote Spike
Hughes, a sad situation—"like a small boy trying to play with his

---

* According to John, Vaughan Williams did not mind how his operas were
performed so long as the performers enjoyed doing them, and considered
Glyndebourne standards excessive. But relations between the two men were
always amicable.

† Gluck was of course German by birth.

trains, which he not only owned but had bought out of his pocket money, and always having them taken away from him". The final catastrophe came in April, when Audrey suddenly became so hoarse that she could hardly speak; she was taken to a nursing home in Tunbridge Wells, where it was soon decided that she could not possibly sing that summer. This was doubly disappointing after her success on the Continent only four months earlier.

★   ★   ★

In July, when Audrey was well enough to travel, she went for a month to Braies, in the Dolomites, to recuperate. John was far too busy to leave Glyndebourne, and the children had of course to stay in England also. She was lonely and depressed, wondering if she would ever be able to sing again. She now had the leisure to reflect upon the life that she and John had been leading. There was so little time or opportunity for private living at Glyndebourne, where the whole year was one continuous round of preparation and performance of, and *post mortems* on, operas and concerts. Delightful and stimulating though it all was—and she suddenly realised "what an amazing thing we've done at Glyndebourne"—it meant that the house was hardly their own. She wrote to John:

> I would have loved to stay peacefully with you at Glyndebourne. I kept feeling what a waste it was to have *such* a heavenly home and so little chance to enjoy it calmly and consciously. Some day, John darling, let's have a month's holiday *there*! Let's do it next summer—both of us giving up our jobs and simply enjoy ourselves at Glyndebourne. It would be heavenly!

Early in August she returned to England, better and more hopeful but in no condition to sing yet.

★   ★   ★

Meanwhile the Glyndebourne season of 1937 had opened on 19th May with *Don Giovanni*. There were a number of changes in the cast, but as before it was Baccaloni as Leporello who stole the show. In *The Magic Flute* the chorus of priests consisted largely of unemployed Welsh miners, tinplate workers and boiler-makers. The absence of "Glyndebourne's own Susanna" in *Figaro* was greatly regretted, but nobody could have wished for a better substitute than Irene Eisinger. *Così fan tutte* was once again a success, and in *Die Entführung* the German bass, Herbert Alsen, showed that his Osmin was in its way as good as the Sarastro which he had taken over from Kipnis.

Perhaps the most remarkable feature of the 1937 season was the final profit of about £2,700. This was due in part to the continued excellent sales of wine, in part to the fact that with no new production in the programme fewer rehearsals were necessary. But against these had to be set certain wage increases, including a rise of fifty per cent in the salary of Fritz Busch.

In August (1937) it was announced that the following year, in addition to *Figaro, Don Giovanni* and *Così fan tutte*, there would be performances of Donizetti's *Don Pasquale* and Verdi's *Macbeth*. It was John who so keenly advocated *Don Pasquale*, which had a fine part in it for Audrey; Busch and Ebert eventually agreed (it was their first great concession to the Christies), but only on condition that if a break were made with an all-Mozart repertoire, a second and more important non-Mozart opera would also be given.

Audrey had often sung in Italian operas (in English translation) with the Carl Rosa Company; but Busch saw that if she was to sing a Norina in *Don Pasquale* that would be up to the high standards of Glyndebourne she would have to go to Italy and put in some hard work there. Four or five months later he was still repeating that it was vital for her to go "as soon and for as long as possible"; but it was not until the following February that she felt well enough to leave for Rome.

Audrey also had a different and quite unreasonable little worry of her own. Busch wanted the part of Ernesto to be sung by a tenor (he had in mind Luigi Fort) much younger than Dino Borgioli, who was forty-seven; but Audrey, now thirty-seven, feared that playing opposite a man younger than herself would make her look old. Ebert thought this nonsense; Busch therefore

went ahead and approached Fort. But Fort had other commitments; it was thus Borgioli who, in the end and to Audrey's
great relief, sang Ernesto.

★   ★   ★

At Braies, the previous summer, Audrey had had no company.
She had not been well enough to do much more than lie in the
sun and think of John and the children and wish that they were
with her. In Rome, of course, she continued to miss them badly
and to clamour for news; but at least her life was full; and for
most of the time she was well enough to work, though she found
that she tired very easily. She took Italian lessons and made some
headway. She studied with Calusio the recitatives in *Figaro* and
her new role of Norina. Erede was in Rome; Ebert suddenly appeared; and the Baccalonis were endlessly hospitable. And of
course she fell in love with Rome.

Calusio worked her hard and she was rather frightened of him;
but she found him an excellent teacher and gradually her voice
began to return. When she discovered that "Glyndebourne
Italian" was a stock joke in musical circles in Italy, she wrote to
John suggesting that it might be a good plan to engage Calusio
for the Festival Company; but nothing came of it.

She often wondered how John was managing without her.
Who, in her absence, was there to persuade him to tear up those
letters written in a moment of irritation? There are several passages in her letters to him which reveal the valuable role she must
habitually have played as a restraining influence:

> Don't hammer your points unduly. You carry enough wait
> [*sic*] now to put your stuff across softly and easily!!!

> Do be careful not to be an operatic "organist"—only con-
> cerned with your own box of tricks.

> You have your stuff so clear in your own mind that you
> don't make it clear to others.

> My fear is of course that you will get too fierce when I am
> not there to act as "grinder down", and that you will set up
> difficulties. which take so much explaining away in order to
> start where you might have begun!

And she learns with some concern, from a friend, that John is "asking the representatives of music in England to your conference in order to tell them what a fat lot of old dunderheads they are—and-always-have-been! But I think you are clever!! I love and admire your tremendous driving force, but I don't want it to swamp your charm or your sound sense—it is *liable* to, I'm afraid. . .!"

The aims of this conference, which was held at Glyndebourne on 5th March, are described by John in two letters that he wrote to Audrey; in them he was using her once again as a sounding-box for his ideas. On 22nd February, after telling her that he had arranged an interview with the Prime Minister's first secretary, he continued:

> I am convinced that the immediate step is the constitution of the musical authority which can represent music and be the contact with Politicians. I believe the Politicians can do nothing until this authority is created, recognised and accepted. The London Opera House [i.e. Covent Garden] is a part of my scheme. Is our success at Glyndebourne sufficient for us to be entrusted with the work? For the first time opera has been properly managed in England. We have proved the organisa-tion. If we can now get the representative Society constituted and accepted, then is the moment with both organisations to start the London Opera House. Music in England will not be respected until the London Opera House is the best in the world. Sadler's Wells would then become the L.C.C. Opera House.

In a second letter, written ten days later, he was clearly re-hearsing his speech for the following day. The most acute prob-lem, he told Audrey, was the lack of good conductors. Munici-palities spent money on concerts of rubbishy music at which the conductor's baton had generally been "bagged by the local organist". Could the critical powers of musicians be sharpened so that they would demand a higher standard? Could a Society be formed, royal or otherwise, which would co-ordinate work, advise Municipalities about their music, and so raise standards? Of course there was the question of money. People never wanted to give money to *found* organisations, but they would probably support an organisation that was proving itself active and effective. "The musicians," he said, "are expressing increased interest in the Conference. We are now twenty-four, including Rhona [Byron], Edwards, Austin and Rudi. . ."

This conference led in due course to John's valiant attempt to establish a National Council of Music (N.C.M.).*

But John's letters to Audrey at this time were not concerned only with Glyndebourne and the salvation of music in England. He wrote to her charmingly about the two children—"Pidge" or "Puff" (Rosamond) now five, and "Gidge", "Dids", etc. (George) now four. He was enormously fond of them and he told her just those little daily nursery happenings that enabled her to picture them.

He told her too of his troubles, especially of his disappointment, indeed indignation, at not being appointed a magistrate; in one letter he described his speech to the Ladies Carlton Club—a speech which clearly contained all those whimsical ingredients that were soon to become so familiar to Glyndebourne audiences. He concluded: "My impression is that it all went well. They laughed and I was well dressed in my tails."

He told her also about his negotiations over the sale of German wines to the King. These negotiations were followed, a little later, by an invitation from the King to him to become official adviser on the general purchase of German wines for the royal cellars; but before the matter had been settled, war had been declared.

One of John's letters about the sale of wines is sufficiently characteristic to justify quotation; it is addressed to the King's Financial Secretary:

Dear Sir,
    I cannot read your signature, and, of course, I ought to know who is Financial Secretary. My impression is that it was Adeane, but I can see a dot over your signature, which makes it impossible. . .

* See Chapter 20.

After discussing the various wines he can offer, and the quantities available, he concluded:

I find that German wines do not taste equally well in all places. Glyndebourne seems to be good; Tapeley is bad. It is the same problem, I suppose, as the German cigar. It is therefore conceivable that Balmoral or Sandringham might be fortunate. I suppose one can only find this out by trial. Red wines are good at Tapeley. It is one of those queer things.

In mid-April Audrey left Rome for Milan and continued her journey to Stockholm, where she sang in a performance of the Brahms *Requiem*. By the end of the month she was back at Glyndebourne and immersed at once in rehearsals for the season which now lay less than a month ahead.

*   *   *

If the casting of *Don Pasquale* had its little difficulties, that of *Macbeth* was to be the cause of a major headache for Busch and Ebert; and to make matters worse, Ebert was abroad throughout the negotiations. This tale of woe will be described in detail, for it is one of a kind that is only too familiar in the operatic world. *Macbeth* was a far more ambitious venture than any Mozart opera, requiring a fuller orchestra and a bigger chorus. It was unknown in England, and the general British public could hardly be expected to rush to hear early Verdi. In particular, Ebert felt sure that "die Snobs" in the audience—which he estimated at seventy per cent of the whole—would almost certainly be bored. Then the casting was far from easy, especially the part of Lady Macbeth which called for a voice of exceptional range but at the same time one which would not be too big for Glyndebourne. Busch began to get cold feet. Might it not be better to do *Fidelio*? Ebert was against it. Or *Idomeneo* (admittedly another Mozart opera, but one which had never been professionally staged in England)? Bing was against it. So the search began for a Lady Macbeth.

A dozen sopranos were considered. For a while Dusolina Giannini was favoured; but after a time Busch began to waver, and he was probably rather relieved when he learned that she could not in any case take the engagement. Other names were proposed. In January Busch went to Italy to hear Iva Pacetti, who had actually sung the part; but he found her voice too powerful and, as Bruno Walter had warned him, long past its best. Marta Fuchs also knew the part and had sung it with Busch in Dresden in 1928; but since then her voice had changed. In any case she was not free. Finally Franca Somigli, an American by birth, was chosen and the contract signed. This was towards the end of January and at the same time another American, Francesco Valentino—who had, said Busch, "the most beautiful baritone voice I have heard for years"— agreed to sing Macbeth. The most urgent problems of *Macbeth* now appeared to be settled.

In mid-February Toscanini announced that he would not appear at the Salzburg Festival that summer, and less than a month later Hitler invaded Austria. Busch and Ebert immediately proposed that the Glyndebourne season should be extended and Toscanini invited to conduct one or two operas there; *The Magic Flute*, *Don Pasquale* and even a new production of Verdi's *Falstaff*, were mentioned as possibilities. But two cables to Toscanini remaining unanswered, the scheme was abandoned. It was eventually learned that Toscanini had decided to conduct no operas in 1938.

Bing had been caught in Austria at the time of Hitler's invasion of the country; only the good fortune that he happened to have in his possession a *Grenzempfehlung*★ which he was taking back to England for an English Member of Parliament, and which he now successfully passed off as having been issued to himself, enabled him to get out of the country. He returned to find all going forward satisfactorily with the preparations for the season as originally arranged. Then, on 22nd March, came a cable from Franca Somigli asking to be released from her contract because she had come to realise that the part was too difficult for her and not suited to her voice.

Busch was justifiably indignant that it had taken her three months to make this discovery, and still more angry when he

★ Permit to cross the frontier.

earned that she had signed a more lucrative contract with the Teatro Colon in Buenos Aires; but he considered himself fortunate, at this late hour, to be able to engage Iva Pacetti. On 11th May, ten days before the first night, Iva Pacetti was suddenly taken ill. He was now even more than fortunate to secure Vera Schwarz, a Yugoslavian who had worked in Vienna and Berlin, and who was prepared to take on this difficult role at such short notice. On 21st May the curtain rose, as had been advertised, on the first performance of *Macbeth* ever to be given in England.

Whatever "die Snobs" may have thought about *Macbeth*—and they did not at first flock to hear it—music-lovers and the great majority of the critics were enthusiastic. The music was a revelation. The direction, the staging and Caspar Neher's sets were considered excellent; and Vera Schwarz made a very favourable impression, especially by her acting. Extensions that had been made to the stage provided the necessary pace for the large choruses, and for the "supers" who were brought up to strength by the addition of Glyndebourne waiters, local Boy Scouts and the staff of the Ringmer Building Works. There were, of course, certain criticisms, but taken all in all the venture proved a triumph which enhanced the growing reputation of Glyndebourne. For John, however, there was a personal disappointment: the visit of the King and Queen to *Macbeth* had at the last moment been cancelled because of the death of the Queen's mother, Lady Strathmore; thus the Queen was deprived of the novel experience of seeing an opera centred on Glamis, the house in which she was born.

Don Pasquale was a *succès fou*; almost too much so, thought John, for the laughter was so continuous that often the singers were drowned. The audience, said *The Times's* critic, "roared and shouted like any shilling gallery". But mirth was intended and inevitable, with Baccaloni and Stabile the perfect exponents of the Italian *buffo* style and (for the amusement of the locals) Mrs Ashton, the Glyndebourne cook, in the silent role of Don Pasquale's house-keeper. Then there was Tuppy, John's current pug, who behaved admirably and took his bow with all the self-assurance of a primadonna. Last, but by far from least, critics and audience alike were captivated by Audrey's Norina.

1938 also saw the first broadcast of an entire opera (*Figaro*) from Glyndebourne, as well as of acts from the other four operas. The season had been a personal triumph for Fritz Busch, and many people must have read with satisfaction the fine tribute to him that appeared in *The Times*; nor should Carl Ebert's great contribution be forgotten. But with two new productions, it was hardly surprising that, successful though the season had been, it ended with a deficit of £7,000.

★ ★ ★

In the middle of July, after the opera season was over, John went fishing with Wells in Norway, where the latter had a tenancy of the Bolstad river. It was a disappointing holiday; "It's so dull here," he wrote to Audrey. "Fishing jaw is worse than any... I want to get home. No more of the bachelor existence for me if I can help it. Wells is a male spinster, full of cranks, but at any rate possessed also of remarkable virtues. Otherwise, I could not stand it and should not be here. He is a very kind friend . . ." John never went fishing with Wells again, but their friendship remained unimpaired until John's death. Wells, his senior by eleven years, lived on until 1963.

In August, at Audrey's invitation, twenty-five children from Bethnal Green came, through the Children's Country Holiday Fund, for a fortnight's holiday to Glyndebourne and were housed in the waiters' dormitory. Little did she then guess that, barely thirteen months later, most of Glyndebourne would be turned into a Nursery School and would remain such for more than six years.

16

Interlude: John Christie *v.* Giacomo Agati

IN HIS Journal for 2nd July 1937 James Agate referred to the
reluctance of the public to visit the theatre, "musical or otherwise", for its own sake:

> Nobody in London [he wrote] goes to any theatre unless it is
> the thing to go to that theatre. Now, just as distance lends
> enchantment to the view, so un-get-atable-ness lends *thingness*
> to theatres. Take Glyndebourne. Does anybody believe that
> these smart audiences would o'er the Sussex downs so freely if,
> when they got to Christie's theatre, they had to see the per-
> formance through leper's squints with their fashionable pre-
> sence unbeknownst to other fashionables? The whole case has
> been put once and for all by Johnson, when Boswell said there
> was not half a guinea's worth of pleasure in seeing the Pantheon:
>
> JOHNSON. But, Sir, there is half a guinea's worth of inferior-
> ity to other people in not having seen it.
> BOSWELL. I doubt, Sir, whether there are many happy
> people here.
> JOHNSON. Yes, Sir, there are many happy people here. There
> are many people here who are watching hundreds, and who
> think hundreds are watching them.*

These sentiments must have reached John, who had already
tried, and failed, to entice Agate to Glyndebourne. On 7th May
of the following year he wrote inviting Agate to his box to hear
Don Giovanni on whichever day suited him. He said that he would
like to have a further talk with him on the subject of Glyndebourne and its aims. He believed that most of those who came

* James Agate, *Ego 3*, p. 165.

enjoyed themselves, though there were inevitably a "few people with cantankerous minds who do not respond to reason. We cannot exclude these." The price of seats had to be high, but "the subscription for all five operas and dinners, costing £11, compares very favourably with what people spend in other directions and for far less value." He concluded, "if you would like to come and see some of the dramatic rehearsal work beforehand you will be welcome. Ebert, our Producer, is a great man."

When, after five weeks, Agate had not even troubled to reply, John's secretary wrote to ask whether he had received the letter. Agate now answered, without any apology for his dilatoriness, "It is very kind of you to renew your invitation to Glyndebourne. I am only sorry that I cannot induce you to believe that I do not care for operatic Mozart."

On 10th July Agate gave to his *Sunday Times* readers a lengthy account of his views on Glyndebourne in general and on Mozart in particular:

> In this [article] will be offered fantastic reasons for the solid unpopular fact of my failure to visit Glyndebourne. Up to this moment I have breathed no syllable against Glyndebourne as an institution, the few wisps of animadversion which have escaped me being directed solely against those who enthuse about Glyndebourne for reasons unconnected with either the country or the music. . . .
>
> But I feel I should now answer a letter from Bere Regis which says: "Dear Mr Agate—*Why* worry about what takes other people to Glyndebourne? Tell us what keeps you away!" Two things keep me away. The first is that I happen not to care for Mozartian opera. . . .

He goes on to say that he was brought up on Mozart, but that with his discovery of Wagner and Richard Strauss he could no longer find satisfaction in the Mozart operas. After the love duet in *Tristan*, the "nursery passion" of "Voi che sapete" left him cold. To turn from the "gorgeous obstreperousness" of *Salome* or *Electra* to the "plain tonic and dominant" of Mozart, "was like asking a boy who had attained to his school XI to return to cricket

14

with a soft ball". Yet, surprisingly, Agate confessed that he could "sit through a concert of three Mozart symphonies and wish they were four". He continues:

> The second thing which keeps me from Glyndebourne is my firm conviction that a theatre is out of place among dewponds. I do not believe in the mingling of art and nature; I do not hold with reading Joyce's *Ulysses* among Hardy's ewe-leases. Art should know its place and keep it . . .

There follows a long and irrelevant quotation from a description he had written, many years earlier, of a round of golf. "That", he says truthfully,

> is vile writing. But it is not viler than the pretence that the beauties of Sussex have any kin with the beauties of Mozart or any other composer. Art, in my view, is escape, and the place for Russian ballet is not the empty steppes but the crowded streets. Thirty Pavlovas, Karsavinas, Lopokovas, would look foolish if they were to tiptoe through *Les Sylphides* at Chanctonbury Ring.
>
> Operatic performances in the Arenas of Arles and Nîmes have made me set my face for ever against any Wotan bawling farewell to Stonehenge. Am I told that Glyndebourne is not an open-air jamboree, that it is as closed-in as a shop? *Tant mieux.* And if it remains a closed shop to me, *tant pis.*

Finally Agate turns to the "Niagara-like arguments" that had been poured forth to persuade him to sample Verdi's *Macbeth*. After a general attack on the opera (which he had heard in part on the wireless but never seen) he says:

> Was it for this melodious pot-pourri that I was invited to file [*sic*] my mind? Was it for this mellifluous brouhaha that I was supposed to get into evening-dress immediately after lunch, catch a train in the middle of my afternoon nap, and at Lewes angle for a taxi? . . .

After some observations on the subject of lighting and a few schoolboy gibes at French and Italian translations of Shakespeare, Agate concluded with the statement that *Macbeth* would "have to carry on *senza* Giacomo Agati".

Supporters of Glyndebourne urged John to answer this attack, and a week later he addressed the following letter to the *Sunday Times:*

It would appear that Mr Agate is using his position as your critic to make a personal statement in your paper about our work at Glyndebourne. . . . If this is merely a personal statement, showing Mr Agate's opinion as an individual, it is of no importance and need not be answered, but it appears to be written under the cloak of his position as your senior dramatic critic. As such it must be taken seriously.

The position then is that your great journal holds itself responsible for the statement that Mozart's operas are dull; that music—and drama too—should be performed only in towns and should, it seems, not even look for the good sites in a town, but in "the crowded streets" for its theatres. Such a policy in musical—and perhaps theatrical—matters has astonished me.

I met Mr Agate a month or so ago and, believing that he would act in his capacity as dramatic critic of the *Sunday Times*, I invited him to come to Glyndebourne to study, and perhaps criticise, the dramatic aspect of our work. I thought he would be interested to see the work of Professor Ebert. His answer was to express disapproval of our work because he thought that the patrons of Glyndebourne—and perhaps I—were snobs; that Mozart operas were boring, and that he was not at all interested in stagecraft or in lighting. Yet he functions as a dramatic critic.

However, believing that perhaps he got out of bed on the wrong side on the day on which I met him, I sent him a letter, again inviting him and endeavouring to show him that our patrons were not snobs, but that they came here at some considerable personal sacrifice because they thought it worth it.

After reporting Agate's initial failure to reply to his letter, and quoting the brief answer that he finally elicited, John concluded: "Apart from this queer incident, Mr Agate is a total stranger to me and to Glyndebourne."

Agate replied at great length. Indeed he was *not* the music critic of the *Sunday Times*, and that paper was *not* responsible for his views on music. He had *not* said that Mozart operas *were* dull, merely that *he* found them dull. He had never said that he was "not at all interested in stagecraft or in lighting"—merely that when he was not interested in what was happening on the stage, he did not care how that stage was lit. And so on. If his friends wanted to get him to *Macbeth* at Glyndebourne

> —and for the last month I have lived in fear of being chloro- formed and waking up in those stalls !—the proper thing to say was: "Forget Macbeth—forget Shakespeare—come and hear some jolly music! To adjure me to come because *as a dramatic critic* I should want to see lighting was nonsense. At the best of times, when I am interested in what is happening on the stage, I do not take much stock of lighting, which is an art or craft or device that even Hollywood knows all about.
>
> Lastly, if Mr Christie will look again at my article he will see that it contained no criticism of the actual performances at Glyndebourne—how could it, since I had not been there? It is my personal misfortune that I prefer Shakespeare to Verdi, and associate theatre-going not with orange-groves but with orange- peel.

And there the matter rested, Agate never went to Glynde- bourne; but Glyndebourne managed to survive without his patronage.

17

1939 and 1940

IT WAS probably largely for economy's sake that it was decided to repeat in 1939 the same five operas that had been given in 1938. There was further talk of trying to persuade Toscanini to conduct *Falstaff*, but in the end the idea was abandoned.

In spite of the worsening international situation, at the beginning of September 1938 various other projects were also under consideration. There was the possibility of an appearance of the Glyndebourne Opera Company at the Lucerne Festival in the following summer. There was (very surprisingly) a scheme proposed by John for co-operating with the Covent Garden that he had in the past so often abused. There was talk of a possible tour of Australia. And, lastly, there was an offer—apparently a firm offer—to appear at the New York World Fair in August 1939.

Then came Munich: the days of deep anxiety followed by the assurance, believed by so many, of "peace in our time". When Glyndebourne had recovered from the shock of preparing to receive, without any previous consultation, two hundred school-children, only the American project remained. In November it was officially announced that the Glyndebourne Opera Company would perform in New York, and in January Bing and Ebert went to America to explore the ground; but difficulties arose and through "sheer impracticability" the engagement was eventually cancelled.

The chief problem of the early months of 1939 was the finding of a Countess to replace Aulikki Rautawaara, who would not be available. John eagerly canvassed an English protégée who had a fine voice but who was exceptionally plain. Busch maintained that half the success of Glyndebourne had been due to the policy of engaging girls who were pretty as well as talented, and John was obliged to withdraw his candidate. Then it was suggested that Audrey's voice might now be ready for the Countess, but in the end she declined the part. Eventually it was given to an Icelandic soprano, Maria Markan. Thus, with the Tasmanian Margherita Grandi who was now engaged to take over Lady Macbeth, the geographical range of the Glyndebourne team had been stretched —and to John's great delight—almost from pole to pole.

★   ★   ★

John and Audrey were extraordinarily innocent politically. With their enthusiasm for all that was Bavarian or Austrian, they found it impossible to realise that Germany and Austria were now under the heel of thugs and murderers, or indeed that there might really be a war. Audrey therefore, in spite of the ill-feeling that her visit to Germany in 1936 had aroused at Glyndebourne, could see nothing wrong in agreeing to sing in Hamburg and Berlin early in the New Year, nor in expressing her willingness to sing Susanna at the Salzburg Festival in the summer. Bing was horrified when he learned of this. He wrote at once to Busch and Ebert for support; did Audrey realise, he asked, that "she would not just metaphorically, but literally, be shaking hands with murderers?" Busch immediately wrote to Audrey imploring her to cancel these engagements.

John was worried but by no means convinced; in any case it was now too late to cancel the Hamburg and Berlin concerts. But he wrote to Lord Halifax asking whether he could take the opportunity, at a reception of the Deutsch-Englische Gesellschaft in Hamburg at which he was to speak, to say anything that might be of use. As a result John had an interview with Sir Robert (later Lord) Vansittart; there is no record of what Vansittart said, but the following day John wrote to thank him for "advice which I feel it easy to accept and which I hope to be able to follow". Then John and Audrey left for Germany, but nothing seems to be known of how they fared there.

There remained the question of Salzburg. On his return John

wrote to Vansittart asking whether he, as representing the
Foreign Office, was prepared to make "a personal comment" that
he wished Audrey to accept the offer; he would also approach the
Prime Minister. Vansittart replied that "on balance"—and as much
as anything because of the damage that such a visit might do to the
reputation of Glyndebourne—he would recommend that Audrey
did not go to Salzburg. Audrey reluctantly accepted his advice.

In March Audrey went to Milan for three weeks, partly to
study and partly for a holiday. She liked Milan far less than Rome
and was not sorry when the time came for her return to England.
In April and early May there was a curious interlude: the Glyndebourne company, at rather second XI strength, gave four performances of *Figaro* and *Don Giovanni* in Brussels and Antwerp.
Audrey sang Zerlina, and Busch, to spare her "bad experiences
with another conductor—as she may discover soon enough at
Salzburg", agreed to conduct.

The Glyndebourne season opened on 1st June, and with thirty-
eight performances was the longest yet given. On 2nd June
Margherita Grandi scored a great triumph as Lady Macbeth, and
the previous year's success of *Don Pasquale* was in due course
repeated. When the curtain fell, on 15th July, on the last opera of
the season, *Così fan tutte*, John came on to the stage to report
"serious news". It had been a month of crises and the audience
feared the worst; some of them, at any rate, must have been
relieved when they discovered that he was referring to Eton's first
defeat by Harrow at Lord's since 1908.*

The following day, in spite of the mounting international tension, the 1940 programme was announced: *Carmen, Figaro, Don
Giovanni, Macbeth* and a revival of *The Magic Flute*. Another
attempt to persuade Toscanini to conduct *Falstaff* at a short Verdi
Festival had failed, in spite of a personal appeal by Erede on
Busch's behalf; although the *maestro* had shown much sympathy
with Glyndebourne, whose *Macbeth* he had heard the previous
year, he simply could not find the necessary time for rehearsals
and performances.

* 1909 was a draw; then in 1910 came Fowler's Match (see footnote on p. 274).

In the event, of course, there was to be no Glyndebourne season in 1940, nor for some years to come. Within less than two months war had broken out, and to many people it must have seemed that this was the end of John's heroic venture. Two days later Rudi Bing (who was soon to find himself working for the John Lewis Partnership in London) might have been seen in Woolworth's purchasing six-dozen chamber-pots for the three hundred evacuee children from south-east London who had just arrived, together with seventy-two adults, at Glyndebourne.

"As long as I live", wrote Edwards, "I shall never forget the arrival of those babies—bus load after bus load being tumbled out on to the lawn—babies in arms (one was only ten days old), crawlers, toddlers and the Nursery School children, who seemed quite grown up." In the foyer where, only a few short weeks ago, the smart opera-goers had discussed Mozart and Donizetti, Rosemary, from the Elephant and Castle, now recklessly rode her new tricycle, and Fat Tommy from Walworth blew bubbles to his heart's content; and a door labelled "Willi Domgraf-Fass-baender" now opened to reveal a bunch of mewling infants.* It was, however, generally agreed, till the novelty wore off, that Glyndebourne was far better than the Old Kent Road.

After the first panic was over, the number of children was reduced to, and maintained at, a hundred, of ages between two and five, with a staff of about thirty-five to look after them.

★   ★   ★

In January 1940 John wrote to Bernard Shaw asking for his assistance in getting a permit for Ebert, who was in Turkey, to return to England to produce films of *St Joan*, *Major Barbara* and Shakespeare's *Macbeth* for Gabriel Pascal, a friend of Shaw's. Shaw replied by return:

> Are you quite sure that it is wise to press for another German conductor just now? Government departments may do any-thing stupid or ignorant; but if I were Home Secretary I should say emphatically that when there are plenty of good English

---

* When Opera was restarted after the War, the artists were surprised to find their dressing-rooms hung with pictures of Little Miss Muffet and the Pied Piper.

conductors available there is no excuse for giving the direction of an English opera to an enemy alien. Glyndebourne has become a leading English institution and should have an English conductor. Busch . . . may have been a pleasant man to deal with, and was irreproachably competent; but he was not better than Malcolm Sargent nor as big as Albert Coates. The B.B.C. seems to have no difficulty in finding conductors. I put it to you that the war may give you a desirable opportunity for making a change. The wireless has made such a difference in musical culture since we formed our musical habits that there must be crowds of young Toscaninis all over the place. Think it over.

But in any case I am not sufficiently *persona grata* with the powers that be, to be a very safe intercessor. The moment we go to war it is always assumed in certain quarters that I must be pro-the enemy.

I should be very glad to help Glyndebourne if I were likely to be really helpful; but on this question I am not to be trusted; I want to see Glyndebourne degermanised. . . .*

Have you ever thought of having a staff of conductors? Busch must be pretty hardworked sometimes.

John replied to this letter at some length. Shaw had misunderstood him: Ebert was a *producer*, not a conductor. But as for British conductors—here John rode for many furlongs his old familiar hobby-horse. As usual, everything was black or white; white at Glyndebourne and black everywhere else. Beecham's *Magic Flute* at Covent Garden was "appallingly bad", Malcolm Sargent's *Messiah* at the Albert Hall "the most impossible performance", and so on. The same, he admitted, went for many continental performances (especially those conducted by men who had refused the Glyndebourne bait); "Toscanini's *Zauberflöte* at Salzburg, I am told, was impossibly bad."

---

* He was not alone in feeling this. His views were put more crudely by a certain "Grace Dane, Sergt.", who wrote from "Arts Club W" to John:

Where are your GERMAN OPERA directors now? Behind barbed wire we hope. But you must find some more if you can. Don't encourage your own country in art—always have Germans—mediocrities or Italians. What you want is a German Bomb under you to knock some sense into you. Not to spend your *UNEARNED* Dividends with the GERMANS.

When, after six days, Shaw had not replied, John wrote again, rather petulantly, demanding an answer. A few days later Miss Patch, Shaw's secretary, wrote to say that Mr Shaw was at present too busy to pursue the correspondence. Finally John was invited to lunch; but of the "most interesting talk" which took place we unfortunately have no record.

As for Ebert, his permit was refused and he remained for the duration of the war in Ankara, building up a Turkish National Theatre.

★   ★   ★

Though the regular Glyndebourne season was cancelled when war broke out, there were soon plans for a War Season—a fortnight in June with two Mozart operas. While this was under discussion, it was decided to tour the provinces with Gay's *Beggar's Opera*, and then take the production to London. Audrey played Polly; Roy Henderson was Peachum and Michael Redgrave Macheath; Frederick Austin conducted and the producer was John Gielgud. Of Michael Redgrave Audrey wrote that his "rather 'Harris-tweed' voice" was quite untutored, but that it was manly and had "definite charm". The tour began at the Theatre Royal, Brighton, in January 1940 and lasted six weeks. It was while the company was playing in Edinburgh that Audrey is said to have prophetically commented that the Scottish capital would be a fine setting for a festival—a "Salzburg of the North".

The tour wound up at the Haymarket Theatre, London, the last performance being on 25th May. Audrey, who confessed to being tired and "on edge", was not sorry when it was over. A week later came Dunkirk, a month later the fall of France. A second tour, which had been under consideration, was of course immediately abandoned, and so too was a project to move the Glyndebourne Opera to Williamsburg, Virginia, and establish it there in a small opera house to be built with Rockefeller money.

18

The Glyndebourne Team

BEFORE dealing with the War years we may perhaps pause to consider the team which set Opera in motion at Glyndebourne, even if to do so involves some anticipation of post-war seasons and the inclusion of judgments not formed until later.

Musicians—and singers in particular—are notoriously temperamental. It is the unanimous opinion of all who have worked at Glyndebourne that the amicable atmosphere that in general prevailed there was largely the result of the genius of its singer-hostess, Audrey Christie. After her death in 1953, many people were to recall what Audrey's presence had contributed to the success of the opera seasons both before and after the War:

> It was Mrs Christie's unforgettable merit [wrote Jani Strasser] that we managed to retain at Glyndebourne the atmosphere of a happy family. . . . She combined a wonderful artistic integrity, when she was on stage or working with her colleagues, with the status of, as it were, Lady of the Manor. There was never any difficulty with her; there was never at any time the feeling that she was not just an ordinary colleague, just one of the cast. But at the same time she had such grace and charm that she could, from one moment to the next, transform herself into a hostess. She was untiring in looking after the singers, who confided their private troubles to her. If anyone seemed to be unhappy, Mrs Christie would invite her into the house, give her a drink and talk with her, and send her away happy and with the feeling that she had found a friend.
>
> But at the same time Mrs Christie was a very important person in shaping and even deciding Glyndebourne's policy.

This she could achieve because not only did she have very great artistic feeling, a sense for standards, and wonderful energy and powers of making decisions; she also had that charm and a way of putting things which made people accept decisions that, coming from others, might have been found unacceptable. . . .

She seemed to have time for everything: time to see that soap and towels had not been forgotten in the guests' bedrooms; time to entertain her visitors; time to give advice and criticism to all who asked it.

She was not only a wonderful hostess [said Moran Caplat*], she was everybody's sternest critic—you couldn't get away with anything with her. She was kindness itself; she knew exactly when a word of praise was necessary or helpful, but she never gave it at the wrong time. She knew, too, exactly when to be quite stern, even harsh, to bring you to your senses. At the same time you knew—as one also knew with Mr Christie—that if you went to her for support and backing in anything you did, or had done, you would always get it. Neither of them would ever have the slightest thought of deserting one of their trusted followers in any of his actions; even if they thought the action that he had taken was ill-advised, they would stand by him—publicly at least.

Yet perhaps Audrey's greatest contribution to Glyndebourne was made through the influence that she exerted upon her husband. For John was an amateur, Audrey a professional. It was she who had saved Glyndebourne from being a second-rate affair, and she continually strove to maintain standards. She was, rather surprisingly, an astute business-woman.

John's enthusiasm, though sometimes undisciplined, was tremendous, his cheerfulness and good temper almost imperturbable; these were, of course, most valuable assets. It was his good fortune to be in a position to finance his very expensive experiment; but it was an experiment that might well have come to nothing without his astonishing flair for finding the right people to realise his dreams. He was, said Moran Caplat, so often right for the wrong

* Who came to Glyndebourne as Assistant Manager after the War, and has been General Manager since 1949.

reason; and Audrey realised this better than anyone. He knew
how to win the loyalty of those who worked for him. He interested himself in every detail of the practical side of the productions; but he also had that rare gift of being able to delegate. And
he always yielded to the superior knowledge of the expert.

Something of what he meant to Glyndebourne has been made
apparent by the gap that has been created by his death. His four-
square beaming figure, with or without his pug of the moment,
was as much a part of the Glyndebourne scene as are the shining
gardens or the gentle brow of the Sussex Downs. One always
sensed his presence and regretted his rare absences.

There were certain matters upon which John was, and remained, wholly unreasonable. Nothing that Covent Garden or the
Arts Council might do was ever right, and if Sadler's Wells came
in for less vigorous attack it was solely because of his great personal regard for Miss Lilian Bayliss. His friends soon learned
that it was best to avoid these topics of conversation. Yet Sadler's
Wells did not wholly escape his thrusts. After seeing one of their
most glittering productions, John said to the producer: "Well,
that was very good; very good indeed. You really must come to
Glyndebourne and do it *for the tenants.*" When Miss Bayliss died
in 1937 John wrote to Audrey: "Dear old Lilian ... I adored her.
She was so honest and trustworthy."

John could be intimidating. To a woman who had applied for
an audition, he wrote: "If you can sing above the average, and act
as well as you can sing, and are tall and reasonably good-looking,
we could give you an audition—*for our chorus.*" Or tactless—as,
for example, when he drafted a letter to the husband of another
applicant for the chorus, informing him that he wanted no
"screechers" at Glyndebourne. ("Why don't you want Mrs Abercrombie for the chorus?" Audrey asked John. "Oh, but I *do*!"
he replied, and was astonished when Audrey made him rewrite
the letter.) But probably Kipnis, whose large bass voice was so
famous, was merely amused when John assured him that "even
the smallest voice" would be audible in his auditorium.

If John had a flair for finding the right men to work for him, he also had some astonishing luck. Had it not been for Hitler, men such as Busch and Ebert would not have been on the market at exactly the right moment. And without those two, Glyndebourne might never have got off the ground. Of Busch, Peter Gellhorn, who was chorus master at Glyndebourne after the War, wrote:

> He was a person of great resilience, tremendous strength of character and quiet authority. He had a lovely sense of humour and seemed always easily in charge of the situation. I remember one particular moment among many, when he was rehearsing the overture to *Don Pasquale*, which has quite a tricky beginning. The entry was a little ragged—not quite together—and perhaps we didn't all realise that he had begun. . . . He quietly put down his baton, waited till all was silent and just said, "Everyone in this wonderful orchestra is invited to play." There was no trouble after that.
>
> Another characteristic of Busch was that he never seemed to be tired. I watched him rehearsing an orchestra from early in the morning until the evening, and we would sit together and have dinner during which he was either discussing interesting professional problems or telling stories from his varied and immense experience. Yet after dinner he would say, "Let's go and play a few duets", and he would take me to his green room and we would sit at the piano and play piano duets until eleven o'clock, both getting very excited and engrossed in what we were doing. And of course there was no sign of fatigue on either side.

At the end of one season the final performance was followed by a dance at which Busch took his seat at the piano and played Viennese waltzes to dance to.

Beecham's celebrated quip, "Mozart, like good wine, needs no Busch", can hardly have been intended to be taken seriously. John Pritchard, while at Glyndebourne in 1950 as Assistant Conductor, was deeply impressed by Busch's approach to the operas of Mozart:

> His rehearsal plan, proceeding from his own very vivid and compelling work at the rehearsal piano, was roughly as follows: As soon as an artist arrived at Glyndebourne he was

called to work with Fritz Busch and perhaps Jani Strasser also. I must mention that the impact upon foreign artists of the particular atmosphere of Glyndebourne was of great assistance, because they were so far removed from the distractions of a big city. They live mostly in small hostels nearby, and the peace of the Sussex countryside gradually sinks into their souls, so that they are far less jumpy and nervy than they would be under rehearsal conditions in London. Fritz always took great advantage of this. He believed in people living on their job, thinking about the particular opera they were working on and being free from outside distraction.

He would sit at the piano and with a great deal of gusto perform the orchestral part. He didn't stick to the score at all; he added all sorts of compelling touches—a little *glissando* or sudden sharp chords which would distract the attention of the singer—almost as if he were trying to put him off. Thus he knew that when later the singer came on the stage, whatever might happen he would be absolutely sure musically.

One day at an ensemble rehearsal I was amazed to see him go round the group of distinguished artists and solemnly whip off their glasses. The singers were no less surprised. "Well," said Fritz, "they don't wear glasses on the stage, and I want to know who won't be seeing the beat." It was very characteristic of him to be thinking already of the finished result.

It is impossible to speak of Busch without immediately recalling his wonderful partnership with Carl Ebert, of whom George Christie has written:

> Ebert had been a famous actor in Germany having studied under Max Reinhardt whose assistant he at one time became. So, when he turned to opera in 1927 as Intendant to the Darmstadt opera house—seven years before starting at Glyndebourne—he was already at the top of the tree in one part of the theatrical profession.
>
> One of the principal reasons for giving up the straight theatre was his feeling for opera as a heightened method of expressing drama. He stated once: 'Die Musik spricht zu mir in einer stärkeren Weise als das Wort.' His extraordinary sensitivity to this other—this most important dimension in

opera, namely music, was always evident in his approach in rehearsals and in the final results. At times he was criticised for excessive interpretation of the notes, of fussiness in his productions; but such criticism was of slight importance when comparing his pioneering work with his great achievement in opera production.

Carl Ebert was the first great producer of opera in modern times. Production, until his arrival, was a poor relation in opera, to which few paid much attention. The singers and, in a few instances, the conductors were the personalities who largely counted.

Watching him produce one had the feeling that he managed to penetrate into the inner significance of a work in a way that seemed to give the work and characters in it a new meaning. Often the meaning he brought out in a given musical/dramatic situation or in a given character was not new and may have been frequently expressed before; yet always, with his power of personality, his productions appeared to be innovations. His *Così fan tutte* at Glyndebourne before the War became a standard production in the world of opera, shamelessly and in a way blamelessly copied in many other opera houses. The same happened to a lesser extent in many of his other productions. His influence in production of opera—his influence in correcting the imbalance which existed as between music and singing on the one hand and theatre and production on the other—was almost certainly more widespread than the influence of any other operatic producer. The fact that Glyndebourne hit upon him and Fritz Busch, and the fact that these two great personalities in opera hit it off together, was a stroke of exceptional and remarkable good fortune.

No one who watched Ebert and Busch rehearsing together is likely to forget the experience. John Pritchard recalls the time when he used to sit in the darkness of the orchestra pit while Ebert explained to the singers exactly what he wanted of them, what he regarded as implicit in the score, what he believed that Mozart expected from the music and da Ponte from the libretto. Busch would continually supplement what Ebert said. They worked together as one man.

Peter Gellhorn develops this:

> Ebert has this amazing ability of taking the printed page of a score and making living things out of it, so that the movement and the action become, for the singer, a part of the score. He made no division between movement and music, which to me is far preferable to the kind of production which is imposed from without, like an additional score to the musical score.
>
> I was present at the first production rehearsals of *Macbeth*, and I still remember the way Ebert rehearsed the chorus, especially in the big banquet scene. He became in turn each one of the chorus, as it were. He seemed to guess what each was capable of, the way he might move and the kind of person he might represent. He started by saying to them, "You must imagine you have come here because you are afraid to stay away. When you drink the toast your hand goes up mechanically, your face becomes like a mask. Only now and then you watch your neighbour to see what he is doing", and so on. He painted the atmosphere so strongly that within five minutes I, sitting in the stalls of the empty theatre, became quite terrified. Everyone who saw this *Macbeth* will remember the sensation that the production caused. . . .

If Busch and Ebert are here singled out, it is because it was they who gave the character to the productions. They, together, with John and Audrey, formed as it were the inner ring. Yet this inner ring must of course also include Rudi Bing—one of John's "Quattuorviri"—whose tireless energy and wise council were invaluable to Glyndebourne, and most especially in the difficult days immediately after the end of the War. It could also be said to include Jani Strasser, the last of the "Founder Members" still in harness, who had worked so long and so devotedly to maintain high standards. But all this is not to belittle the invaluable contributions of Erede and Oppenheim, and of all the members of the general staff, not forgetting that tower of strength, the stage foreman and general factotum, "Jock" Gough.

As John once said, Jock and Sock (the pug) really ran Glyndebourne. Jock could turn his hand to anything, from the building and plumbing of a lavatory to the most intricate construction on

15

the stage. He feared no man, and many a time he and John "sacked" each other. "If you do *Don Giovanni* like that, then I'm off," Jock said on one occasion. He was; and it took the combined persuasion of John, Busch and Ebert, who had pursued him to his cottage in Ringmer, to prevail upon him to return. John made Jock the present of a dog. "What is he like?" asked Audrey. "Just as obstinate as Mr Christie, Ma'am."

Such, then, was the Glyndebourne pre-war team—a team which continued after the War also. It was unique in the history of Opera.

PART IV

19

The Years of Separation

DURING THOSE radiant, anxious weeks of June 1940, as the Germans marched through France and the threat of invasion grew from day to day, John trembled for the safety of his young family. What ought he to do? At last the decision was taken and the passages booked; on 19th July Audrey, with her two children, the young daughter of a friend, and the governess Miss Morgan, boarded at Liverpool a Canadian Pacific liner bound for Quebec. Audrey had not wanted to go.

John, at Glyndebourne, was "bewildered, but not yet depressed. . . . I sit in your stage dressing-room," he told her, "look at the photographs and restlessly go out. . . ." Then, as he wrote on, his mood changed and he grew "seriously alarmed; all my eggs in one basket, and what destitution it would be! I could not contemplate another marriage and could not imagine the replacement of these darlings." Again and again, during the separation which finally lasted for almost four years, he was to ask himself whether he had decided rightly, whether the risk he had taken and the years apart had not been too big a price to pay.

Meanwhile Audrey and the children were sailing, safely but uncomfortably, across the Atlantic. The ship was crowded with mothers and small children; there was even a pair of two-year-old twins travelling unaccompanied. Some of the mothers, accustomed to the services of nannies, were utterly helpless on their own, and stewards who were family men were summoned to explain and assist in the changing of nappies. The heat was intense in the cabins, whose ports had to be kept closed. Discipline was lax, everything chaotic. Even the minutest infant might never for a moment be separated from its life-belt. Audrey managed well but found it all, even with Miss Morgan to help her, terribly exhausting. After ten anxious days the ship reached Quebec, where she, her trio of infants and Miss Morgan took the train to Toronto.

Audrey was more fortunate than some of those who had emigrated at short notice: she had about five thousand Canadian dollars at her eventual disposal. Moreover she had learned, during her childhood in Canada, how to manage on a bare minimum. But it was, as John said, "a gallant effort arriving with only £50 and enough luggage to sink the ship". After staying for a short while at an hotel in Toronto she rented a cottage on the edge of Four Mile Lake, Burnt River, about 130 miles from the city; the cost was only $100 for the rest of the season—which meant so long as she could survive in the face of winter.

John wrote constantly to Audrey and to the children. Fortunately he was very busy with his great new project: the foundation of a National Council of Music designed to put an end to "the bungling amateur approach to musical performance in England". It kept his mind occupied and, for a time, stopped him from brooding. One evening in September he watched, in pyjamas, the bombing from the roof of Grosvenor House, enjoying the sirens "like growling tigers, defiant rather than frightening. . . . Darling, I am really sorry you and the children could not experience that with me. I could easily have made you enjoy it as a sport. . . . The danger is quite negligible." In the street he ignored the warnings and taunted those who ran for safety; he never knew what fear was,* and could not understand that others might not be so fortunate. "Frightened?" he wrote. "Bosh! It's children's fireworks. The children would enjoy the bangs; so would you, and of course I do and always did." Finally, he "got rather bored with the bombs and wished they would come nearer", gratefully recording "quite a decent air raid at last".

During the first year of separation from his family he was much

* He even looked forward to having a tooth out. "I love gas," he told a friend. "It *interests* me."

in Devon. "At Tapeley he was unable to find suitable wartime occupation", wrote Miss Belshaw, who was in charge of his Estate Office. "He was lonely and restless. He spent a good deal of his time digging into family history." Trivial little occupations, such as dead-heading the cannas, slaughtering black beetles or searching the local shops for vaseline to prolong the life of his razor blades, helped him to pass the long hours. "I saw him almost daily", added Miss Belshaw. "He talked incessantly of his early life. I gathered that at one time there had been a strong bond between him and his father. Of his mother he was always critical, although often, after talking about her, he would add, 'My mother was a good woman.'"

From time to time he had to go to London to canvass support for his N.C.M. When in London he was often to be seen taking tea at the Ritz, where he would stuff his pockets full of lump sugar—already a rare commodity—to feed any horses he might come upon in the street. He was also occasionally at Glyndebourne making little improvements to the Theatre. But wherever he was he thought lovingly of his distant family, and like a *leitmotiv* there runs through all his letters to Audrey the cry, "My darling, I admire you, I respect you and I love you and I want you . . . and I want those babies; the dog★ is not enough."

★   ★   ★

Meanwhile all was going well on the shores of Four Mile Lake. The cottage was a success and the children's cheeks grew rosy in the good country air. Rosamond and George had some simple lessons from Miss Morgan, who became a most loyal supporter of Audrey; and the following dialogue suggests that the boy, though at times a bit out of hand, was developing on sound lines:

> George: "Adam and Eve were the very first people in the world, weren't they, Miss Morgan?"
> Miss Morgan: "Yes, darling."
> George: "And was Mozart the next?"

He rowed on the lake, watched the chipmunks at play, helped

★ See p. 215.

in the house, collected beetles and brought home tiny fish in jam-jars, and grew very proud of his fine Canadian accent. Rosamond too helped where she could, fetching wood and water with her brother and in her leisure moments making "little presents for Jesus" or for her earthly father. Audrey began to practise again. In September came the news of the serious illness, and soon after of the death, of the faithful Childs. John wrote to George:

> I am so sorry about Childs. He was with me for about 30 years. He died peacefully in Lewes hospital. He was cremated and a bunch of roses from you with the inscription "from his loving godson, George" was placed in front of the earn [*sic*]. I know you were fond of him. I was. And he adored both you and me. He was a witty man and a very good man. I hope you will try to remember Childs with respect and affection. In your work and doings try to be as good a man as he was. . . .

In October the first snow fell at Four Mile Lake, and the little party packed up their belongings and returned to the town. Though everyone was astonishingly kind, Audrey did not like Toronto. A Finnish girl was engaged to help in the house; this left Audrey with more time to work seriously at her music, and for her innumerable social engagements. She did a Radio test and gave one or two concerts. In February, thanks to strings pulled by John, she was invited to sing at Government House in Ottawa, and in March she was in New York seeing agents; she knew that if the War went on for long she would be obliged literally to sing for her supper. While there she heard Beecham conduct. To John she wrote that she did not actually have any conversation with him at the reception given in his honour, but that when he was told that she was present he described her to another guest as "a nice little woman married to an awful fool of a husband".

★   ★   ★

In England the long winter dragged on. All hopes of a short war and a swift victory had died, and the country braced itself to face the "blood, sweat and tears" that now lay ahead. Tapeley was full of paying guests. The Saunton Sands Hotel had been taken over by the War Office for the Duke of York's School, and suffered accordingly. The Golf Club House became the American Headquarters for the area, and the American Army reduced the new course to a battle-field. Most of Glyndebourne was still occupied by infants.

John without his family was like a lost soul. Again and again he played through the records of *The Beggar's Opera* in order to hear Audrey's voice. Sometimes he picked up a stray soldier or airman, near Tapeley or near Glyndebourne, and brought him home for a few hours of civilised living—for decent food and wine and good music on the gramophone. He continued to fiddle with little tasks in the Theatre, helped by the invaluable Jock Gough. He did his stint of fire-watching. When a land-mine fell somewhere on the estate, he ordered that the crater and the damaged trees should remain untouched so that the children, on their return, would be able to see the fun they had been missing. But he was confident that the house and theatre would escape damage: "I don't think Hitler would bomb Glyndebourne," he said. "I'm sure he *respects* us."

At Christmas he acquired a new pug, Bimperl—named after Mozart's dog but soon renamed Pumperl on account of his regrettable refusal to become house-trained. Pumperl figures in almost all of John's letters, and in many cables; he was fed upon the fat of the land—mushrooms, grapes and asparagus—and so fared better than did most of the human race at that time. He also shared his master's taste for milk puddings: "You should see him eat tapioca; it clings to his mouth and he tries to eat it without closing his lips. He loves it—throws it about, makes voluptuous sounds, swallows and licks. But as an exhibition of sheer pleasure it is marvellous. . . ."

Between July 1940, when Audrey had left England, and the end of that year, she had written some fifty letters to John and had received an equal number from him; but in April 1941 she wrote sadly that she had only had four letters from him in as many months. He was deeply penitent, and thereafter gave her little cause for complaint. In the summer and autumn of 1941 she sang at a number of concerts in Canada and the States—in Philadelphia, in Halifax, and in Vancouver to an audience of ten thousand. John, anxiously awaiting news, provided her with a kind of musical " correspondence course":

> I am so certain of your success, but I must warn you of three things. (1) You must be calm and confident as I am. You have every reason to be so, so no more nonsense about your working yourself up and getting nerves. . . . I am absolutely confident. Hurrah! (2) Don't let your voice go white. It need not do so. (3) If you are singing English, make the ends of the words clear: love, not lo— . . . Oh! yes, and (4) do rest and don't talk before your concerts. Remember that Melba would not speak to anyone beforehand.

But in spite of what Audrey earned by her singing—and in February (1942) she reported that she had made $1,550 in three weeks from concerts in Seattle, Edmonton and elsewhere—she was often hard put to it to make both ends meet. John sent the pittance that could legally be exported; he even went so far as to suggest that she might make some money by selling her name to Columbia to advertise face-cream, but happily she was never obliged to. All who knew her in Canada and the States are agreed that she behaved with great courage throughout those difficult years.

In the autumn of 1942 she was in Kelowna (British Columbia) where she had lived as a child, and George sporadically attended a boarding school there. John sent the eight-year-old boy a cable to hearten him, *three* copies of *Tom Brown's Schooldays*, and later a sensible letter of advice:

> I have not had much news of you, but I expect you find school life absorbing and almost all-embracing. I have no doubt that you will make a success of it, though in finding your feet you are sure to make mistakes. Your successes are more important. Preserve your sense of right and wrong. Fight your own battles and learn to depend on yourself. Make good friends. Find someone you can ask advice of in a friendly way.
>
> And don't forget Mummie and Rosamond and even me. . . . We are here to help you and to offer you our experience. You will find in Rosamond a very wise little woman who, being of

your own age, will understand better than Mummy and me what you want to do. Write to her, ask her advice. . . .

He had also written to Rosamond:

I realise that you will miss George during these next few months. You must expect him to develop by his contact with other schoolboys. Some developments you will like and some you won't. Beneath the changes on the surface you will find the same George. Don't be disappointed if there are things you don't like; try to see them in relation to his growth in experience. Be patient and try to help him and make him understand that your help is at his service. Be amused: you will find that the best way of understanding each other. . . .

In November 1942 John was considering the possibility of joining Audrey in the spring in Canada, where he hoped to persuade the Ontario Government to build a Glyndebourne at Niagara Falls or City; and a fortnight later, after Rommel's defeat in North Africa, he suggested the alternative of her bringing the children back to England. Permission for him to go to Canada was, however, refused, and in February both the children fell ill. Audrey was almost at the end of her tether.

But with the coming of spring the children recovered their health and Audrey her spirits. In April she wrote to Miss Marguerita Fowler, one of John's secretarial staff who was living at Glyndebourne during the War:

George and Pidge are quite pathetically anxious to get home. . . . However, I don't think the Atlantic is a fit place to risk children at the moment. They are both growing tremendously. Pidge's latest craze is a skinning knife, which she has bought herself; it is really a dangerous weapon. She wears it on a short string around her neck (it is in a leather sheath fortunately) and searches every walk for a couger [puma] to kill. She really looks charmingly ridiculous when, knife in hand, and bent quite double, she sets off!!

Audrey was now singing again, and in a warm-hearted cable

from Beecham on 27th May John learned of her triumph in
Figaro in Montreal:

> HAVE JUST CONDUCTED TWO PERFORMANCES MOSTLY WITH
> METROPOLITAN SINGERS OF MOZART'S FIGARO FOR MONTREAL
> FESTIVAL IN WHICH AUDREY AS SUSANNA HAS SCORED A BRILLIANT
> AND SPECIAL SUCCESS WHICH I THINK WILL HAVE FORTUNATE
> RESULTS—BEECHAM

Little could either John or Audrey then have foreseen that these
were to be her last appearances in Opera.

The Beechams seem to have been very kind to Audrey, and in
August they offered her the use of their flat in New York. John
wrote to her on 27th August (1943):

> I am in favour of your using the Beecham flat, and I think
> you should borrow £1,000 if it is convenient to your friend;
> you must have money to finance this Audrey–Glyndebourne
> scheme. I am, to my indignation, not allowed even to recognise
> such a debt; but no regulations will prevent one in due course
> from behaving like a gentleman.
>
> I want you to make a success of this New York business. You
> must establish your own name there and so make Glynde-
> bourne's at the same time. During this period you can't live on
> nothing, and you must behave like an artist. If you could get
> one performance of Susanna you might make, and would and
> should make, a great hit. Get a contract for one performance,
> get and pay for publicity and then demand $1,500 for the next
> performance and spend it all on publicity. If they won't pay it,
> advertise that your fee is $2,000. Stay at the best hotel and leave
> New York in a huff. Do something outrageous (and funny if
> possible). . . .

In view of John's objection to behaviour of this kind on the part of
artists engaged by or under negotiations for Glyndebourne, his
advice to Audrey is very surprising.

In the autumn of 1943 John attempted to get permission for
George to return to England, first in a bomber and then, when
that had failed, in a warship. The sea journey, he told Rosamond,

"would be thrilling for George. With a bit of luck he might look forward to some shooting; it makes a good rattle but he would like that, and I am sure he would be a great success with the officers. . ." But this too was refused.

In fact the first of the Christie household to reach England was Beanie, Rosamond's beloved wire-haired fox terrier. John visited Beanie regularly while he was in quarantine, and refused to be intimidated by his hostility because "dogs never bite me". But, for all his intelligence, Beanie was unable to associate John with his family in Canada. "Would you send me a stocking of Rosamond's?" John wrote to Audrey. "I will at once take it to Beanie and I expect he would recognise it. I pray every night that God will explain to him and bring him safely to his happy home. . . ."

In November Audrey fell ill. The strain of her protracted and difficult exile was telling on her. She longed, beyond everything in the world, to be back in England, back at Glyndebourne with John at her side. But depressed though she was, she saw that the end of their separation was now in sight. The Allies had taken Naples and were poised for their thrust towards Rome and the North; there were more and more devastating air-raids on Berlin; everyone was saying that a landing in France would come with the spring. It was in fact towards the end of May (1944), a week or two before D-Day, that Audrey and the children finally arrived in Lisbon and so reached England in time for the flying bombs—possibly the most disagreeable of all the experiences to which British civilians were subjected during the War.

* * *

For the first year after the departure of his family, John had been chiefly at Tapeley, but towards the end of May 1941 he returned to Glyndebourne. Chastened by Audrey's reproaches, he had resumed writing to her with the greatest regularity, and in such volume that it brought on a return of his "tennis elbow". In his letters he described in detail his negotiations with the N.C.M. and other matters of importance, but he also told her of the little trivial happenings that would enable her to picture his day-to-day life. Sometimes we learn of him improbably employed:

> This evening I heard a baby crying in the sick room (the old nursery) and I went up, as I always do. It had stolen some sweets and was in bed today with a stomach-ache. It was sitting on its pot in its bed with one of the girls watching it. So I applied my remedy. The pot was removed. The baby, aged I should think three, lay down and I lifted its feet high above its head for half a minute, laid the baby down again and tucked it up, and it immediately went to sleep again. Magic! The story has run round the nursery.

John was devoted to small children and enormously enjoyed having the Nursery School in his house. His friend and neighbour, Rhona Byron, recalls:

> Rudi [Bing] was then living with John at Glyndebourne, and they had a wonderful time together. John loved teasing the nurses—and, in particular, two middle-aged sisters known as "Wizz" and "Hem". After Rudi had begun working daily from Glyndebourne at John Lewis's store in London, John would often bring in one or two of the toddlers to tea with him. After dinner, Rudi and I used to go and sit in the Organ Room (in the dark because there was no blackout, and with rugs wrapped round our knees because there was no heating) while John went off to collect as many nurses as he could. He would then explain to them the story of *Der Rosenkavalier* or *Figaro*, etc., with excerpts on the gramophone; the fact that the nurses had no idea what he was talking about did not worry him in the least.

Miss Fowler, too, has many recollections of Glyndebourne in wartime: of fire-watching, of skating on the ponds in the hard winter of 1940, of country dancing and the periodic grand dance in the winter for the nurses and the Canadian soldiers stationed in the neighbourhood; and above all, of the great Christmas parties for the children, at which John always played a big part.

Of course the principal function, for John, of the infants at Glyndebourne was that they reminded him of his own children,

so sadly far away. His darling children! He thought of them incessantly. He sent them bicycles and books and penknives and
music cases. He sent them fiddles, and further fiddles when the
first consignment was lost at sea. He sent them anything and everything that he could get a permit to export. Being well supplied
with clothes—"I have 180 handkerchiefs, 132 pairs of socks and
stockings, 110 shirts, etc., of all kinds; I am a dressy man", he
rather absurdly told Audrey—he used his clothes' coupons to buy
what they needed in their cold climate. He sent of course every
penny that it was permissible to send, and devoted long hours to
the exploration of ways and means to exceed the permissible.

For his admiration of Audrey's courage he could find no adequate words. On 10th July 1943 he wrote:

> I am determined that when you return you shall have every-
> thing. I will do all I can to make your life happy and to help the
> children. You will find me very unselfish. . . . We shall both be
> several years older, but what of that; I am not at all an old man.
> The children won't find me old. I am handicapped, as far as
> they are concerned, by my blindness . . .; my lame foot does
> not matter much. . . . My blindness will make it difficult for me
> to play games with them, which I could otherwise do with
> ease. . . .
>
> My darlings, I do want you so much! I go for walks alone. I
> sit alone. I eat alone. Nobody comes here. But it won't be too
> long now, and then for many years of happiness and perhaps
> success. . . .

In December 1941 he wrote:

> I go to London wearing my thin tropical dark grey suit, with
> nicks [trousers] pressed, and no waistcoat, vest, overcoat or hat,
> and find other people shivering in vest, waistcoat, winter things
> and overcoat, and making a fuss if there's a draught. . . . I sit in
> draughts. I have never been so well.

Whenever he was well he was convinced that he could never
be ill again, and attributed his immunity from sickness to a sensible
regimen or to the genius of his masseur. But shortly after this
boasting he had to report a sharp and inexplicable attack of

lumbago. "There *must* be some cause", he informed her, "and I must find it out."

In the spring of 1942 he sold at Restell's some 13,000 bottles of the stock of wine that he had laid in for the Festivals. He told Audrey, "I feel that the patrons of the Festival after the War will prefer to see, say, iced lager on the tables around them rather than the expensive wines which they used to be able to afford. I regard this sale as a gesture to them." This wine realised nearly £20,000 —almost twice what he had been led to expect and many times what he had paid for it. The task of packing up and despatching this enormous quantity occupied him and Jock for many weeks.

Audrey must often have wondered how John was faring when she was not there to vet his wilder letters and the drafts of his more provocative speeches. He was in fact frequently helped in this matter by Dr H. C. Colles, who had been Music Critic of *The Times* since 1911. When Colles died in 1943, John wrote to Audrey, "I am very sorry indeed. In your absence he had always done what you did so well—check and guide me; and I was conscious of it. He gave me great strength—in the background, as it appeared to be, but actually in leading me."

But from time to time, as can be seen from John's letters to Audrey,* she reminded him of his especial weaknesses. In August 1942 he wrote:

> I am taking note of your suggestions about my blowing my own trumpet. I am not arrogant or conceited, but I know Glyndebourne has been a marvel and it seems silly to pretend otherwise. Yet there are those who, out of envy or jealousy, have buried their heads in their hands or who deny its success. All the same, I will take your hint. I never mind you saying or writing these things.

He did not wholly lack the faculty of self-criticism; "I don't think I have great brains", he told her, "but I have an unusual brain and something of my mother's persistence and tenacity. I

---

* Many of Audrey's letters to John are missing.

think I have the capacity for success, but I think bigger than my neighbours. I fancy I am generally too far ahead. People are always looking to their own careers; we don't care about that. We are like wing three-quarters at 'Rugby' who don't get the ball. . . ."

His mood varied, but gloom predominated. Sometimes it was the War news that depressed him, sometimes the enormous "unjust" taxes he had to pay; sometimes the loneliness and the boredom became almost unbearable. He was "fed up" with England. All his best laid schemes for a better world seemed to go agley. He thought of selling Glyndebourne after the War or of handing it over to the National Trust. He thought of giving up Tapeley and moving into a much smaller house on the Devonshire estates—Saunton Court; but Audrey was strongly opposed to this, fearing that he would vegetate there. He even considered the possibility of emigrating to Canada. He owed perhaps more than he realised to the kindness and sympathetic understanding of Rhona Byron, who was always at hand when he could no longer bear his own company.

The possibility of having to give up Glyndebourne brought him up sharp against a new problem—the problem of what would be in the best interest of the children:

> I feel—though it is terribly difficult for me—that the children must have a new outlook on life and that they must dissociate themselves from the past; to be tied to a derelict past will be the worst thing for them. It seems that all my hopes are killed, and killed at any rate by having done something fine. . . . But Canada may be better. We should be able to transfer money out to Canada.

The mood of gloom persisted for many months, but, even when he was at his lowest, John often enlivened his letters with an anecdote. In April 1943 he sent her a graphic account of a scrap he had had with two poachers:

> They paused and we met. One then bolted and I closed with the second; but he got free, pointed his rifle at me and said he would shoot. We both had our blood up; but I had a bad shoulder and had to go slow, so after a bit he escaped. . . . My hand was covered with blood.

Two of John's men were now seen approaching, but the poachers unwisely returned to the attack:

> So I went in again for another scrap, and got first one rifle away and then the other, saying that I was not going to be shot at again. . . . Later they were being examined in the office and I took them in cake and tea. . . . It took from 3.30 to 6.30; I thoroughly enjoyed it, and today am a bit stiff; still, I should like some more incidents.

★   ★   ★

A perpetual problem at this time was Audrey's father, Aubrey Mildmay, who was now living at Ringmer. For Audrey's sake John was remarkably kind to, and patient with, his eccentric and difficult father-in-law;* but in the end he was forced to admit that it was impossible to help him. On 7th November 1943 he wrote:

> I saw your father this morning after church. He was well. Yesterday being cold and a nasty wind he went out for a walk; the next warm day he will be in bed. Oh! he is starting to use his battery on his deaf apparatus, and he said he could hear me read the lessons. Probably he has not switched it off, and when it is run down he will say that the battery does not help and will discard it. . . . He is painting cows, that is, pictures of cows.

On 30th January 1944 he wrote again:

> I saw your father for a moment. Edwards and I have practically given up trying to work with him; he is absolutely hopeless. He is always in a muddle and always gives everyone trouble and doesn't mind giving them trouble. . . . I am leaving him to stew in his own juice. . . .

★   ★   ★

The year 1943 saw the deaths of two women who had played

* The only letter from Aubrey Mildmay to be found among John's papers certainly suggests a mild eccentricity. It begins: " 'Darling' John—I feel like that because I suddenly realise that perhaps there never was anybody like your sundered Audrey—my far-flung sundered Audrey—for love and wit, and touching the spot, in thought and word and execution . . . including intimate letter-writing. . . ."

very important roles in John's life—his aunt Lady Margaret
Watney, and Fanny Mounsey. The former had been almost a
second mother to him during his difficult early years, and to the
latter he owed his discovery that music did not begin and end
with Wagner. John attended Fanny Mounsey's "Quaker memorial
service and found most of our friends from here [Glyndebourne]
at it. She was an amusing woman. I had not seen her for about a
year. . . ."

When 1944 dawned, it seemed to many people, John among
them, that there would be peace—in Europe at any rate—before
the year was out; one thing, however, now appeared certain:
that the spring would see him reunited with his family. He realised
that he had much to be thankful for. He, his wife and children
had so far come unscathed through the holocaust. Not a pane of
glass had been broken at Glyndebourne or at Tapeley. Even his
businesses were flourishing, and he told Audrey:

> The Building Works' profits for last year are a little over
> £14,000, of which we distribute a bonus of I think about
> £2,000. This is the first of the results to come out. Hill's and
> Calnorth will do better than last year. I wonder whether we
> shall get our income up to £50,000—not that it matters as it is
> all taken in taxation. . . .

But even after his family's passage had been booked, and it
might have been expected that his optimism would have returned,
he still suffered from moments of depression; and in almost the
last letter that he wrote to Audrey before she sailed, he confessed
that he still saw no future for the Festival Opera:

> Darling, I feel I want to live quietly with you and the child-
> ren. Our businesses should go on well. I want not to embarrass
> ourselves and the children with any more Glyndebournes. We
> have proved our case, and if we are wanted we shall be ready to
> serve. . . .

But happily Glyndebourne was to be wanted again; little more
than two years later, on 12th July 1946, its curtains were to rise
upon the world première of Benjamin Britten's *The Rape of
Lucretia*.

16

20

Planning a Better World

"THE DAY is not far off when the Economic Problem will take the back seat where it belongs, and the arena of the heart and head will be occupied, or reoccupied, by our real problems—the problems of life and of human relations, of creation and behaviour and religion." This might well have been written by John; the passage in fact is taken from a book by a man whom he came to look upon as the chief opposer of the National Council of Music: Lord Keynes, Chairman (from 1942 to 1946) of C.E.M.A. and of its peacetime successor the Arts Council.

C.E.M.A. had been started in the early days of the War, by private aid, to provide cultural entertainment under the difficult conditions then prevailing; it was soon to be sponsored by the Board of Education and entirely supported by a Treasury grant. Thus, almost unnoticed, State patronage of the arts came to Britain at a time when it might least have been expected. In June 1945 the wartime experiment was made permanent under its new name of the Arts Council of Great Britain—a name carefully chosen, said Keynes, as having initials (A.C.G.B.) which could not be converted into an acronym.

It was in the spring of 1938 that John had taken the first steps towards the foundation of his National Council of Music. Gradually it developed into a vast project to build a better world after (or indeed during) the War—a Utopia in which greed and self-seeking would be no more, in which the things of the mind and the spirit would predominate and in which Britain would lead the way. Though he did not yet say it in so many words, it was to be a world in which he hoped to act as a kind of benevolent artistic and spiritual dictator. He could "think big", as he so often told Audrey, for he believed that to *do* big things this was necessary. But in the absence of Audrey's restraining influence he soon came to think enormous.

John had managed to enlist for his Council a considerable amount of support from the musical world. Professor Edward Dent, Sir Adrian Boult, Dr Malcolm Sargent, Sir George Dyson, Dr Ralph Vaughan Williams, Sir Walford Davies and Miss Myra Hess* were among those who were prepared to co-operate, though Dyson found much to criticise. In particular, Dyson failed to see how the work of the Council would differ from that of C.E.M.A. or the aid given to music by the Carnegie and Pilgrim Trusts. The B.B.C. took offence at a thoughtless statement by John about "England's four famous orchestras"—a quartet which did not include theirs. But at first the real opposition came from Sir Hugh Allen, Director of the Royal College of Music and the secretary of the Incorporated Society of Musicians (I.S.M.).

Allen wanted the Council to be controlled by the I.S.M., but was prepared to concede that non-professionals—e.g. John— "should not be wholly excluded". John foresaw what would happen: "This gallant body will go to the Government and ask them for a large sum of money which they will spend among themselves." Allen exasperated John: he would not answer letters; and when a meeting was finally arranged—a meeting which involved John in nine hours of train journeys—he failed to turn up. John wrote angrily: "I get helpful letters from other people in connection with the Council. I get no replies from you and only that ridiculous visit† when you tried not to co-operate. Allen you must do better!" Again, if only Audrey or Dr Colles had been at hand to stop the posting of this petulant letter, much unpleasantness might have been avoided.

A number of committee meetings of the N.C.M. were held during the winter of 1940–41, and the Council was duly founded. An undated list of members shows the name of Sir Hugh Allen,

* I use their styles at the time.
† I do not know to what this refers.

who presumably in the end agreed to co-operate, and of Sir Henry Wood, who had also at first shown himself reluctant to help.

Throughout the War John wrote incessantly to men of distinction in the political, literary, musical and artistic worlds, pouring out his ideas to them and begging them to help create a better England—and thus a better world. Some—Sir Edward Bridges and Sir Kenneth Clark, for example—replied warmly; some alleged interest in John's Utopia but pointed out that first of all there was a war to be won; some passed him on to others; one or two rebuffed him; many of the replies are missing.

It is impossible to give more than an indication of his innumerable schemes at this time to defeat mediocrity, inefficiency, indolence and corruption. One project, conceived in a moment of high optimism, was the formation of a Glyndebourne Society. On 2nd September 1941 he told Audrey: "I want 20,000 people to take a £10 subscription which we will invest in War Loan: total £200,000. They then get it back after the War in tickets for Glyndebourne, and so preserve Glyndebourne for the future."

A month later he wrote to her again to tell her that he was about to see Mr (now Lord) Butler, the new President of the Board of Education, to enlist his support for the Glyndebourne Society. He wanted "the Cabinet to join first of all. Then I want it supported by all the Press, by all professional organisations, Clergy, Lawyers, Scientists, Accountants and Learned Societies. I want it to stand for Music, Art, Literature, Architecture, Drama, Science, all of which will deal with Glyndebourne through their own learned societies ... It's a grand scheme—one million members. . . ."

On 31st October 1941 he wrote to Mr Anthony Eden, then Secretary of State for Foreign Affairs. His letter, he said, dealt with "Reconstruction and the New World". He asked that Churchill should send him, officially, to Roosevelt and Mackenzie King to start the N.C.M. immediately in America and Canada. "This scheme gives Roosevelt and the Federal Government just what they want—a Council in America of sufficient standing, representing the art of Music. I want to link up the whole world in due course with it. . . . We have a scheme for building a Glyndebourne in Canada and repeating over there our English Festival of seven weeks. We must get the festivals of the world in future into the British Empire. The British Council supports me; will you?" There is no reply to this letter among John's papers.

John was never afraid of saying exactly what he thought; on 4th February 1942 he wrote to Robert Foot, Joint Director-General of the B.B.C., a letter which, though all too true in substance, is patronising in tone and reads almost like a school report on a boy who has been doing badly:

> I am not satisfied with much of the musical side of the B.B.C.'s work—good music and rubbish. You have got an excellent man in Adrian Boult, who is ideal to work with. But many of the performances are very poor (not his) and not worth what they cost. The key to the situation lies in the Conductors. . . . Because of them and because of the conditions in which they work in England, the soloists are not good enough. The B.B.C. Opera performances are decent but not good enough. You have all the money that is wanted; you can pay decent salaries, and, so far as I know, do. You have good orchestral players, and yet you are not electrifying England with the conductors you are finding or making. Something is wrong. . . . It seems to me that you want a Director of a Committee of Cultural Reconstruction. . . .

In other words, what the B.B.C. needed was (thought John) a John—and his friend Sir William (later Lord) Jowitt thought the same and tried to get John appointed to the Board.

In March John gave Audrey his views on England—a materialistic England run by "the Machine"—and on Winston Churchill:

> Churchill to my mind is in many ways a great man, but I don't like him and am shy of him. I suspect that he is dangerous. I don't think he is interested in a better world, and I suspect him of being contemptuous of those who are. On the other hand, suppose Australia proposes to leave the Empire I should expect Churchill to be the one man who would and could prevent it. Yet I don't like his friends; I hate Beaverbrook and regard him as being totally evil.
> Churchill has fought the Political Machine all his life, and

bobs up here and there in prominent position, finally doing marvels as Prime Minister but I suspect being responsible for grave errors not yet announced or attributed to him. I don't want to see a world planned by him.

"I am depressed," John wrote to Audrey two months later. "I see no signs of ideals anywhere, only people thinking that others must make sacrifices and are to blame. . . . The Machine which controls us here is intolerable. We are being strangled. Taxation must be severe, but we have trickery and pious fraud on top. . . ."

In fact, John remained, as has already been said, deeply depressed for many months. He wanted to win the Peace; he seemed reluctant to admit that it was necessary first to win the War. Taxation would, he saw, eliminate the rich:

I don't know that I mind a new world without personal riches, if it is based on ideals—but that is where I think it fails. It aims only at mediocrity. For some time taxation will be crushing, and you will see that there is no kind of gratitude from the Government Machine for any effort we make. I don't feel inclined to make any more efforts. I feel inclined to live without any more problems. I want peace with you and those children. . . .

On 6th June John wrote a long letter to Sir Stafford Cripps, at that time Minister of Aircraft Production. In it he begins to show signs of a zeal, not far short of megalomania, which, in the absence of Audrey's steadying influence, now temporarily replaced the amiable eccentricity of pre-war years and which was to return after her death:

I have several problems which may perhaps interest you, because they concern the building of the New World in the matter of the mind and the spirit.

First, the Future of Glyndebourne. I do not think I am in the position to guarantee this Festival in the future, nor do I see why I should do so. I have proved it; now the New World should carry it on. I want an audience which is passionately keen on our work. I have never had any Government subsidy for this work. Owing to my enterprises I pay considerable taxes and am always short of cash. I am by birth a considerable landowner.

I turned into businesses, which my office runs, everything which is done in connection with my estates; and I employ about a thousand men in consequence, and with financial success. I started all these businesses. I was actuated in this purpose by idealism. I now propose to induce the Government of Ontario to build a new Glyndebourne to my designs at Niagara City. . . . But it depends in the first instance on the support for which I ask in the first paragraph above.

After discussing in detail his plans for a Canadian Glyndebourne which, he said, could only be realised if he received financial help for his Sussex festival, he turned to the N.C.M. and then proceeded to outline a fantastic scheme for curing all the nation's ills:

I want to crystallize the National Conscience by giving it a constitution and a home (Glyndebourne). The Slums and Poverty of the past would not have been tolerated if the National Conscience had been made aware of these problems. Party Papers and Party Politics aggravate these problems instead of curing them. I want a succession of conferences, some thirty strong, on all problems, attended by the right people who will come down here and sit until they have found the problem and perhaps its solution. Then the result of such a conference must appear in the Conscience's own journal called *Glyndebourne* . . .

He continued:

We are bursting with enthusiasm and ideals. If our schemes are right, we want backing. We want finance. I think we should not depend on the backing of a rich man or a rich Trust, but on the Government. We want a better World and we offer service. I know you are busy, but these are National problems. We are idealists (I mean my wife and I), but our results show that our feet are on the ground. Ideals pay. I want to base the New World on Ideals. Can we meet?

Nearly three weeks elapsed before John received an answer from Sir Stafford's personal assistant. Sir Stafford was "extremely interested" in John's proposals and had given them "careful consideration". "He feels, however, that the question of State aid to the arts is so important that it should be the subject of an enquiry which would include within its scope not only the splendid work which you have done at Glyndebourne and your ambitious proposals for the future, but also the work and plans of other appropriate bodies such as C.E.M.A. and the Royal Colleges of Art and Music." He hoped that John would keep in close touch with Lord Keynes, and regretted that the pressure of War Cabinet and Parliamentary business would be likely to make it difficult for him to devote any of his time to these matters during the next few months. In other words, he had no intention of doing anything.

John's gloomy mood persisted throughout the autumn and winter. He saw himself as the only really sane man, the only man activated by ideals, in a world of crooks and imbeciles, and such a discovery is inevitably depressing. He now turned to the Church to persuade it to give a moral lead. He visited the Bishop of Chichester (Dr George Bell), who expressed interest and passed him on to the Archbishop of Canterbury (William Temple). John and the Archbishop had two things in common: the latter had inaugurated a somewhat similar crusade during the First World War—the National Mission of Repentence and Hope*—and both he and John claimed descent from Lady Godiva. Temple expressed himself "not only interested but *keenly* interested" and passed John on to the Archbishops of York and Westminster. Nothing happened.

In a letter to Lloyd George John sketched a Utopian plan for voluntary fuel rationing which, like many "voluntary" schemes, was to be enforced on all who did not co-operate. He told Lloyd George that both Chamberlain and Churchill had turned down his offer to form a Ministry of Economy to stop waste. He again urged the formation of such a ministry. "I wanted no compulsory powers", he wrote. "I believe that I would have been backed by every organisation in the country and that I would have succeeded, because my case is based on what every man in his own conscience knows is right. . . . The refractory people would have been dealt with by regulation and punishment through the ordinary force of law . . ."

* See *Life and Letters* by William Temple, p. 208.

Lloyd George's answer is missing. But, as John told Audrey, waste still went on everywhere: "Up to a week ago we had strikes; now we have soap rationing. The members of Brooks's just waste soap. They have been given rubber bristle mats, but they don't use them and leave the soap in pools of water. Today I found the gas oven left on. . . ."

John was also at this time still indignant at the way he had been treated over taxation. "My taxation appeals have all been turned down by the Treasury," he told Audrey. "Now I fancy I am free to bring it all out in a book in which I come right out into the open and challenge all this humbug which goes on." The book was never written.

★   ★   ★

Lord Keynes had recently become Chairman of C.E.M.A., and it was soon clear that he proposed to extend its scope; it also now seemed likely that C.E.M.A., originally designed to fill a wartime need, would become a permanent institution. John not unreasonably felt that, so far as music was concerned, it was pirating his ideas, and that the villain of the piece was Keynes. The two men, contemporaries at Eton, fell out; though subsequently they often found themselves travelling between London and Lewes in the same train, they pointedly entered different compartments.

On 20th November (1942) John told Audrey that, rather than temporise with the enemy, he would "sooner throw a violent incendiary bomb into the whole lot of them and cauterize the rubbish and littleness out of their minds. I believe I am right. I know I am. . . ." The following day he wrote to Keynes:

> Thank you for your letter of the 19th inst. I gather from it that it is the intention of C.E.M.A. to enlarge itself to do the work that the N.C.M. set out to do, and for this reason I propose to withdraw my efforts to help by creating the N.C.M. . . .

Many weeks passed and there was still no reply from Keynes. "I feel that I am thwarted", John told Audrey. "I feel so bitter about the way in which I and my work have been treated that

I am disinclined to do anything more for this blasted country."

John now turned to Lord Esher, President of the British Drama League, to whom he wrote a long letter at the beginning of February (1943). After criticising the constitution of C.E.M.A. and some of those who had been chosen to serve on its Advisory Panels, he continued:

> The overwhelming danger is that of mediocrity. C.E.M.A. up till now has done nothing but mediocrity, which it has persistently described in its own bulletins as being "the finest possible", etc—thus proving that it is incapable of doing the work that has to be done. Keynes has shown no sign of burning with artistic sense; in fact, he told me in a letter that he had only undertaken the work on condition that he had to give no interviews. He also told me that he had not the foggiest idea of what I wanted. . . . In my opinion it is vital that either the Chairman or else the essential driving force of the Council should be literally burning with artistic fire. . . .
>
> The N.C.M. seems to us to be almost ideally constituted, and a group *such as* our Board of Management might just as well manage drama in addition to music. . . . What seems to be happening is that Keynes is making a copy of our N.C.M., and, being a copy, perhaps a bad copy. . . .

Lord Esher's reply is not among John's papers.

In June John told Audrey: "I personally think the N.C.M. is dead, though I expect that Keynes will bag most of the ideas for C.E.M.A." In October he wrote that he was soon to see Sir George Schuster, at that time a member of the Select Committee on National Expenditure, about "my scheme for a Ministry of the Mind or whatever it might be called—the National Conscience. The series of Government Departments or Ministries is wholly materialistic. Make out your list of the finer things of this world and the next world; they are concerned with the mind and the spirit. The Government has no contact with them. . . ."

Presumably Schuster was too busy to see John and therefore invited him to put his views in writing, for five days later Schuster wrote:

I am passing on the letter to Assheton* and will let you know when I hear from him. I have written a very strong personal plea, which I do with complete honesty since, as I said to Assheton, I feel that we as a nation owe you a debt—a debt of which I personally am reminded whenever I get pleasure and peace after a wearying week by playing over the Glyndebourne records on a Saturday or Sunday evening—as I do very often.

"At any rate that's a very charming letter", John told Audrey. "I can't expect anything to be done for me. I have had nothing but kicks and noes."

But John was by no means down and out yet. The more he was rebuffed, the more extravagant became his ambitions. He now had the idea of buying the freehold of Covent Garden, for which he was prepared to pay £100,000, and making it the focal point of a vast enterprise, with Bing as General Manager. On New Year's Eve he wrote to Audrey:

I went to London on Wednesday and dined with Boosey, Holt, Hawkes† and Rudi [Bing] at the Café Royal—an excellent dinner with a magnum of champagne (costing probably £10) and oysters, until we were turned out at 11 p.m. We discussed the whole problem in a most friendly and informal manner. Boosey is very much on my side, and so I think is Hawkes. Holt has an old-fashioned approach, and when he arrives at the right thing has the wrong reasons. The satisfactory thing is the tale he told of a meeting of their old supporters with a view to doing something during the War. Result £6,000 and then afterwards A saying he won't be associated with B. Then Pomeroy‡ said, "What do you want? I will find it, but it must be in my name." "Not at all", says Holt, and it all breaks down. But note that they are thinking in terms of £6,000! The last words I repeatedly drilled into their ears were, "Think big!"

I said I wanted £100,000. We would begin with an operetta which would astonish London with its perfection, and with all

* Ralph Assheton, now Lord Clitheroe; Financial Secretary to the Treasury, 1943–44.
† Boosey and Hawkes, Music Publishers, etc. Harold Holt, Musical Agent.
‡ Jay Pomeroy had recently sponsored two financially unsuccessful seasons of Italian opera at the Cambridge Theatre in London.

the auxiliary details right and with the house looking the same but the atmosphere changed: to be a People's house. I want the stalls to be cheap and the people's seats, with a new foyer of their own. . . . Reseat the stalls; keep very few boxes. Run the operetta for three months (you in it, doing of course the chief part). Follow with four months of ballet, two months of staggering good opera, one month Russian government opera, one month Russian government ballet. . . . But this, darling, is all rather fiddling. Total cost say £180,000. Here comes the important development. Bring Foot from the B.B.C. on to the Board. Capitalise their broadcasting and television, the B.B.C. to contribute £250,000. Bring Rank from the Films on to the Board. Further contribution £150,000. City Guilds and Business Houses £100,000. Total £½ million. I to be Chairman, salary £5,000, and the other Directors £1,000. . . .

There would of course be superb orchestras, and these would be sent abroad ("Bring the Foreign Office in") to advertise Britain. "The N.C.M. would be wanted in the background. . . . Bring Guthrie in as Rudi's assistant. The N.C.M., the Theatre, the £100,000 Trust are my ideas. All the rest is Edwards's flash of genius in the night. We shall lead; the Musicians' trouble comes because they think small. . . ." It was, he yet again reminded Audrey, necessary to "think big", and he cabled to her on 20th January 1944:

> GOOD INTERVIEWS ALL PLANS LONDON ENGLAND WORLD MUSIC DRAMA ARCHITECTURE CULTURE IDEALISM ALSO MUSIC TRUST AND CORPORATION AND NCM PROGRESSING BUT STILL STRICT CONFIDENCE ALOUD LONDON MUSIC AWAITING BEANIE VERY WELL MUCH LOVE= JOHN CHRISTIE

But the B.B.C. showed little desire to be incorporated in John's mammoth enterprise. In February John went with Edwards and Rudi Bing to Broadcasting House, where he was received by Haley, the Deputy Director, and two of his staff: "A sticky beginning," he told Audrey, "but things improved. . . . After three-quarters of an hour I suddenly fizzed. I just let fly. Haley's eyes sparkled. I have rarely created such an effect. . . . A few days later I got a letter which to my mind turns the whole thing down."

It was hardly surprising. In the end the scheme collapsed and Boosey and Hawkes acquired Covent Garden.

In a letter to the new Chancellor of the Exchequer, Sir John Anderson, John now suggested that he would need a million pounds a year to put the music of England on its feet. Only an undated draft of the letter exists, but it was presumably written in the early part of 1944:

> I feel I cannot avoid or delay in taking up the matter of music with you personally. I regard the position as almost wholly unsatisfactory. I am sure that I can put it right and that I can carry the artists among the musicians with me; the rest I care, relatively speaking, little about. The Government has got to act. It is necessary to back one man. I believe that man must be I. I have no motive of profit or self-advancement in my purpose. I have refused, and still refuse, a title, having this in my blood (my grandfather* refused to be made a Marquis and an uncle refused a peerage). . . . I stake my reputation on making this work not only a success, but an overwhelming success; Glyndebourne has given me the necessary credentials. . . .

He then went on to describe, yet once again, the deplorable state of music in this country and the need for "State aid pure and simple. . . . I should expect to spend £50,000 *per annum* on the composers, and they would receive the strongest inspiration and attention and criticism in addition." There must be further opera houses, perhaps in Manchester and Glasgow. "We are thwarted by the Treasury, by Keynes and by C.E.M.A. . . . Keynes refuses to see me, and I believe that he is there, with the satisfaction of the Treasury, in order to keep me out."

After further criticism of C.E.M.A. he concluded: "I am thinking on much bigger lines, but I am prepared to be judged by results. Apart from buildings, I think of £1,000,000 *per annum* for music. We now have to pay for the past; we are miles below scratch. . . . Don't hesitate. I can deliver the goods and I want nothing in return."

* Lord Portsmouth.

Presumably Anderson could give little encouragement, for on 6th March 1944 John told Audrey:

I don't think there is any question of doing the opera again and I feel I don't want to do it. I am too angry at the way in which I have been treated. But I am interested in the Glynde-bourne orchestra all the year round. You were right when you said we should not just copy what we did before the War, but we should look at the problem from a different angle. . . .

But his optimism returned, and before the month was out he was again "thinking big". On 29th March, at a time when the purchase of Covent Garden was still under consideration, he wrote to Audrey:

My idea is to collect a large sum of money for a National Glyndebourne Trust to control a Corporation which shall run Covent Garden, the Haymarket [theatre] (with new stage and dressing rooms), the National Theatre, the New Queen's Hall —large, smaller and tiny for opera, operetta, ballet, music and drama—all to be on superb lines and to link up these with the National Gallery and National Portrait Gallery and the other Galleries and so become the Headquarters of England's Art. . . . We might get one of the Royal Houses in St James's Palace as our Headquarters. . . .

He really was incorrigible; it was high time for Audrey to be back again at his side.

★   ★   ★

Less than two months after this letter had been written Audrey and the children were back in England. Thanks to the good offices of a friend, Admiral Sir Francis Tottenham,★ they completed the journey from Lisbon in a small Dakota full of V.I.Ps, landing at a small airport near Bristol. John did not come to the airport, as Audrey was expecting, but met the train in London. Always assuming that he knew the place and time of arrival of the Dakota's secretly scheduled flight, this was an error of judgment

★ It was Sir Francis's daughter who had accompanied Rosamond and George to Canada.

on his part; and Audrey's display of irritation somewhat marred the happiness of a reunion after nearly four years of separation. But Audrey was very exhausted; and probably she was also showing the first signs of the long illness which, in the closing years of her life, was so often to make her difficult and unreasonable.

21

Glyndebourne Reopens its Doors

"IN THE years immediately following the war", wrote Spike Hughes, "Glyndebourne was like a huge kitchen, where ideas, hopes, plans and proposals bubbled busily on the stove fired by the Christies' energy, ideals and ambitions." Many of these ideas, hopes, plans and proposals had been bubbling busily throughout the War; after Audrey's return fresh enterprises were considered, and yet further enterprises when peace came at last. Not all of them bore fruit.

After his failure to buy the freehold of Covent Garden, John also unsuccessfully attempted to join forces with Jay Pomeroy. Another project, inspired and warmly advocated by Bing,* was that of an International Festival of Music and Drama at Oxford; it was discussed in detail by various committees, but came to nothing through the lack of the necessary financial support. Audrey's pet child—a Children's Theatre—did however materialise.

It was in April 1944 that the Children's Theatre, a non-profit-making organisation designed "to introduce children to the living theatre through full-stage performances of classical and contemporary plays"—had been founded under the Chairmanship of Dr J. J. Mallon, Warden of Toynbee Hall, with Mr John Allen as administrator and producer. In March the following year it passed under the management of Glyndebourne, in association with Toynbee Hall (where the first performances were staged). John and Audrey joined the Council of the Children's Theatre, Bing

---

* After rising to the rank of a manager of Peter Jones in Sloane Square, Bing returned in the autumn of 1944 to his job of General Manager of Glyndebourne.

took over the administration and Edwards joined the Executive Committee.

Miss Fowler, who had been appointed secretary to the Theatre, recalls "a hilarious evening" when Dr Mallon came to Glyndebourne to discuss the collaboration: "This lovable and quite inimitable figure, with his india-rubber face, bounced up and down on the sofa as he enthusiastically discussed everything from Trade Boards in Manchester to Ballet at Toynbee. Whether it was the hock or the ginger ice-cream sundae during dinner, or the port that followed, that made the Warden of Toynbee Hall such a warm-hearted raconteur, I shall never be quite sure. . . ."

Both John and Audrey helped with money from their own pockets to get the Theatre launched. The L.C.C. sponsored various London performances, and local education authorities gave assistance to some highly successful provincial tours. But before long the Authorities were required by the Ministry of Education to cut their budgets, and the Theatre found itself in financial difficulties. Hope of an "organic relationship" with the Ministry and the Arts Council did not materialise, and an appeal in the summer of 1947 for an annual grant of £5,000 from the latter was rejected. There was talk of approaching the Carnegie or the Pilgrim Trust, the Lord Mayor of London, or one of the City Companies; but if any such approaches were actually made, it would seem that they were rejected. In 1948 the Arts Council relented to the extent of a donation of £3,000, but it made it quite clear that this was not to be thought of as an annual grant. The following year the Theatre again appealed to the Arts Council, only to learn that "unsatisfactory reports of the work of the Children's Theatre had been received" and that no more money would be forthcoming. Finally Mr Allen, disapproving of three plays which the L.C.C. wished him to produce, sent in his resignation, and soon afterwards the Theatre closed down.

It must not, however, be imagined that the Children's Theatre had been a failure. In the four years of its existence more than a thousand performances had been seen by over half-a-million children and enormous interest had been aroused. Hundreds of letters told of their enjoyment and of the critical attention they had given

17

to the details of production. (One boy wrote to demand "a much bigger splash" in future when Tobias, in James Bridie's *Tobias and the Angel*, was fighting the mud-fish in the Tigris.) Taken all in all, the Theatre had been very well worth while.

John himself had never been closely involved in this project, his chief contribution—other than financial—having been an attempt to impose artistic standards in scenery and so on that were quite inappropriate to a company that for the most part played in school halls.

Another venture which materialised, but which did not prove profitable, was the participation of Glyndebourne in the so-called "Company of Four" at the Lyric, Hammersmith. The idea was to produce a series of straight plays, unfamiliar and of high quality, using actors recently demobilised. Each play was to run for about a month. The first production, *The Shouting Dies*, by Ronda Keane, opened on 5th October 1945; it was followed by plays by Thornton Wilder, Jan de Hartog, William Saroyan, John Coates, Sean O'Casey, Jean Cocteau and others. In June 1946 came *The Brothers Karamazov*, adapted from Dostoevsky's novel by Alec Guinness. The final production was Walter Macken's *Galway Handicap* in February 1947.

In all these ventures Bing was indefatigable. He found a fine ally in Audrey, and it was to her that he wrote regularly and in great detail about his various negotiations; as he explained to her, he could count on her showing John any letters addressed to herself, whereas John might easily forget to show her letters addressed to him. Together Audrey and Bing guided John's hand, conspiring to prevent him from posting rash letters and persuading him to eat humble pie when it became necessary. The latter was not always easy, for it was one of John's weaknesses that he could not forget and would never forgive.

A letter from Bing to Audrey, bearing no date, clearly refers to John's bitter quarrel with Lord Keynes and C.E.M.A. and Bing's hope that John would try to patch it up. This quarrel had of course originated in John's anger that C.E.M.A. had, as he saw it, stolen his idea of a National Council of Music. It came to a head over a proposal by John for a joint season at Covent Garden, with Bing as General Manager. This was very brusquely turned down by Keynes, now also Chairman of the Royal Opera House. Bing's letter runs:

> Dear Audrey—If you think this is a quite stupid idea please don't even show it to John. But if you should feel, as I do, that the moment may be ripe. . . .
> But if it is to be done it must be done at once, spontaneously, gracefully and not grudgingly—without recriminations, *genuinely* looking ahead and not to the past. The N.C.M. and all that was a long-drawn-out game, and John is and ought to be big enough to acknowledge that the other man has won. All right, let's shake hands and have a fresh start.
> I know he feels bitter—and rightly so; but can he rise above it? I feel if he could get himself to write one of his really inspired letters, *genuinely* not trying to "pique" the other man but *acknowledging* his deserved success—then all may still be well!

Among John's papers is also the undated typescript draft of a letter from him to Keynes. Neither the style nor the reasonableness of it suggests that it was his own compilation. Possibly Audrey and Bing composed it between them; or possibly it was this that Bing submitted to Audrey to give to John, if the moment was propitious, to serve as a model upon which he might compose a letter of his own. Was this letter, or one like it, ever sent? We do not know, but it seems unlikely. As Bing told Audrey: "I fear John is *so* determined to be angry with the Arts Council that not much can be hoped for."

Keynes was, in John's eyes, not the only villain of the piece: there was also Miss Mary Glasgow, Secretary-General of the Arts Council; and more particularly there was Steuart Wilson, its Musical Advisor. John and Steuart Wilson met by chance at a musical luncheon. "Smilingly [John wrote to Lady Violet Bonham Carter] I told him that I had heard he had opposed our amalgamation, but that in future he must be careful to get his facts right. He then flew into a violent rage and I laughed. . . ."

Bing was horrified when he heard of this encounter and at once wrote a joint letter to John and Audrey, imploring them to see that such incidents, which could easily wreck the delicate negotiations he had in hand, did not occur again: "I know of course that John doesn't mean to upset anybody, but the fact remains that he does—largely perhaps because his peculiar sense of humour, which I share and enjoy so much, is not equally understood by others."

The quarrel continued for several months, John calling Steuart Wilson a liar and Steuart Wilson calling John a fool and proposing (though doubtless not seriously) a duel; what is surprising is that John did not accept the challenge. A letter from John to Steuart Wilson, written on 11th April, seems to conclude the correspondence.

★   ★   ★

The major question that was exercising Bing, John and Audrey in the autumn of 1945 was of course the restarting of the Festival Opera at Glyndebourne. Edwards recalls an earlier and "most memorable" talk with Bing over lunch at the Cadogan Hotel at which it had been decided, on John's suggestion, to reopen the Opera Office in London. This had been provisionally set up in a house in Cumberland Place; then the unexpired portion of the lease of 23 Baker Street was purchased for £10,000.

With the return of peace the immediate problem was the choice of operas to be performed and, since Busch and Ebert were still abroad, of the team to direct them. There now appeared a new possibility. With the appointment of Karl Rankl as Musical Director of Covent Garden, the rejected Beecham found himself almost as it were thrown into the arms of Glyndebourne: in October he offered to collaborate in a Glyndebourne season for the following summer, and to conduct without a fee. Glyndebourne readily accepted, and it was eventually agreed that the operas to be given would be *Carmen* (in French, in the original version with dialogue), *Figaro* (in Italian) and *The Magic Flute* (in English or in German).

So far, so good. But nobody familiar with John and Beecham— "that amusing but bad man", as John called him—could possibly have imagined that trouble did not lie ahead—trouble that all Bing's diplomacy, all Audrey's tact and charm, would be unable to overcome. The concluding round of the contest took the form of a Ladies' Final in which Lady Beecham (Betty Humby) "served", at her husband's request, Sir Thomas's point of view in a letter written on 3rd November to Audrey; long though it is, it deserves quotation in full:

Dear Audrey,
  ... I shall now endeavour, to the best of my capacity, to be my husband's mouthpiece; indeed he has requested me on this occasion to function as a scrupulously faithful medium of his reflections on the Glyndebourne question.
  What I am first desired to emphasise is that never at any moment has my husband wished to act as a kind of musical dictator. The best evidence of this is that he discussed at great length with all of you on several occasions the comparative merits of a considerable number of singers. In order to make our attitude sufficiently clear, I must ask you to recall the first general talk we had together at Glyndebourne many weeks ago. On that occasion my husband endeavoured, and I think successfully, to state without any ambiguity the conditions on which he would be prepared and pleased to link himself with your organisation.
  He first indicated the declared policy and plans of Covent Garden, an institution with a considerable subsidy in the offing. He pointed out that this enterprise is committed to the exploitation and development of what is called euphemistically in the Press "British Talent". You may also recall that in the opinion of my husband this alleged talent hardly existed today, and that he advocated strongly that the policy of Glyndebourne should be nothing more nor less than the most perfect representation of Opera from the purely artistic angle without regard for any subsidiary consideration. This declaration on his part met with the completest agreement from you and John, and it was upon the basis of the acceptance of it that my husband announced his willingness to throw in his operatic lot with you.
  Apparently this is all to be changed, and he, after forty-three years of operatic work carried on in every country of importance in the world, brought up as a child with the great artists of the time, the friend of all the leading composers of the past fifty years, the sponsor of one half, if not more than one half, of the prominent singers before the public, is now asked to be a kind of nurse in a species of musical kindergarten.

Now so far as I know he has agreed in the most complacent [*sic*] fashion to everything suggested to him up to a certain and critical point:—namely, is one of the greatest musical master-pieces in the world, *Carmen*, to be treated with the respect due to its beauty and grandeur?

Upon a communication from Mr Bing that a conference was proposed to consider Miss Kathleen Ferrier as a likely interpre-ter of the principal role, my husband pointed out (1) that all the great Carmens of the world from 1875 to the present year have been sopranos, (2) that only two mezzo-sopranos have ever sung the role with a fair measure of success, and (3) that no contralto has ever succeeded in doing anything with the role but make a complete ass of herself. At the seance held at Mr Dino Borgioli's studio my husband gave vent to these universally known facts in language that admitted of no misunderstanding and Miss Ferrier's singing-master wholeheartedly agreed. In view of this, one is entitled to ask why it is necessary to waste one second of the time of a very busy man in discussing something which everybody who knows anything at all about Opera has long ago excluded from the area of practicability.

On the strength of another audition in this same seance we are invited to consent to the choice of an embryonic tenor for the strenuous role of Don José. Evidently it must have escaped your observation that this gentleman has a very distinct ten-dency to sing off the key, is not particularly musicianly, and, most important of all, has not yet had the upper part of his voice placed adequately by his instructor. In all probability, after about one half hour of solid singing he would, in his pre-sent condition, peter out and dry up decisively.

And, mark you, because my husband, who has a thousand times more experience of these matters than either you or John, places a note of interrogation against these two rash proposals, he receives a letter suggesting that he is failing to understand the true inwardness of the Glyndebourne gospel or tradition.

Both of you seem to be under the impression that the patron-age of British artists is an invention or discovery of Glynde-bourne. I must therefore inform you that as far back as 1902 my husband conducted a long season of opera in which only British artists were employed. Between that date and 1920 he gave approximately 1600 performances of Opera in which none but

British artists were employed. Between 1920 and 1939, with the exception of the all-Russian season in 1931, he has made a point of engaging for every season of Opera at Covent Garden or elsewhere never less than fifty British singers. It may be true that very few of them have played leading roles, but in his view, as well as that of the public and the Press, they were not fit for them.

You have spoken of the singers discovered or developed by Glyndebourne who have, as the result of your influence or training, made names in the world. We should very much like to know who they are. Such artists as Heddle Nash, Ina Souez, John Brownlee, etc, all sang for Tom at Covent Garden and elsewhere long before they appeared in your theatre.

When you endeavour to press the claims of young artists over highly experienced exponents of certain parts, it is fair to enquire why you ever felt obliged to make use of such veterans as Stabile and Andresen, both of whom were in an advanced state of decline. And certainly neither Baccaloni nor Borgioli could be classed as Freshmen in your organisation. This does not appear to me as altogether consistent or square with the recently declared policy of Glyndebourne. At any rate, there is one thing about which no one should remain for a moment in uncertainty: without adequate and, indeed, distinguished singing there is no longer the slightest possibility of obtaining a recording contract with any Company known to us. The day for any other kind of operatic reproduction has gone by.

My husband is more than a little interested in what John has described as the modern approach to music. He thinks he knows what is meant by this but is not quite certain. If it means the production of Opera with equal regard to the various elements of singing, playing, acting, scenery, etc, this so-called "modern approach" is one of the oldest things known to history. The Greeks developed it to a very high point of perfection; the Florentines of the latter part of the sixteenth century experimented with it by no means unsuccessfully, and the great Monteverdi, aided by the equally great Palladio, combined to produce an entertainment which nothing we have done here in the last twenty years can even begin to rival.

In this country the elaborate masques of men like Jonson, Fletcher and others, married to the music of Ferraboschi, Lawes and others, were without question a synthesis of the various arts on a scale of luxury and magnificence compared with which our efforts of today are just little parlour games. And what of the great Gluck, the so-called reformer of the Opera, who laboured all his life to achieve, and succeeded in achieving according to the verdict of all musical history, that which Glyndebourne considers to be its goal? And coming down to more recent times, for what purpose other than the most complete realisation of his aim, did Richard Wagner build a Festspielhaus at Bayreuth?

Not outside many persons' recollection is the artistic collaboration of Verdi and Boito over *Otello* and *Falstaff*, in which the parts of Iago and Falstaff were created by my husband's old friend Victor Maurel. From him he derived the information that for the production of *Otello* eighty-five stage rehearsals were held, and for *Falstaff* ninety-three. Can anyone imagine for one moment that something highly unusual was not the result of the co-operation of the most successful writer of Opera in the world and the most knowledgeable personality in Europe?

The Opéra Comique of Paris, during the period 1880–1910, saw the production of sixty new works of which at least twenty have found their way into the permanent repertoire of the world; and every musical historian knows that no more highly finished performances than those given in this theatre have yet been heard anywhere.

Let us now consider what has been done in England. When my husband began to give the works of Mozart on any large scale thirty-six years ago, this composer had a very small public. Between 1910 and 1920 he had given nearly eight hundred performances of the Mozart operas. Each one of them had a preparation more arduous and extended than any others elsewhere, before or since. For instance, for the revivals of *Figaro* and *Il Seraglio*, the greatest authority on the theatre of the eighteenth century, Nigel Playfair, was engaged to superintend the productions. He rehearsed these two works with the singers every day for five months in action only and without the music.

At least fifty other operas given during this period received the same laborious preparation. And we should like to know what anyone thinking and talking about opera today has to say about the all-Russian seasons given in 1913 and 1914 in London. I have never met any competent judge of this matter who does not assert with emphasis that for magnificence of decoration, unapproachable chorus-singing, elegance and distinction in the principal performers and the most perfect ensemble ever seen on the operatic stage, these representations have made all coming after them something in the nature of amateur theatricals.

Yet it was John's opinion that "we have had practically no experience of Opera in England"*! Betty Humby's letter continues:

What does all this amount to? Nothing more than that this so-called modern approach to music is something that the best musical and dramatic minds of the past three hundred and fifty years have agreed should be the one and only method of presenting Opera. Furthermore, they have most of them succeeded in doing so.

But there is one important difference between these great and distinguished persons and yourselves. There is not one among them, be it Monteverdi, Handel, Mozart, Gluck, Rossini, Verdi, Wagner, Puccini, Massenet or Richard Strauss, who has not emphasised in the most pointed way that Opera is, as to fifty per cent of it, singing; and there is not one of the great masters that Tom has known personally who, given the choice of an accomplished and experienced singer on the one hand, and an unknown and incalculable beginner on the other, would not only select the former without a moment's hesitation, but have a great many pungent comments to make upon the alternative proposition.

Now if Glyndebourne has got anything new to tell my husband about the art of production in Opera, he is willing to learn; but if he is right in assuming that that which you imagine to be an epoch-making discovery is nothing more than the genuine old method with which he has been acquainted since he was a child, then he has only one observation to make, which is this: that this new-old approach should function in exactly the same way that it has always done. There is nothing in the art of the theatre known to Mr Ebert or any other producer that was not present in the minds of the great men of the Renaissance, the 18th century, the 19th century, and the early part of the 20th century. Not one of the distinguished men who have worked

* In a letter to Malcolm Sargent, 4th November 1940.

with Tom in days gone by had anything to learn from these so-called modern approaches.

To sum up—my husband is prepared to co-operate with Glyndebourne upon one condition: that the performances are, from the musical angle, of the highest excellence. Anything less than this will not do. He is willing to admit that talent, and even genius, can be found in the very young. He has been lucky enough to encounter it on a few occasions in his long career. But with mediocrity and with embryonic material he will have nothing to do. He still feels that with Professor Ebert, whom he finds to be in every way a kindred spirit, something very remarkable could be achieved at Glyndebourne, but only in the way stated.

As a final word, as this was the policy agreed upon by all of us at our first meeting, it cannot be imputed to my husband that he has committed one single act or uttered one single thought that has not been wholly consistent with it.

with affection from
Betty

To this powerful and lucid letter Audrey replied:

My dear Betty,

. . . It seemed to me that the major part of your letter was based on a wrong understanding of what John meant by "modern approach". Everyone who is interested in the history and development of Opera is aware of what has been done from the time of Monteverdi through the time of Gluck and so on. I admit Thomas made it good reading!

When John and I went to the operatic festivals on the continent or to Covent Garden in the early 1930s we found that each opera billed was performed, on an average, two or three times in the season. Sometimes the houses were full—but not always. On the other hand, revue, musical comedy and other intrinsic trash could run to full houses for months, sometimes years. The answer seemed to be that the trash was rehearsed until it gave the illusion of co-ordination, whereas the operas, though conceived and written by "Masters", were hurtled on to the stage willy-nilly. More often than not, singers with international names arrived from the ends of the earth, each with his own particular conception of the role he was to portray; with any

luck the conductor could in a minimum of time give a few co-
ordinating ideas to the so-called "ensemble". He could then indulge in the thrill of steering them through the perilous rapids
of public performance. Histrionically it was more often than not
in the nature of an impromptu charade. The audience admired
the names, the voices or the orchestra, but rarely had any idea
what was going on—bar what they could mug up from programme notes by the gleam of a cigarette lighter! We felt it
hard that Mozart, for instance, should come off second best to
Mr Cochran!

We did not propose to apply Cochran methods to Mozart,
but John did design a stage capable of being used in modern
representations, and we were fortunate in getting Charles Ebert.
He took an "infinity of pains" over getting every aspect of his
half of the affair.

You say we failed musically.* I maintain that in performance
we did not. Our singers, whether famous or more or less known or
unknown, were chosen for their capacity to portray the "spirit"
of the character, as well as for their capacity to *sing*, *act* and *look* the
part. Musical preparation was such that there was "ensemble".

Thomas criticises our recordings of *Figaro*, *Don Giovanni* and
Così. We criticised his stage representation of *Zauberflöte*, when
in our opinion Husch had in no way the spirit of the part fey,
part earthly creature that Mozart makes Papageno. Berger was
a bird-like child's voice but not a mother, and far less the evil
spirit that the Queen of the Night must become. . . . Recording
has never been our chief aim. It was the Gramophone Co's idea
originally, not ours.

All this is but detail, but relevant. What is difficult to know
is whether all this storm-in-a-teacup really means that Thomas
regrets his very splendid offer last summer to throw in his
"operatic lot" with ours.

Your husband has made a terrific "to-do" about Miss Ferrier
and Mr F——. He came to hear them at an audition; it was
merely for him to say whether or not he would consider them.
He suggested Miss B—— for Micaëla when we dined with you;
was she a better suggestion? All his other suggestions were of
singers unfortunately unknown to any of us; naturally we made
what enquiries we could regarding them. We made no storm!

* Lady Beecham had not said this.

They were all left open to discussion or agreement. A festival, however short, takes—as we all realise—much planning and discussion; but it is going to be doubly difficult if we are all to get "worked up" instead of trying to arrive at conclusions!

So much for Thomas's letter. John and I wanted to meet you at lunch mainly to tell you that we are greatly worried that the problems of doing a season at Glyndebourne in 1946 become more and more insoluble the deeper we probe. Also the expense of the season, as it has developed since our first proposal in the summer, has enormously increased. There are now under consideration three operas and one of them a major new production, the whole season running into at least four weeks. In existing conditions John does not believe that we can get, in the time, sufficient public money to safeguard us; therefore we personally must be prepared, not only for the certain loss on the season, but also, in the event of some catastrophe such as crippling strikes, etc., to underwrite the total commitment.

Therefore we have come to the conclusion that we must return to our original suggestion of a "token season" of two of our former productions. There is the possibility of doing such a season (of, say, fourteen performances) in London. We believe we might transfer our intimate performances to Sadler's Wells with success; also there seems a fair chance of our being able to get the Theatre. I don't know what Thomas's reactions to this change of plan would be. We are encouraged to think that such a project could be successful with the public, in view of the present difficulties in getting to and from Glyndebourne. Could Thomas let John know as soon as possible what he feels about this? If he agrees, then there are urgent matters to be dealt with immediately—for instance the engagement of certain singers. ... Soon they will be unavailable for the necessary dates, or we will have to pay competitive fees.

We have not forgotten your suggestion of Delius; but as none of us know it[*] we cannot but suggest that it should be discussed between Thomas and Ebert during the collaboration of the first season. This would ensure its having much worthier treatment in a following season. ...

Yours ever affectionately
Audrey

[*] Probably *A Village Romeo and Juliet.*

Bing read Audrey's reply, which he considered "absolutely first-class"; it was then passed by John and duly despatched. All idea of *Carmen* was now abandoned, and there was further talk, at Glyndebourne, of holding a season of the two Mozart operas at Sadler's Wells. It seemed very unlikely that Beecham would collaborate in this, and indeed any hope of his participating rapidly faded. It is the great tragedy of post-war Glyndebourne that John and Beecham could not hit it off. Glyndebourne was logically the final answer to so much that Beecham had lived and worked for; and he, our greatest conductor, would have been—musically—the ideal successor to Fritz Busch.

★   ★   ★

John still favoured a season at Glyndebourne, but Bing was very apprehensive. "I get more and more frightened about it," he wrote to Audrey on November 13th:

> I am not able to ignore completely the stage-hand position—to mention only one major worry—and just to say, as John does, "Oh, I am not worried—the neighbours will see us through." It does not solve the problem at all, and I am afraid this is stressing the amateurish touch to such an extent that it may be disastrous. Also the orchestra question is by no means clear; but what *is* clear is that it will be infinitely more difficult and expensive to get an orchestra for Glyndebourne than for London. However, we will have to reach a decision at the meeting on the 22nd.

For a time there was talk of "week-ends of music" at Glyndebourne during the summer of 1946, but Bing was very doubtful of the wisdom of this. Would people really be ready to make the pilgrimage to Glyndebourne, he asked, unless the musical fare was something that they could not possibly obtain in London. "Why not a cycle of 'Opera through the Ages'," Jani Strasser suggested, "with soli, orchestral items, big excerpts with chorus, etc.—surely very unusual, very attractive and very Glyndebourne? Connecting link between excerpts could be made either by talk or in programme notes. Grouping could be made either chronologically or, if that seems too monotonous, according to type or countries. . . .

Then one could do a concert or two with 'French Opera' and bring a few singers over for the occasion. Once that is achieved, I think that Londoners will pounce upon them and engage them for their concerts, so that the cost of bringing them over would be lessened. . . . Well, it's just an idea. . . ."*

*   *   *

But there was yet another project which, in 1945, Bing was energetically pursuing: an amalgamation of Glyndebourne and Sadler's Wells, to include "what is commonly known as the *Peter Grimes* group—Crozier, Britten, Peter Pears and Joan Cross mainly: all the people who have left Sadler's Wells and whom a section of the Governors is most anxious to win back". In November Bing had a very satisfactory talk with Eric Crozier, who a month later sent him the Group's proposal for a new "Opera and Play Company", independent of Sadler's Wells but possibly to be associated with Glyndebourne. The scheme was, of course, the outcome of Britten's remarkable success that summer with his first full-length opera, *Peter Grimes*.

The Company was to commission and undertake the performance of new operas and plays, giving an annual season of seventeen weeks in London, the provinces and the Continent. For the first season there were to be three productions: Britten's new full-length opera, *The Rape of Lucretia*, to a libretto by Ronald Duncan; a programme to include a short classical opera (Pergolesi, Gluck, Mozart), a chamber work and a short play with music; and a new full-length play. Bing wrote enthusiastically to Audrey on 18th December:

My own impression is that the scheme is extremely interesting: here at last is a really constructive idea which seems

---

* Mr Strasser comments on this passage, which is quoted verbatim from a letter he wrote at the time: "This does not quite tally with the recollections I jotted down for myself. My suggestion, as you quote it, was the alternative of two, the other being 'talks or lectures by eminent musicologists or musicians about the development of opera illustrated, not as is now customary with records, but by a team of singers with piano accompaniment or, where the character of the works would allow it, a small orchestra'. I wonder if this could be added to make the paragraph quite complete and authentic."

economically possible. It centres round two creative artists of real importance: Benjamin Britten and Ronald Duncan (the poet, whose latest work at the Mercury had an extraordinary success). I have very little doubt that the scheme will go through and will cause very considerable excitement, and I feel we ought to consider very carefully indeed before we turn it down. After all, John has for years advocated the commissioning of new British works, and also that such works should be written in close consultation with the stage. Both is happening within this scheme: composer, author and producer are working together on the creation of a new work which is specially devised for particular circumstances practical and economical. . . .

As I told you over the telephone, a private individual has promised to put up £3,000. . . . Crozier further told me that the Arts Council has promised £5,000 if he succeeds in obtaining another £5,000 from other sources. The total capital investment required is £10,000.

The main question to decide, once you and John have in principle made up your minds, is whether or not the scheme should be put on at Glyndebourne, or by Glyndebourne in London. Crozier wants the Lyric Hammersmith for it, but it seems possible to me to have perhaps one week at Glyndebourne. . . .

Yours ever,
Rudi

P.S. I tried Beecham again five times last night—I am afraid I have to give up!

It was finally agreed that there should be a season of fourteen performances of *The Rape of Lucretia* at Glyndebourne, with its world première there on 12th July 1946. On 6th May Bing wrote to Audrey:

This is just to tell you that on Saturday night Ben played his whole Opera, which he had finished that afternoon. I really was enormously impressed, and think we need not have any fear about the quality of the work, which, as far as I could judge from this very rough performance, may be among the really important works of our time. It is brilliant, full of inspiration and, for John's benefit, full of some lovely tunes. Of course I know nothing about the scoring but think that Britten has always been very clever with that too.

For the Britten season, Ebert, who had been brought back from Turkey by John, acted as Artistic Director, Bing as General Manager and Eric Crozier as Producer; the sets were designed by John Piper. Ernest Ansermet and Reginald Goodall conducted, on alternate nights, two different casts of singers who were soon to form the nucleus of The English Opera Group and subsequently of the Aldeburgh Festival. The performances of the first team were chiefly memorable for Kathleen Ferrier's superb singing of the part of Lucretia; this was her first appearance on the operatic stage in a career so soon and so tragically to be cut short.

At the end of the Glyndebourne season *The Rape of Lucretia* toured the provinces and was also taken to Holland. Bing went with the Company to Holland, but he did not enjoy himself. He wrote angrily to Audrey about "the incredibly unfriendly attitude of the Group" towards him—an attitude that he could attribute only to the fact that he had felt it his duty to "stand up to them in Glyndebourne's interest".

The financial loss incurred by the Britten season, of which Glyndebourne bore its share, was described by John as "startling"; and though later he was often heard to say that he had "never taken a penny" of public money, he was glad enough to accept £3,000, which had been guaranteed by his old enemy the Arts Council, to put towards the deficit. "One of the difficulties with the Britten group", said Bing, "arose from the fact that the English tour with *The Rape of Lucretia* was a box office disaster and, as usual with artists, they did not accept the fact that the English provinces at that time did not want to hear a contemporary opera and tried to put all the blame on the unfortunate manager who, in their view, had failed with publicity, etc."

Though the 1946 Glyndebourne programme had announced that the 1947 season would again include *Lucretia*, together with "a new contemporary opera" (which eventually proved to be Britten's *Albert Herring*), John made it plain that this time he was not going to be in any way financially responsible. Secretly he

13 (*Above*) Audrey, George, Rosamond and John Christie, 1936. (*Left*) George, John and Mary Christie (holding Hector) at Hector's christening in 1961

14 (*Above*) Fritz Busch, John Christie, Carl Ebert and Moran Caplat, 1951.
(*Below left*) Jani Strasser and (*right*) Rudi Bing

would probably have been glad to have been spared any further Britten operas; the trouble with *Lucretia*, he told his friend Mr Oliver Lyttelton* after the première, was that there was "no music in it". Not only did he dislike the opera, he also disliked the sets and costumes; he disliked most of the singing and regretted that the work had not been done "properly"—in other words, with an international cast. Mr Lyttelton was unable to agree; he was in fact soon to become Chairman of Britten's English Opera Group and to find the money to launch it.

It was obvious, as Anne Wood (of the English Opera Group) says, that "there were acres of ground on which there could be no agreement between what might be called the two parties—one grounded in continental tradition and opera in foreign languages (and all that that implies); and the other, young, very English, immensely creative and out to establish a whole new era of English opera and music—which indeed they have succeeded in doing in the most brilliant way, not only for themselves and by themselves but by releasing the creative energies of a great many other people as well. . . ."

In October (1946) Britten and Crozier wrote a joint letter to John, at the same time sending a copy of it to Bing, saying that they intended to set up a non-profit-making company of their own, and to collect private capital to launch their next season. They would like to consider buying Glyndebourne's production of *Lucretia* if Glyndebourne was prepared to sell it. They would be willing for *Lucretia* and *Albert Herring* to be staged at Glyndebourne, but this would mean their engagement as an independent group, for which Crozier, not Ebert, would be the producer. A little later, however, Crozier informed Audrey that he was after all agreeable to a joint season of Glyndebourne and the Group, with Ebert producing. He added that they all hoped that Audrey would agree to becoming a Trustee of their new Company.

Bing was suspicious. The Group had "quite frankly disclosed its financial instability", and he doubted whether the Arts Council would give financial support to performances at Glyndebourne with two guinea seats. He begged Audrey not to become a

---

* Now Lord Chandos.

18

Trustee. Ebert, now back in Ankara for the time being, was equally apprehensive, believing that there was as yet no guarantee that the opera had real merit and that the Group had turned again to Glyndebourne because they had not found the financial backing they were hoping for; but Britten's subsequent triumphs were to show how groundless were his doubts as to the quality of the work, and it was in fact for the *theatre*, rather than for the money, that the Group wished to return to Glyndebourne.

In the event, the 1947 Glyndebourne season consisted of nine performances of Gluck's *Orpheus* (sung, to John's great relief, in Italian rather than in French) with Kathleen Ferrier in the title role, and a number of splendid performances of Britten's *Lucretia* and *Albert Herring*, presented by the English Opera Group who came "as visitors to Glyndebourne". But later in the year Eric Crozier wrote a polite letter to Bing, saying that the Group would present its 1948 season independently, though he wished to make it clear that this decision did not rule out the possibility of amalgamation at a later date. No amalgamation was, however, to take place, and in due course the Group started its own and most successful Festival at Aldeburgh.

22

Edinburgh and After

EDINBURGH HAS not inaptly been described as "the Salzburg of the North", and it may be remembered that Audrey, on a visit there in 1940, had exclaimed, "What a place for a Festival!"

Bing had not forgotten this chance remark. Soon after Audrey's return from America he had reminded her of it and proposed that the possibility of such a Festival should be seriously explored. In February 1945 he approached the Lord Provost of Edinburgh, Sir John Falconer, on behalf of Glyndebourne, with a scheme for the formation of an Edinburgh Festival Trust, to establish the first European post-war International Festival of Music and Drama there in the summer of 1947. Salzburg, Munich, Bayreuth and other famous Festival Centres would, he pointed out, be out of action for several years; Edinburgh should seize the opportunity to fill the gap, and Glyndebourne, Britain's leading pre-war Festival, would be willing to offer its experience and provide the organisation.

Bing then went on to elaborate his scheme for a three-week Festival, using (if the lease could be obtained) the King's Theatre, the Lyceum and the Empire for opera and drama. He proposed nine concerts (orchestral and solo recitals) in the Usher Hall, chamber music or small-scale orchestral concerts in the Free-masons Hall, and open-air entertainment which might include Scottish dancing, and serenades like those formerly given in the courtyard of the Munich Residenz and at Salzburg. He discussed finance, though he stated that the figures he gave must at this stage inevitably be very rough and that Glyndebourne was not to be in any way responsible financially.

Edinburgh was much interested, and the Lord Provost friendly and very helpful; committees were formed, and in November the decision was taken to go ahead. Collaboration with the Arts Council and the British Council was to be investigated. Negotiations were to be begun with organisations such as the Sadler's Wells Ballet, the Old Vic and the London Philharmonic, and Beecham was to be sounded. During 1946 and (according to John) in spite of the opposition of Keynes,★ the Festival took shape. In the early months of the following year there was feverish activity and much coming and going between Glyndebourne and the northern capital, with Bing receiving great support from his two new assistants, Moran Caplat at Glyndebourne and Ian Hunter in Edinburgh. Ian Hunter also found himself in the role of personal assistant to the Christies—a job that was far from being a sinecure.

On 24th August the first international Festival of music opened. Eighteen performances of *Macbeth* and *Figaro*, produced by Ebert, were given in the cramped surroundings of the King's Theatre. Audrey had hoped to share the role of Susanna "with Seefried (or whoever)", but she was not well enough to sing; she had never been really fit since her return from America.

Bing, in his Report to the Directors on the 1947 seasons at Glyndebourne and in Edinburgh, wrote that *Orpheus* (at Glyndebourne) had been "not too unsuccessful, though the ballet was an outstanding failure"; the opera had in fact been a great success with the audiences, though some of the staff did not like it. Glyndebourne had been left with a deficit of more than £8,000; in Edinburgh, however, where an opera deficit of £13,000 had been anticipated, the actual loss to the Edinburgh Festival Society amounted to only £9,500—a figure which the authorities considered very satisfactory. The Festival had indeed been a most remarkable achievement within two years of the cessation of hostilities, and a personal triumph for Rudolf Bing. The Festival Society helped Glyndebourne with a handsome grant

★ On 9th May 1959 John wrote (to Sir William Haley): "Then Keynes tried to stop the Edinburgh Festival, three months after the Scots had decided to come in. The Lord Provost showed me the letter. The Arts Council copy has been destroyed." Lord Keynes, already a very sick man, died on 21st April 1946.

towards its deficit and much welcome publicity, and "after great initial difficulties agreed to invite Glyndebourne to act as Artistic Management also for the next Festival in 1948".

★   ★   ★

Meanwhile John was still seeking support for a Glyndebourne Trust. On 3rd June, in a letter to Sir Edward (now Lord) Bridges at the Treasury, he drew attention to what he considered the deplorable start made by the State-aided and recently re-opened Covent Garden:

> Covent Garden have had a run of seven months. Their first opera, *The Fairy Queen*, has been dropped and forgotten; the second, *Carmen*, has been dropped and cannot be forgotten or forgiven; the third, *Manon* was poorly attended; the fourth, *Zauberflöte*, is monstrously bad★. . .

The remedy, he said, was obvious: the amalgamation of Covent Garden and Sadler's Wells, with Glyndebourne "the expert executive acting as the servant of the Board of Trustees" and Ebert "the key to the whole of this problem". Sir Edward's reply is not among John's papers, nor is the reply to a letter to Sir Edward in October, in which John makes mention of the fact that Glyndebourne has been invited "by Paris, America, Palestine, Spain and Holland" to give seasons in these countries. It would seem that the last three of these were in the nature of tentative inquiries rather than definite proposals.

Without some kind of amalgamation or State aid it certainly looked as though Glyndebourne could not survive in its existing form. In November (1947) John sailed to New York; his immediate objective was to try to arrange one or more operatic seasons in America, but he also still hoped that it might be possible to set up "Glyndebournes" on the further side of the Atlantic, in America or Canada. "Be successful—be happy—don't talk too much," Audrey wrote to him, "and whatever you do *don't* let them think you are unwanted in England or no one will want you!" In the following May he paid a second visit, during which

★ He had said the same of both Beecham's and Toscanini's pre-war productions of *Die Zauberflöte* (see p. 201).

he arranged a season at Princeton University for the autumn of 1949; but so-called "ill health" prevented his going on to California to discuss something similar for Berkeley: the truth was that he did not like America.

He also found time in New York (and money, advanced by his kind hostess, Mrs John Macrae) for a gigantic shopping spree to buy clothes and other things for his family—shoes, hats for Audrey ("one is a little flat straw bowler with a large ball of fluff in front—or behind if you prefer that"), collars and under-wear and stockings in enormous quantities. Food purchases in-cluded a 60-lb keg of honey, and among miscellaneous purchases there is mention of a "little gadget for wetting envelopes—the Customs people use it".

Just before the Queen Mary was due to berth at Southampton, Audrey received a cable asking that the ship should be met with the biggest available lorry. Mystified, but obedient always, she did as he ordered. The explanation was that, at the last moment, John had succeeded in buying a ton of sugar and rice. This was far beyond the permitted quota for an individual to import, but he managed to persuade a large number of his fellow travellers on the ship to take handbags of it through the Customs. This illegal hoard (for there was, of course, still food rationing in England) was concealed in a store-house excavated under one of the cellar floors at Glyndebourne.

In January (1948) George Christie went to Eton to Mr Nigel Wykes's house. It meant a great deal to John that his son was thus following in his footsteps and also showing, as he had done, keenness in games. The choice of housemaster was an appro-priate one, for Wykes was keenly interested in opera; and he too was fortunate in that John each year extended an invitation to him to bring parties of boys to Glyndebourne as his guests. John's visits to Eton, dressed in clothes very unlike those worn by the average Eton parent, might have embarrassed many boys; but George soon came to realise that his father was "a notable character" and took it in his stride. Meanwhile Rosamond ("Pidge") had been at Southover Manor School, where she had worked at the piano and the violin and done a good deal of riding. After leaving Southover she spent six months in Paris, followed by a season in London.

In February John was invited to serve on the Arts Council's new Opera and Ballet Panel; he accepted and so effected some kind of a reconciliation with a body which he had formerly considered as his enemy. But he was still hoping for a Treasury Grant to put his own house in order. In April he wrote again to Bridges, thanking him for much help and sympathy in the past, and now asking directly for "A Treasury Grant—to the extent of something like the amount of my losses". But no grant was made.

Glyndebourne Productions Ltd were not in a position in 1948 to provide, on the home ground, more than a few Mozart concerts, with Beecham conducting his Royal Philharmonic Orchestra (which continued its association with Glyndebourne until 1963). They were, however, again active elsewhere—first at Bath, with *Die Entführung* in English at what was soon to be called the Bath Festival, and then in Edinburgh with *Don Giovanni* and *Così fan tutte*, the former conducted by Rafael Kubelik and the latter by Vittorio Gui.

In the autumn it was officially announced that there would be a season at Princeton in October 1949; then came a postponement, and finally the news that, for some unexplained reason, the season had been cancelled by Princeton. In the spring of 1949, Sir Thomas Beecham, now established in style in one of John's houses in Ringmer, conducted at Glyndebourne a series of concerts of works by Mozart, Haydn, Schubert, Schumann and Brahms. These included a divertimento for two hurdy-gurdies by Haydn, and much publicity was given in the Press to the news that John would himself be playing one of the hurdy-gurdies. But when he discovered that more was involved than just turning a handle he stepped down, and the public was informed that he had poisoned his finger gardening. He is, however, remembered for his appearance on the stage, at the beginning of that particular concert, with his pug, Bimperl, under his arm, its stern towards the audience. While he delivered his introductory speech he twisted the pug's tail as though it had been the handle of a barrel-organ.

In May, Bing lunched with the Beechams and had a long and frank discussion about Glyndebourne and its problems. Beecham, (he told John and Audrey)

> disapproves of the overweight which in his view the production side is getting at Glyndebourne, and he fundamentally disapproves of what in his view is a waste of money in the way of rehearsing the dramatic side.
>
> Beecham, and I believe quite rightly, thinks that Glyndebourne's future can only be assured if it expands its operations and ceases to be a small luxury organisation, necessarily too expensive for a wide audience and therefore not in line with present trends, whether we like them or not. He thinks (and I personally agree) that Glyndebourne must widen its operations and, while of course if at all possible it should perform at Glyndebourne, it should also tour and use the machinery of the British Opera League (Beecham's old organisation). He feels that this could be revived at a moment's notice, and be of enormous use in administrative ways—and, of course, financially.

But there were problems. How, for example, would Ebert—a perfectionist—react to the improvisation and other difficulties unavoidable when a company was on tour? Bing thought that he would probably be willing to accept that in the post-war world the luxuries of pre-war days could not be afforded. He thought the whole scheme "entirely workable" provided that John was "prepared to accept a rather drastic change of Glyndebourne's attitude to touring and rehearsal arrangements".

But nothing came of this, and it was perhaps only natural that Bing, who had worked so heroically and so long on behalf of Glyndebourne, felt depressed and discouraged. Doubtful now of the future of Glyndebourne, and finding (as he later told Audrey) that "the happy atmosphere of pre-war days" had vanished, he soon after accepted the important post of General Manager of the Metropolitan Opera House in New York. He was succeeded at Glyndebourne by Moran Caplat. John, though he generously blamed himself for putting Bing in a position which obliged him to leave Glyndebourne, was understandably rather hurt by what he felt to be Bing's defection.

Bing's departure was Glyndebourne's loss; its gain at this time was the return to the fold of Fritz Busch, who had kept away as a result of a stupid quarrel eight years earlier. This had arisen over Ebert's production of *Macbeth*, which Busch had appropriated without acknowledgment. Busch was entirely to blame. There had been further trouble during the War, when Busch had shown what to John seemed ingratitude, by inviting another artist, rather than Audrey (who so badly needed the money), to sing Susanna in America. But as Bing has pointed out,* "Busch was at that time fighting to establish himself in a strange country used to the best singers the world had to offer. Audrey was a delightful artist as long as she was surrounded by the love and care she received at Glyndebourne; she was not a great singer and I don't know whether at that time she could have stood up to the cold eyes and ears of New York and the competition that was then around. . ."

Moran Caplat, who had not in any way been involved in these matters, was selected as mediator, and with the help of Frances Dakyns persuaded Busch to come back.

At the beginning of August, as soon as the Eton holidays had begun, John had taken his son to Norway for a short fishing holiday. In spite of bad weather, poor fishing and the absence of Audrey; in spite, too, of John's hip which prevented his walking any distance and was often painful, they both enjoyed themselves. It was George's first visit to the Continent, and it proved to be John's last fishing expedition. They returned to England in time for John to go with Audrey and the children to Edinburgh for the Festival, where Ebert's admirable production of Verdi's *Un ballo in maschera* joined further performances of *Così fan tutte*.

In November Audrey went for several weeks to Germany and Austria. While she was away her father, on the death of his brother Harry, inherited the family title and became the Rev

* In a letter to the author, 28th March 1967.

Sir (Aubrey) Neville Mildmay, tenth baronet. His new rank did not make him any easier to deal with: "Your father is being utterly tiresome", John wrote when he gave her the news. "I think there is a fair sum of money to follow the baronetcy. He won't listen, and blackguards everybody. . . He wants to take a flat in London. He hates Sussex. . ."

*   *   *

Hardly had Bing abandoned Glyndebourne when there was a favourable change in the fortunes of the Festival Opera House. Plans for the Festival of Britain, to be held in 1951, were in hand, and Glyndebourne was now offered a Treasury Grant to enable it to stage four Mozart operas there. Glyndebourne, conscious of the difficulty of doing four new productions in the same year, proposed that it should receive one half of the grant in 1950 to put on two of the operas; but this was refused. It was then that Mr John Spedan Lewis, of the John Lewis Partnership, who had long been a generous supporter of Glyndebourne (and who had indeed thrown a life-line to its General Manager on the outbreak of War), came forward with the offer to underwrite the 1950 season to the extent of £12,500.

Thus it came about that in 1950 Glyndebourne once more found itself with its own Festival in its own Opera House.

*   *   *

July came. For the first time since the War the afternoon Special carried its oddly attired posse of passengers to Lewes. All seemed to be back to normal; but how long could it last?

The Glyndebourne season consisted of *Die Entführung* and *Così fan tutte*. In the latter, the Jugoslav soprano Sena Jurinac began her valuable connection with the Festival Opera House. After a short but successful season the Company moved to Edinburgh, where eighteen performances were given of *Figaro*, and of Richard Strauss's *Ariadne auf Naxos* in its original version. For all these operas except *Ariadne* the scenery had been designed by Rolf Gérard, who came in for some sharp criticism for his frivolous Mozart sets and was soon dropped. On the other hand, Oliver

Messel's staging of *Ariadne* was rightly admired. *Ariadne* was conducted by Sir Thomas Beecham in what proved to be his only
operatic association with Glyndebourne.

In October, John had his left eye removed; it had been of no
use to him for many years, and there was a danger of its affecting
the other. "Apparently I have to go to hospital for it!" he informed
Miss Belshaw. "I don't know why; the General's dog here had
his removed and next day was rabbiting. . ." John maintained
that the removal of his eye improved his health, and subsequently
recommended Mr Gow and other of his friends to have one out
too. However, not long after his operation John had a mild heart
attack at Victoria Station; but he made a full recovery from it.

★   ★   ★

The prospect for 1951, with a State guarantee of £25,000 to
fall back on, looked rosy, and after the end of the 1950 season
various alterations and extensions were carried out in the Festival
Opera House whose seating capacity now became almost double
what it had originally been.

In May Audrey was ill and in hospital, where John kept her
posted with news of rehearsals and difficulties over the painting
of the scenery, and any little titbits of news that might interest
or amuse her. His pugs, past and present, were often in his
thoughts:

> I was running to hide from Sock this evening and turned
> into the Gents' place in the house. My feet shot away from me
> and I fell, but with one hand caught hold of the door architrave
> and with the other held my spectacles (unbent), and I landed
> gently on my fore-arm, which is now a bit sore—not bad. Sock
> did not follow me. He created a scene at supper. I picked him
> up and he fought me furiously. He bit Michael Northen in
> the face. All conversation stopped. It was a magnificent per-
> formance—for seven minutes. "If you think pugs are soft,
> you see this one", he shouted; and they watched. . .
> Darling, I miss you very much. I walked out alone tonight
> and thought of you and George (the pug). I have got to get
> you better. So you must be calm. . .

Though he tried to keep up her spirits, he had no illusions as to the seriousness of her condition.

The 1951 season opened with Mozart's *Idomeneo* which, though to some extent known in England through amateur performances in the thirties, had never been professionally staged in this country. John, who had found the opera rather tedious when he had heard it in Munich before the war,★ was forced to change his tune when he saw Glyndebourne's magnificent Busch–Ebert–Messel production with Jurinac as Ilia and Richard Lewis in the title role. *Figaro, Così fan tutte* and *Don Giovanni* followed, the last-named with décor by John Piper. *Così fan tutte* was televised by the B.B.C. from Glyndebourne in its entirety, and in spite of protests in the press at this "affront to ordinary viewers" the Company has courageously continued to televise operas annually from Glyndebourne.

Don Giovanni was taken to Edinburgh, together with a new production (to mark the fiftieth anniversary of Verdi's death) of *La forza del destino* with a wholly non-Italian cast and some noticeably non-Italian accents. *La forza del destino* may not have been an entirely successful production, but there was surprise and indignation, both in Scotland and at Glyndebourne, when it was announced by the Edinburgh Festival Society that the Hamburg Opera, and not Glyndebourne, had been invited to take part in the 1952 season. It was an ungenerous gesture, indeed a calculated snub, to the founders of the Edinburgh Festival, attributable, it has been said, to "a matter of cost and Scottish parsimony† allied to what might be termed a 'natural break' in a love-hate relationship".

In June, John was prosecuted for driving on the wrong side of a narrow road. He was convicted and fined £25. His licence was also forfeited—very possibly because of a letter to the Bench to the effect that he could not attend as he had more important matters on hand—and anyhow he was innocent. Mr Quintin

★ See p. 146.
† Edinburgh has still not built an adequate Opera House.

Hogg was briefed for an appeal, which resulted in John's fine being reduced to £5 and his licence being restored. Moreover he was awarded costs. John wanted to prosecute the Police Inspector for malicious prosecution and/or giving false evidence, but was dissuaded.

The episode remained a lifelong grievance to which John often referred with much bitterness. And understandably: he had been unjustly accused, as his almost complete vindication showed. But there was a further point: he had particularly wanted to attend the original hearing (in Devon); but the date chosen for it coincided with the opening of the Glyndebourne Festival, and the Bench refused to change it. John had felt that he was being persecuted, and that the reason for this was that there was still feeling against him in Devon as a result of the will case.

On 14th September 1951 Fritz Busch died suddenly in London of a heart attack; he was sixty-one.

The appointment of Busch in 1934 had been a very great stroke of good fortune; without Busch, and without Ebert whom he brought to Glyndebourne, the Festival Opera House might well have foundered almost at once. It is impossible to estimate what Glyndebourne owed to him, and what, in spite of the troubles there had been, it lost by his death. It was the end of an epoch. To what has already been written of him (on p. 206) may be added John and Audrey's joint tribute to him in *The Times*:

> Fritz Busch is gone—a fact hardly to be believed by those who but a matter of days ago heard in Edinburgh or by wireless his magnificent performance of *La forza del destino*... Glyndebourne has lost the man who set its original musical pulse, who worked tirelessly in those original days to assemble the artistic personnel who brought our initial success. We and all those who through the years have worked with Busch in Sussex and now in Edinburgh wish to pay tribute to one whom we respected and admired for his musical integrity as well as for his unsurpassed ability to collaborate inspiringly and successfully in an artistic venture of the delicacy of opera. Collaboration with Busch also implied efficiency, the prompt

answering of letters, and the ability to make wise decisions. His work, too, has shown an unusual combination of humility with greatness, and it is for this that we shall remember Fritz with admiration and affection. His audiences will remember with respect his constant resistance of Hitler's efforts to get Busch (a true Aryan) to return to his native land until the political air had been purged.

★   ★   ★

The Treasury Grant and John Lewis's generous guarantee had made it possible to start Glyndebourne up again; but what of the future? Where was the money to come from, to keep it running? John had good cause to be worried.

It was at this juncture that a *deus ex machina* descended in the person of Mr (now Sir) N. T. Sekers, a Hungarian who was director of the West Cumberland Silk Mills and a great lover of music. He had already generously presented the materials for the dresses of *Don Giovanni*; he now came forward with a proposal which was to bring valuable financial help to Glyndebourne at this critical moment in its history. This was to replace the ordinary programme by a handsome programme book, lavishly illustrated, in which leading British industrialists would be persuaded to advertise. He proposed aiming at forty advertisers, and a gross annual income of £20,000.

Mr Geoffrey Herrington, Director of High Duty Alloys, was the first to be enlisted; he was soon followed by Mr Arthur Gilbey and in due course by sixteen other Directors of big British firms, all willing to take a page in the Glyndebourne Festival Programme Book for 1952 and to pay handsomely for the privilege. Through the years the number has gradually increased until it has today almost reached the target set by Mr Sekers.

Out of this venture there grew the Glyndebourne Festival Society—a kind of "Friends of Glyndebourne" with corporate, individual and associated memberships entitling the contributor to various privileges. By the time the 1952 season opened, the Society had a total of over eight hundred members. It has continued to flourish.

On 15th June a special performance of *Idomeneo* was given in memory of Fritz Busch; John Pritchard conducted, and during the interval a bronze bust of Busch was unveiled. Three days later came the official first night, with Vittorio Gui conducting Rossini's *La Cenerentola*; thus a new composer and a new conductor, of both of whom Glyndebourne was to hear more in the future, made their début at the Festival Opera House.* Sesto Bruscantini's splendid Dandini set the seal of success on what was unanimously declared to have been one of Glyndebourne's most sparkling productions. Gui also conducted performances of *Macbeth* and *Così fan tutte*, while John Pritchard remained in charge of *Idomeneo*.

Membership of the Festival Society contributed the sum of £3,200 towards the expenses, and the sale of the Festival Programme Book another £4,750; but at the close of the season John found himself saddled with a deficit of nearly £18,000. His thoughts turned again, and now more urgently, to an idea which had occurred to him during the War: the formation of a Trust to run Glyndebourne.

Audrey had always viewed such a Trust with suspicion, fearing that Glyndebourne might thereby lose the peculiar qualities that had made it unique. In one of the last letters she wrote—to Mr Sekers on 4th February 1953—she thanked him for his "unbelievable kindness" in a hundred ways, and in particular for his quick appreciation of the grounds for her anxiety over the Trust. She felt that the whole thing had been in danger of being "rushed through". George was now eighteen, and had always been given to understand that he would carry on Glyndebourne. "If the Trust had gone forward in the form in which I first heard of it, he might have been faced with the fact that he was only one of a number of people" controlling it, not all of whom might have wanted to retain "the ideals and essence of Glyndebourne as created". She continued:

I feel that you have expressed a very clear understanding of

---

* Gui had of course already conducted Glyndebourne's productions at Edinburgh in 1948 and 1949.

my point of view when you compare our hopes for Glynde-bourne.... with what the Wagner family created and appear to be maintaining [at Bayreuth]. I think one does not want to hamper the growth of Glyndebourne by sticking to too old traditions—as D'Oyly Carte has done for Gilbert and Sulli-van—but year by year to give it fresh "fertilisation", yet al-ways repolishing and improving the original idea. . . . Personally I only want to know that Glyndebourne may continue in its best form as long as there is any need for it, *and* that, if George is capable of improving on what we have started, his initiative may not be frustrated or hampered. . . .

If this continuity for Glyndebourne, plus the opportunity of developing the children's possible talents for guiding and controlling it, can be achieved, I would feel very differently over the whole thing. . .

Though the Trust was not in fact to be set up until 1954, a year after her death, Audrey lived to know that it would be so constituted that the Glyndebourne she loved and believed in would be preserved.

★   ★   ★

To the great grief of all visitors to Glyndebourne in 1952, Audrey had been ill during the whole of the season. Several operations to relieve very high blood pressure effected only tem-porary alleviation. These were tragic and difficult days for John, for illness and severe migraines often made her unreasonable, and even unkind to him; but he understood and forgave, and his loyalty to her never wavered. On 31st May of the following year she died at Glyndebourne; she was only fifty-two. After crema-tion her ashes were interred in Sussex; but later a part of them was removed to Devon.

If Fritz Busch and Carl Ebert, as conductor and producer res-pectively, had realised John's dream of Opera at Glyndebourne, Audrey had been the guiding influence of its destiny in the early days. The perfect hostess, she had herself created, perhaps almost without being aware of it, the unique atmosphere which she

15 John Christie, 1954

16 Family group at Glyndebourne, 1959. John Christie, Rosamond, Mary and George

and all who came to Glyndebourne were so anxious should not be destroyed. "We should aim at the sky," John had urged, "but have our feet on the ground." Audrey had urged her husband to aim high, to "do the thing properly"; but probably her greatest contribution to their joint venture had been that innate sense of proportion which had restrained him when his feet began to leave the ground.

Her death was not only a personal tragedy to John and to their two children; it also left, at the Glyndebourne Festivals, a gap that no one else could hope to fill. She had lived bravely, uncomplainingly setting about the remaking of her life after her singing career had ended. Her friend Mrs Edwin Fisher wrote:

> From that time onwards there was always the threat of ill health to haunt her; she never gave in and fought valiantly to overcome it, even when she began to lose her sight. Whenever she was with people, she made the supreme effort to be her old gay self; but what could have been her thoughts when she was alone? After her two grave operations she told me how she would fight against taking the drugs which were given her to relieve the great pain she had to endure; how she would count the hours till the next dose was due and then say, "Not yet; I'll bear it a little longer." I think she was one of the bravest people I have ever known. . . .

23

The Last Decade

THE DEATH of Audrey affected John deeply. He had been lonely during the War, but then he had been able to look forward with confidence to a reunion with her; now, at the age of seventy-one, he had to face his declining years alone. George Christie wrote:

> After my Mother's death there was a gradual tendency for my Father to vegetate more and more. He continued to be militant, but the fights he concerned himself in became increasingly out of date the more he cut himself off from current events by hibernating at Glyndebourne all the year round. Depressingly his dog became almost as important to him (or so he liked people to think) as his battles.

The winters especially were long and dreary for him, though he continued to find some occupation and some interest in structural alterations of various kinds at Glyndebourne. Hanging about these building operations, in all weathers and usually in the lightest clothes, did no good to the jaundice from which he suffered regularly every winter. From time to time he was forced to go into hospital, but he was an impossible patient and within forty-eight hours had invariably made his escape and returned home.

His social life was limited, but Rhona Byron and other of his faithful friends continued to visit him. He slept a good deal. He talked much of the past—of Audrey and of his mother, of Eton days and of C. M. Wells;* and "Fowler's match"† constantly

---

* When John realised that he might not outlive Wells, he wrote a glowing obituary notice of him and sent it to *The Times*. It was not used.

† A famous Eton *v*. Harrow match in 1911 when R. St L. Fowler, who captained the Eton eleven, saved his side from what appeared to be certain defeat

recurred in his flood of recollections. To those who saw him holding court in the foyer during the Opera seasons he seemed little
changed, for he put on a brave face in public and never shirked
the duties of a host. His children were a great comfort to him.

But the story is not yet over: his life had still nine more years to
run, and there was still much to be done. There was the Glyndebourne Trust to be established, and in a form that Audrey would
have found acceptable. There was the planning of the Festivals,
and though John played each successive year an increasingly
minor part in the choice of operas and singers, he none the less
liked to have his say. And there were still one or two little battles
ahead—battles which he was to fight with all his old tenacity
though often from ill-prepared positions.

It had been Audrey's last wish that the 1953 season should go
ahead as planned. It opened, only a week after her death, with
Gluck's *Alceste*, conducted by Vittorio Gui and with décor by Sir
Hugh Casson. This was the first opera to be sung in French at
Glyndebourne, and there is no evidence that John protested. *La
Cenerentola*, *Ariadne auf Naxos* (second version), *Die Entführung* and
Così fan tutte completed the season's bill. Ebert produced through-
out, as brilliantly as ever.

Edinburgh, perhaps rather ashamed of the ingratitude it had
shown in 1952, had recalled the Glyndebourne company to its
1953 Festival. To *Idomeneo* and *La Cenerentola* there was now added
a rather startling novelty: Stravinsky's *The Rake's Progress*, with
sets by Osbert Lancaster. John found the work too advanced for
his taste: "I don't like the music," he said, "and I can't imagine
hearing the overture* played on a concert platform—and what
use is an overture if it can't be played in a concert? But I am told I
may come round to it."

He never did. Wagner and Richard Strauss were really almost
as far as he was able to go towards the "music of the future". He
still clung to the hope that one day he would hear *Parsifal* on his

by taking eight wickets for 23 runs. Eton's victory took the heart out of Harrow
cricket; for many years thereafter the Harrovians not only never won, but played
as though a draw was all they aimed at.
  * It has no overture.

own stage. In the latter part of 1953 he was in correspondence with Wieland Wagner, whose sister had recently visited Glyndebourne, and there was talk of staging *Tristan* under Wieland's direction. But once again the project came to nothing. The only Wagner John was ever to hear at Glyndebourne was the *Siegfried Idyll* and the semi-amateur performance of a scene from *Die Meistersinger*.

In 1953, too, after more than thirty years with Glyndebourne and its multifarious activities, Edwards felt that the time had come for him to retire. He had been John's right-hand man, and it is impossible to estimate what John owed to his business acumen, his energy and his unswerving loyalty. He was succeeded by Mr E. S. Norman, who in his turn was to keep a finger on the pulse of all John's enterprises, and in whom John placed a great deal of trust and responsibility.

1954 opened auspiciously with the award to John, in the New Year's Honours List, of the Companion of Honour.* His first reaction had been to refuse: "It's just a sop from Whitehall to stop my negotiations with the Treasury," he cried. Then, very characteristically, he attempted (but without success) to have it awarded posthumously to Audrey instead of to himself. But in the end he was persuaded to accept. Later in the year he was presented with the Mozart Medal of the Vienna Mozart Society— the first time that it had been given to an Englishman. It was posthumously awarded to Audrey at the same time.

On 31st May of the same year the Glyndebourne Arts Trust was formed and the following announcement made:

> Mr John Christie has conveyed to the Trust, on a long lease at peppercorn rent, the Opera House, the mansion, the grounds and the gardens, which together make up Glyndebourne.

The Trustees will be responsible for the general supervision

---

* John had at one time been fond of saying that he wanted nothing for himself; but his attitude changed, and towards the end of his life he was heard to express surprise that Cambridge had never given him an honorary degree. By then it was too late for his friends there to put his name forward.

of these properties and of the Glyndebourne Festival Opera. They have made an agreement with Mr Christie that he and his colleagues, who have brought the Festival to its present high level of distinction, shall continue to be responsible for its direction and administration.

Glyndebourne does not receive any subsidy from public funds. It has to maintain itself out of its own receipts together with such resources as the Trustees can create from the donations of persons and institutions who believe that it is of importance to preserve, at the highest international standard, this Festival of Opera presented in the distinctive setting of an English country house. The Trustees are anxious to emphasise that the formation of the Trust makes it no less essential for Glyndebourne's present friends to continue to give their increasing support.

Sir Wilfred Eady was appointed Chairman of the eleven Trustees. The Glyndebourne Executive, acting on behalf of Glyndebourne Productions Ltd, was to plan the seasons and submit its budgets to the Arts Trust. Ebert alone of the Executive was not also a member of Glyndebourne Productions Ltd; the former therefore soon became merged in the latter, Ebert of course playing his part as sole Artistic Director.

Two new productions were added for the 1954 Glyndebourne season: Rossini's *The Barber of Seville*, and Busoni's *Arlecchino* which joined *Ariadne* as a curtain-raiser. *Arlecchino* was produced by Peter Ebert, Carl's son, who had been his father's assistant since 1947; this was the first Glyndebourne opera not produced by Carl Ebert. With Vittorio Gui, now largely responsible for musical policy at the Festivals, as conductor, the *Barber* became one of Glyndebourne's most brilliant successes, and Oliver Messel's décor was exactly right. Rossini had in fact now established himself, along with Mozart, as Glyndebourne's principal composer, and his *Le Comte Ory* was produced for the Edinburgh Festival. In the autumn the Glyndebourne Festival Opera took *La Cenerentola* to Berlin for the West Berlin Festival.

Those who wish to read a full account of Opera at Glyndebourne will of course turn to Spike Hughes's book; here there is space only for a steadily accelerating survey of each season's principal novelties.

1955, the year in which Glyndebourne came of age, provided a new production of *Figaro* with a strongly Italianate flavour, and *The Rake's Progress* which had already been heard in Edinburgh. At the Edinburgh Festival came Verdi's *Falstaff* with Osbert Lancaster's witty scenery and costumes; those in the audience who were "in the know" enjoyed recognising, in the ancestral portraits on the wall of Ford's house, unmistakable resemblance to some of the Glyndebourne staff.

1956, the year of the Mozart bicentenary, saw his six principal operas performed at Glyndebourne. It was the longest and most ambitious season yet held, marred only by "that awful Glyndebourne ballet" (as *The Times*'s critic called it) in *Idomeneo*, which never ceased to jar. The effort of producing these six operas would in any case have made it impossible for time to be found for a new production for the Edinburgh Festival; in fact Edinburgh could not afford to issue such an invitation and it was to be five years before Glyndebourne returned there.

However, the Company went in September to the Royal Court Theatre, Liverpool, for a successful fortnight's season of *La Cenerentola*, *Don Giovanni*, and what a critic of a national newspaper termed "Mozart's melodious Bedroom Farce"—i.e. *Figaro*. While in Liverpool, Moran Caplat revealed to a reporter of *The Liverpool Daily Post* his great ambition: to buy up an old aircraft carrier and convert it into a circulating Opera House. As a former Lieut-Commander R.N.V.R., Caplat would have been in his element as General Manager of this floating Glyndebourne.

In the late summer of 1956 John had a prostate operation at Guy's Hospital, and in the winter a second and more serious heart attack. "I was rung up at Cambridge," said his son, "but told that I should not come until the following day; he was dangerously ill and might not survive for long. I went up to London the first thing next morning and on entering his room found him scuttling back into bed, thinking I was a nurse and much relieved to find that I wasn't!"

About this time there began, too, a gradual deterioration of his sight which was to lead, in the very last months of his life, to almost total blindness. Though he might complain when he was sent to hospital, he never complained of his disabilities or spoke of himself with self-pity. Courage had always been one of his qualities, but patience had not; it was something that he had gradually acquired over the years.

1957 opened with Rossini's *L'Italiana in Algeri*, which turned out to be one of the least popular of Glyndebourne's novelties. *Ariadne* (second version) was this year preceded by Mozart's little *Der Schauspieldirektor*, and Glyndebourne audiences saw for the first time the production of *Falstaff* that had delighted Edinburgh in 1955. Some of the southern critics were less enchanted, and the rather ponderous horse-play introduced by Ebert amused them less than it did the audiences; but *The Times* found the production "perfect".

In 1954 Edinburgh had had to make good a deficit of £35,622 after a season that had cost £63,699, and the following year both the cost and the loss had been even greater. Though a return of the Glyndebourne Company in 1958, with *Carmen*, came under discussion, Robert Ponsonby, Artistic Director of the Edinburgh Festival, could not budget for an expenditure in excess of £50,000, and Glyndebourne again stayed away.

But in May Glyndebourne went to Paris to take part in the international *Théâtre des Nations* season at the Théâtre Sarah-Bernhardt. Four performances each of *Le Comte Ory* and *Falstaff* were given—the latter, in particular, to enthusiastic audiences who were amazed at the perfect ensemble achieved by a cosmopolitan team. At Glyndebourne itself, the only novelty was Wolff-Ferrari's *Il segreto di Susanna*, which was chosen as a curtain-raiser to *Ariadne*.

In August 1958, a week after the end of the Opera season, George Christie married Mary Nicholson, the daughter of Ivor Nicholson (of Ivor Nicholson & Watson, the late Publishers). The wedding took place in Witley Church, Surrey, with the

Glyndebourne Chorus as choir and a number of soloists, including Richard Lewis and Geraint Evans, also taking part—a fine demonstration of the affection of everyone at Glyndebourne for the Christie family.

That same autumn John handed over to his son the Chairman-ship of Glyndebourne Productions, remaining however on the Board of Directors. It was a stroke of good fortune that George Christie was well equipped to carry on the work that his parents had begun. He was naturally musical, and he had grown up with music going on all around him; he had at least a working know-ledge of one instrument—the violin; and he had read modern languages at Trinity College, Cambridge. His knowledge of languages was to be valuable to him, not only in his dealings with the foreign artists at Glyndebourne, but also when he was visiting the Continent in search of new talent.

Where John had shown his genius principally in the realm of construction and design (his last great achievement was the build-ing of a full-sized stage for rehearsals), George was to prove the artistic Chairman who saw the musical future of Glyndebourne in dramatic and exciting terms. It must have warmed the heart of John to see his ship, which had so nearly foundered in the forties, now set on a straight course in a calmer sea.

*   *   *

It had seemed to John for some time past that the Press, and in particular *The Times*, had not paid sufficient attention to Glynde-bourne while Covent Garden was constantly in the news. On 3rd November 1958 he addressed a letter to the Editor, his friend Sir William Haley, pointing out that the first ten years of the new Covent Garden had been "just lamentable" and that Glynde-bourne alone was able to provide first-rate operatic performances. Four months later he wrote again, deploring the fact that Glynde-bourne's new rehearsal stage had been ignored by the Press and suggesting that this continued conspiracy of silence, together (of course) with the "malice" of Keynes, had been largely responsible for Bing absconding to America:

Should I be writing to you, or to Howes,* to ask him to come
and look at it and write about it? I think not. I think that if he is
any good he would be doing so on his own. . . . Something is
wrong. This little, baby jealousy seems to me to be too childish. We are surely all of us above it; if not, we had better clear
out. . . .

In the same letter to Haley of 9th May, partly quoted in the
footnote on page 260, he refers again to the "ingratitude" of
The Times, which ignored Glyndebourne while giving Covent
Garden uncritical praise. But *The Times* had done even worse in
his eyes: it had just "written up" Keynes—still unforgiven after so
many years.

Sir William replied on his return from the Continent. He said
that it was inevitable that Covent Garden, the main Opera House
in the heart of London, should receive a good deal of attention
from the Press, though it should of course be criticised when its
performances fell short of what they ought to be. He regretted
that John had not been given the chance of helping to shape its
destiny, but it was no use crying over spilt milk. "I cannot see any
way in which it could benefit Glyndebourne for *The Times* or any
other paper to be constantly reiterating that it is better than Covent
Garden."

He was, he said, an old friend of John's. He had always tried to
show his admiration for John's efforts, both while he was at the
B.B.C. and since, and he would continue to do so. "The point is
that I do not think it really will support them to decry Covent
Garden. . . ."

John, who liked Howes personally and admired much of what
he wrote, gratefully acknowledged this "friendly letter" and
turned his attention to the Festival, which was opening on the
following evening.

1959 was the year of Glyndebourne's Silver Jubilee, and the
weather furnished it with a summer that was unforgettably
golden. But it was clouded by the news that Carl Ebert, who had
been with the Festival Opera House ever since its inauguration,

---

* Frank Howes, Assistant Music Critic of *The Times* from 1925 until 1943 when
he became "Our Music Critic". He retired in 1960.

felt that at seventy-two the time had come for him to retire. To mark his departure he had chosen, for the gala first night of the season, Richard Strauss's *Der Rosenkavalier*.

Ebert had always opposed John's desire to present *Parsifal* at Glyndebourne; what he was now about to undertake seemed almost as temerarious. But Ebert was confident, and on 28th May the season opened with the first of thirteen performances of *Der Rosenkavalier*. The principal singers were Elisabeth Söderström (Oktavian), Régine Crespin (Feldmarschallin), Oscar Czerwenka (Ochs) and Anneliese Rothenberger (Sophie).

The orchestra had been cut down to sixty players in a version authorised (though not arranged) by Strauss; this reduced the volume of sound to bearable decibels, but in the opinion of many people it created an imbalance—particularly, of course, between strings and wind—when assessed against the effect that Strauss had originally intended. The stage did not prove, as some had feared, unreasonably crowded; indeed the total cast was considerably smaller than that of *Macbeth*. The production and performances were undoubtedly exceptional by any standards. What was lost by the reduction in the size of the orchestra and the consequent imbalance of sound was compensated for by the feeling of intimacy in the inter-relationship of the characters—something which was intended by the librettist, Hofmannsthal, but which was precluded by Strauss's "Grand Opera" orchestration and consequently virtually unknown in full-scale performances given in bigger opera houses.

At the end of the performance John came on to the stage to present Ebert with a silver rose-bowl. In a twenty-five minute speech he found a good many uncomplimentary things to say about Covent Garden and the Arts Council, whose representatives were his guests for the evening, but omitted to mention Ebert and his bowl until his memory was tactfully jogged by Moran Caplat.

Der Rosenkavalier was generally considered to have been one of Glyndebourne's successes. However, Mr Frank Howes thought otherwise. In particular, he deplored the volume of sound which, in his opinion seemed "to sear the ears like a whiplash". John wrote immediately, and indignantly, to Haley. Once again it was, he said, Howes defending Covent Garden by decrying Glyndebourne. "His criticism of the Feldmarschallin is hotly resented. . . . I sent a note of protest round to our first night audience, and they are supporting it vehemently. . . . I am fighting against musical politics. I thought it better to be quite open about it all, because this ought not to happen again."

It is extraordinary that John had never learned that critics are entitled to criticise, and even to hold views that differed from his; nor could he understand that editors would not reprimand them for doing so. As Spike Hughes says, the writing of such letters "was a practice which might well have done more harm than good had it not been for the personal affection felt by Fleet Street for their regular indignant correspondent". *

Two days later John returned to his old hobby-horse, the building of a better Britain—though this time he was using very small bricks. On 9th June he wrote to the Prime Minister (Harold Macmillan) a letter which suggests that his mind was no longer what it had been. In it he explained at considerable length how he had missed a turning in Brighton because of a misleading signpost. What was needed, he said, was "a new Ministry—of Efficiency" to put this signpost and other such inefficiencies right. . . . If only Audrey had been at his side to keep a watchful eye on his wayward pen !

The other novelty of the Jubilee season at Glyndebourne was *Fidelio*, an opera which Ebert had long opposed on the grounds of unsuitability but whose immediate success proved that his fears had been groundless. Günther Rennert, who produced *Fidelio*, the following year, joined Gui, who conducted it, as one of the two "Artistic Counsellors" and so became Ebert's successor. With the unscheduled entry of bats in the prison scene in *Fidelio*, and the designed appearance of one of the Glyndebourne pugs in the first act of *Der Rosenkavalier*, the 1959 season was unusually rich in animal life.

For August there had been announced a Handel–Haydn Festival

---

* Throughout his life John had written frequently and often whimsically to *The Times* on a variety of topics, though his letters were not always published.

of Concerts and Operas conducted by Sir Thomas Beecham; but once again this collaboration with Beecham came to nothing, with the result that the regular season could be extended till it reached the record total, to date, of sixty-eight performances.

Finally, the Jubilee was marked by the award to John of the German Bundesverdienstkreuz, and of the Great Silver Honorary Medal "for services rendered to the Austrian Republic"; and soon afterwards Ebert received an Honorary C.B.E. To the West German President, John wrote:

Dear Herr President,

I am very much indebted to you for the Honour you have presented to me. It has occupied my mind persistently during the few days since your Ambassador conferred it on me. I have always liked the Germans, and in the First War I saved the lives of several who were taken prisoner in our trench, and I have often recollected this occasion.

Our work here was undertaken, not out of personal ambition, but because it was necessary to bring to this country what was normal on the Continent and yet hardly existed here. This, thanks to two Germans, Busch and Ebert, and to the genius of my wife, has been successful.

We must build the new world and your action helps to bring our two countries together. Thank you very much.

1960 saw a further new composer, Bellini, conquer the Glyndebourne stage with *I Puritani*, which had not in fact been professionally produced since 1887. The part of Elvira proved a fine vehicle for the wonderful voice of Joan Sutherland. Largely as the result of a vigorous campaign by Mr Eric Linklater, Glyndebourne returned to the Edinburgh Festival in August with *I Puritani*, *Falstaff* and a triple bill which included Poulenc's *La Voix Humaine*—the first purely French opera performed by the Glyndebourne Company.

Before the opening of the 1961 season, Lady Violet Bonham Carter unveiled a bronze bust of John, the work of Oscar Nemon, which had already been seen in its plaster state by the audience on the last night of the 1960 season; it was the gift to John of the Glyndebourne Festival Society. The original design had, at John's urgent request, also included Sock, but he had finally consented to the removal of his beloved pug. The bust, said Lady Violet, was "a little larger than life . . . but the subject is a man whose personality has outgrown that of normal men". It now stands in the walled garden, behind the covered way.

Neither of the two experiments of 1961 was an unqualified success. Some of the critics found Franco Zeffirelli's production of Donizetti's *L'elisir d'amore* fidgety and "mannered", and much of the singing was below the standard to which Glyndebourne audiences were accustomed. The world première in English of Henze's *Elegy for Young Lovers*—a brave choice in view of the conservative tastes of Glyndebourne audiences—provided the first booing ever to be heard at Glyndebourne, and was followed by a spate of advertisements inserted in the personal column of *The Times* by those who now wished to change their *Elegy* seats for anything else whatever. The story is told that John came one day upon two strangers in the grounds and commented upon the "dreadful work" that was at that moment being rehearsed in the Opera House. When he discovered that they were in fact W. H. Auden and Chester Kallman, joint authors of the libretto of the *Elegy*, he was delighted to have had the opportunity of telling them personally what he thought of it. However, the production and sets received praise from the critics and the cast was on the whole good.

If there was no Glyndebourne novelty at Edinburgh that year, there was at least a London novelty: a whole evening of a Promenade Concert at the Albert Hall devoted to a concert performance of Glyndebourne's *Don Giovanni*. It was intelligently received by an audience appreciative of the chance to hear the Glyndebourne Company for a mere three shillings.

In the middle of the 1961 season there had occurred an event which gave John enormous pleasure: the birth of his first grandchild, Hector Thomas Clevland Christie. John had always strenuously maintained that his son had been named after George the pug; jocularly he now lamented that the new infant was not to be called Sock.* But he doted on the child, dandled it lovingly

* At Tapeley there is however the tomb of a dog named Hector (d. 1916).

in his arms, often slipped out of his box during a performance "just to see if Hector is all right", and wished only that Audrey could have lived to see the day. The continuance of the line seemed assured, though he trembled—"*all* my eggs in one basket!"—when George and Mary drove off with Hector beside them in the car; perhaps he remembered that he had said the very same thing when, twenty years before, his wife and their small children had sailed for Canada.

French opera, if Poulenc's little one-part *La Voix Humaine* can really qualify as such, had reached Glyndebourne in 1960 and had clearly confirmed John in his dislike of everything French; it was therefore somewhat surprising that two years later he agreed, apparently without protest, to the production of Debussy's *Pelléas et Mélisande*. Gui conducted, and Ebert, who had retired from Glyndebourne three years before, returned as producer. It was perhaps the greatest triumph of their long and successful partnership, and one of the finest productions ever staged at the Festival Opera House.

Monteverdi's *Orfeo* had more than once been proposed for Glyndebourne, but for some curious reason the suggestion had not been adopted. However, in 1962 Monteverdi did reach the Festival Opera House, but with his *L'incoronazione di Poppea*, a work which had never been given a fully professional production in England though it had been heard at Oxford in 1927. This rather hazardous venture was a considerable success.

For the first time John had not been in his box on the opening night. Some weeks before he had had an operation for cataract. The operation was doubtfully wise, but he had ruined its chances by rubbing his eye and was now almost completely blind. He was, however, able to hear the performance relayed to the house, and in the interval he appeared in the foyer. Those who saw him hardly recognised him; no longer able to shave himself, and rejecting the services of others, he had the previous autumn grown a patriarchal bushy white beard.

His courage during the last months of his life was astonishing. "I never heard him once complain of his blindness", said Rhona

Byron, "even when it was acute and one knew he was often pretending to see more than he did." George and Mary watched over him devotedly, wheeling him out in the garden and helping him to pass the long hours of waiting for the end that all knew could not now be far away.

Devoted to him also was Dennis, the butler. "He had been marvellous in helping to look after Audrey when she was very ill", said Rhona Byron, "and he was just as marvellous in looking after John. Though John had nurses and there was really nothing that Dennis could do, he sat with him constantly; John very much appreciated this and would never disturb him by ringing for him in the night if he could help it. There was an occasion when John fell out of bed, and rather than call Dennis down he stayed on the floor all night. John had an incredible capacity for making people fond of him. . . ."

While the opera-goers, unaware of the full seriousness of his condition, were listening to *Figaro* or *Poppea* or cheerfully picnicking in the lovely grounds, John lay patiently awaiting death. To those who gathered at his bedside—his children, Rhona Byron, Jock Gough and other of his old friends—he spoke at the last, not of Glyndebourne, not of his mother or even of his wife, but of his days as a master at Eton: of what had been, he always maintained, the happiest time of his life. On 4th July, just as the first guests were beginning to arrive for the evening's performance of *Così fan tutte*, he died. He was in his eightieth year.

It had been John's wish that the Festival should continue in its normal way, and on the following evening, before the curtain rose, the audience stood in silence to honour his memory. The opera chanced to be *Figaro*, and it was appropriate: it was the opera with which, nearly thirty years before, Glyndebourne had first opened its doors.

A Memorial Service was held in Westminster Abbey on 3rd September. Though the Abbey organist, Sir William McKie, played Bach while the congregation was arriving—and on an organ which had been built by Hill, Norman and Beard—it was Mozart that had been chosen for the service itself; not even now was John to be allowed his Wagner. Vittorio Gui, with the Royal Philharmonic Orchestra, the Glyndebourne Festival Chorus and soloists who had often trodden the Glyndebourne boards, conducted Mozart's Requiem Mass; Lord Hailsham★ read the lesson and the service ended with the solemn march from the third act of *Idomeneo*.

It was, inevitably, a sad occasion; yet it could also have been regarded as a happy one. For though John Christie, the man, was dead, his life's work lived on and flourished. Not many men live their lives for an ideal; fewer live to see their ideals realised, and yet fewer die in the knowledge that what they have fought for will outlive them.

John died knowing that his long and often bitter battles had not been fought in vain, and that the Glyndebourne Arts Trust, and Glyndebourne Production Limited under the Chairmanship of his son, would carry on the work that he and Audrey had begun.

★   ★   ★

The careers of many men who achieve a measure of fame in life follow, almost from their beginning, a predictable pattern. There is no cause for surprise in the able young subaltern finally achieving the rank of Field Marshal, in the clever young politician graduating in due course to Cabinet rank. But John was forty before his interest in music became serious, and nearly fifty before he embarked upon the venture which was to make his name a household word in the world of music.

The reason for this is plain: as a schoolmaster he led for many years a life that seemed to be wholly satisfying. Yet all that time there was, at the back of his mind, the nagging feeling that he had not yet found himself, that he had something more important to give to the world. But what was it? He did not know. He wanted to live for an ideal, but the ideal eluded him. Had he stayed at Eton and taken a boys' house, he would have found his little niche among the Eton eccentrics: nothing more. But, happily for music, his interest in teaching faded and he left.

Even now, there was still no sign where his search for an ideal

★ Now Mr Quintin Hogg again.

was to take him. Then—out of the blue, as it were—appeared Fanny Mounsey.

A widely disseminated Glyndebourne myth alleges that John's marriage to an opera-singer led to his becoming interested in music and so to his building an opera house for her to sing in. This is of course untrue. The real turning-point in John's life was not his marriage with Audrey, but the advent of Fanny Mounsey:

> There is a tide in the affairs of men,
> Which, taken at the flood, leads on to fortune;
> Omitted, all the voyage of their life
> Is bound in shallows and in miseries.

Without Fanny Mounsey, John would most probably never have turned seriously to music; and without music he would not have found Audrey. Had Fanny Mounsey been a garden-lover and not a musician, Glyndebourne might have become a second Bodnant. Had she been a zoologist, it might have become a private Whipsnade; and indeed it is not too difficult to imagine John, with his passion for pugs and his fearlessness of bulls, stocking his park with wild animals, leading his trembling visitors into the lion's den, and denouncing on every possible occasion the inefficient running of the London Zoological Gardens.

It was Fanny Mounsey who helped to change the course of John's life and gave it its new direction. But she was, as it were, no more than the steering-wheel; as yet there was no motion. Then came Audrey to provide the driving force to set him on his way. With his own single-minded devotion to a goal once recognised; with his inherited wealth, his vision, his enormous vitality and his wonderful obstinacy; with his brilliant team of experts and with a fair measure of good luck—with all these but, above all, with Audrey at his side to support him, he thus achieved at last his long-sought goal: the miracle that is the Glyndebourne Festival Opera.

W. J. W. B.
25th July 1967

20

Index

Note: Operas are entered under their own titles, not under the composer.

Adenauer, Konrad, 284
Agate, James, 192–6
Albert Hall, the, 285
Albert Herring, 256, 257, 258
Alceste, 275
Alington, Dr Cyril, 96
Allcock, C. H., 25
Allen, Sir Hugh, 227–8
Allen, John, 240, 241
Alsen, Herbert, 184
Anderson, Sir John, 237
Andresen, Ivar, 177, 247
Ansermet, Ernest, 256
Antony Vicarage, nr. Devonport, 28–9
Ariadne auf Naxos, 148n, 154, 266–7, 275, 279
Arlecchino, 277
Arts Council of Great Britain, 205, 226, 241, 243, 255, 256, 257, 260
    and *n*, 263, 282
Ashton, Mrs, 190
Assheton, Ralph (Lord Clitheroe), 234–5
Auden, W. H., 285
Austin, Frederick, 202
Austin, Sumner, 178

B.B.C., the, 180, 191, 227, 229, 236, 268
Baccaloni, Salvatore, 180, 183–4, 185, 190, 247
Barber of Seville, The, 277
Barbier von Bagdad, Der, 148n
Barlow, Sir Thomas, 27, 28
Bavarian Alps, the, 117–18
Bayliss, Lilian, 205

Bayreuth, 33–4, 50, 116
Beard, Donald, 104–10
Beaverbrook, Lord, 229
Beecham, Sir Thomas, 158, 160, 161, 164, 176, 201, 206, 255, 260, 284
    in U.S.A., 214, 218
    collaborates at Glyndebourne, 244–53, 263, 264, 267
Beecham, Lady (Betty Humby), 245–50
Beggar's Opera, The, 141, 202, 215
Beilke, Irma, 179
Belcher, John, 85–6
Bell, Edward, 93 and *n*
Bellasis, Charlotte (Mrs Daniel Christie), 3
Belshaw, Margaret, 213, 267
Benson, Sir Rex, 46
Bettoni, Vincenzo, 167
Biggs, William, 120, 121
Bing, Rudolf, 100, 165, 182, 189, 197, 198, 209, 210, 235, 236, 240,
    241, 242–4, 253, 254–6, 257–8, 259–60, 264–5
    in World War II, 200, 220
Birch, Frank, 119
Blakiston, C. H., 62
Bonham Carter, Lady Violet, 243, 284–5
Boosey and Hawkes, 235, 237
Borgioli, Dino, 184–5, 247
Boult, Sir Adrian, 227, 229
Bowden, Mr, 148–9, 150
Brewerton, Elmore, 48–9
Bridges, Lord, 228, 261, 263
Bridgewater, Mrs Violet, 144
Britten, Benjamin, 254–8
Broke, P. V., 41
Brookes, Charlotte, 2*n*
Brooks's Club, London, 101, 233
Browning, Oscar, 95
Brownlee, John, 179, 247
Bruscantini, Sesto, 271
Busch, Adolf, 162–3
Busch, Fritz, 162–6, 170, 176, 177, 180, 182, 184, 188–9, 191, 197–8,
    201, 208, 209, 244, 271
    quarrel with, 265
    tributes to, 206–7, 269–70
Busch, Hans Peter, 165
Butler, Lord, 228

Butterwick, Cyril, 45–6
Byron, Rhona, viii, 100, 187, 220, 223, 274, 287

C.E.M.A., 226, 227, 233–4, 237, 242
Calusio, Signor, 185
Capell, Richard, 162
Caplat, Moran, 204, 260, 264, 265, 278, 282
Carey, Clive, 121
Carl Rosa Opera Company, the, 140, 141, 142, 159
Carmen, 144, 244, 245, 253
cars, John Christie's, 30–2, 33–4, 37, 51, 106–7
Casson, Sir Hugh, 275
Cenerentola, La, 271, 275, 277
Chichester, Countess of, 145
Children's Country Holiday Fund, 191
Children's Theatre, the, 240–2
Childs, 43, 48, 62, 72–3, 82, 101, 106–7, 145, 177, 214
Christie, Agnes (née Clevland, grandmother of J.C.), 3, 4, 8–9
Christie, Audrey (née Mildmay, wife of J.C.)
    marriage of, 140–8, 149–58
    at Glyndebourne, 165, 173, 175, 179, 180, 181, 190, 198, 202, 203–4,
        240–5, 250–3, 257–8, 271–3, 289
    audition of, 166
    away, 183–8, 198–9
    in U.S.A., 211–19, 265
    home, 238–9
    illness of, 267–8
Christie, Augustus Langham (father of J.C.), 4–12, 16, 17–19, 25, 51–3,
        54, 56, 59, 65, 73, 85, 86–7
    illness of, 87–91, 125–32
    will of, 132–8
Christie (Christin), Captain Daniel Béat, 1–3
Christie, George William Langham (son of J.C.)
    childhood of, 173, 213–14, 216–17, 218–19, 262, 265, 271–2
    manhood, vii–viii, 84, 278, 279–80, 287
    quoted, 73–4, 207–8, 274
Christie, Hector Thomas Clevland, 285–6
Christie, Langham, 3, 56
Christie, Margaret, 3
Christie, Lady Rosamond (née Wallop, mother of J.C.), 29–31, 34–5,
        38–9, 47–8, 49, 51, 53–6, 59, 61, 65, 67n, 69, 70–1, 73–9, 85–91, 95,
        125–33, 137–9, 145–7, 148–50, 156–8, 169, 174

Christie, Lady Rosamund—*contd.*
early years of marriage, 4–19
contests husband's will, 133–9
writings of, 13 and *n*
J.C.'s tribute to, 139
Christie, Rosamond (daughter of J.C.), viii, 158, 173–4, 213–14, 216–217, 218–19, 262–3
Christie, William Langham (grandfather of J.C.), 3, 4, 29, 33, 46, 51–3, 54–5
Christie Unit Organ, the, 109
Churchill, Mr, Headmaster, 15, 16
Churchill, Sir Winston, 228, 229–30, 232
Clark, Sir Kenneth, 228
Clevland, Archibald, 3*n*
Clevland, Col Augustus, 3
Cole, Molar, 35
Colles, Dr H. C., 222, 227
Collier, John, 34
"Company of Four", the, Hammersmith, 242
Comte Ory, Le, 277
Conybeare, A. E., 69
Cornbury Park, Oxfordshire, 17, 21, 32, 38, 50, 59
Così fan tutte, 163, 167, 170, 171, 177, 180–1, 184, 199, 208, 266, 268, 271, 275
Covent Garden Opera House, 33, 170, 175–6, 178, 186, 197, 205, 243, 245, 247, 261, 280–1, 282
J.C. proposes at, 145
J.C. tries to buy, 235–7, 238
Craig, Matthew, 119–20
Crespin, Régine, 282
Cripps, Sir Stafford, 230–1
Crozier, Eric, 254, 255, 256, 257–8
Czerwenka, Oscar, 282

Daily Express, 161
Daily Mail, 178–9
Daily Mirror, 176
Daily Telegraph, 162, 171
Dakyns, Frances, 162–3, 265
Dane, Sgt Grace, 201*n*
Daniels, Georgina, 83, 145, 156–7
Davies, Sir Walford, 227

de Havilland, R. S., 24–5
Dennis, the butler, 287
Dent, Prof Edward, 118 and *n*, 119, 227
Domgraf-Fassbaender, Willi, 167, 176, 179
Don Giovanni, 155, 159, 160, 161, 179–80, 183–4, 199, 263, 268
Don Pasquale, 184, 190, 199, 206
Douglas, Johnstone, 140, 141
Dresden Opera House, 118
Duncan, Ronald, 254–5
Duncombe, Sir Edward, 32
Durnford, Dick, 39–40
Dyson, Sir George, 227

Eadie, Noel, 176
Eady, Sir Wilfred, 277
Ebert, Carl (Charles), 164–5, 170, 172, 176, 180, 182, 184, 185, 188–9,
    191, 197, 198, 201, 206, 244, 249, 250, 252, 257–8, 260, 261, 264,
    275, 277, 279, 281, 283, 284, 286
  in wartime, 200, 202
  tribute to, 207–9
  retires, 281–2
Ebert, Peter, 277
Eden, Anthony (Earl of Avon), 228–9
Edinburgh Festival, 202, 259–61, 265, 266, 268, 275, 278, 279, 284
Edwards, W. E., viii, 80, 81, 101, 110, 112, 121, 147, 149, 151, 187,
    200, 224, 236, 241, 244, 276
Eggesford, N. Devon, 7
Eisinger, Irene, 167, 176, 177, 179, 184
Elegy for Young Lovers, 285
Elisir d'amore, L', 285
Elizabeth, Queen, the Queen Mother, 190
Ellerslie school, nr. Barnstaple, 14–15
English Opera Group, the, 256, 257–8
Entführung aus dem Serail, Die (Il Seraglio), 112, 116, 119, 120, 121, 123,
    140–1, 173, 177, 181, 182, 184, 275
Erede, Alberto, 165, 185, 199, 209
Esher, Viscount, 234
Eton College, 4
  J.C. pupil at, 20–6
  J.C. master at, 36–7, 38–57, 72, 73, 95–7, 287
  J.C.'s speech at, 69–70
  Harrow matches, 199, 274*n*

Eton College—*contd.*
Officers' Training Corps, 46–7
Evans, Geraint, 280
Evening News, 160

Faerie Queene, The, 64, 69
Falconer, Sir John, 259–60
Falstaff, 166, 167, 182, 278, 279
Farjeon, Herbert, 172
Ferrier, Kathleen, 246, 251, 256, 258
Festival of Britain, *1951*, 266
Fidelio, 114, 283
Figaro, 120, 163, 167, 169, 170, 171, 177, 180, 184, 191, 199, 260, 266,
    268, 278, 287
Fisher, Mrs Edwin, 273
Flanders, active service in, 62–71
Foot, Robert, 229
Fort, Luigi, 184–5
Forza del destino, La, 268
Fowler, Marguerita, 217, 220, 241
Fowler, R. St L., 274*n*
France, visit to, 73
Fuchs, Marta, 189

Gardiner, Hunter & Co, 148–9
Gellhorn, Peter, 206, 209
George VI, King, 187, 190
Gérard, Rolf, 266
Giannini, Dusolina, 188–9
Gibbs, Dr Armstrong, 115
Gibson, Thornely and Dolly, 114, 118, 119, 120, 121, 140
Gielgud, Sir John, 202
Glyndebourne Arts Trust, 272–3, 275, 276–7
Glyndebourne Manor, 3, 50, 56, 72–3
    history of, 56
    modernization of, 75–84, 91
    Organ Room, 76, 77, 103–4
    visitors at, 92–6, 100–1, 122–3
    first operas at, 109, 110, 112, 115, 119–22
    Opera House built at, 151–2, 155, 158–9
    in World War II, 200, 215, 220
    1938 conference at, 186–7

Glyndebourne Festival Opera
  First season, 160–73; *1935*, 175–7; *1936*, 179–81; *1937*, 182–4; *1938*,
    188–91; *1939*, 197–8, 199; *1940*, 199–200; in wartime, 202; *1946*,
    244, 252–6; *1947*, 256–8, 260; *1948*, 263; *1949*, 263–4; *1950*,
    266–7; *1951*, 268; *1952*, 271; *1953*, 275; *1954*, 277; *1955*, 6, 278;
    1957, 8, 279; *1959*, 281–4; *1960*, 284; *1961*, 284–5; *1962*, 286–7
Glyndebourne Festival Society, 270, 271, 284
Glyndebourne Festival Programme Book, 270, 271
Glyndebourne Productions Ltd, 263, 277, 280
Glyndebourne Society, projected, 228
Goldsbrough, Arnold, 122, 156
Goodall, Reginald, 256
Gough, "Jock", 165, 209–10, 215, 287
Gow, A. S. F., viii, 39–40, 43–4, 72–3, 78, 96
Grandi, Margherita, 198, 199
Gregory, Sir Roger, 129*n*, 133, 150
Gui, Vittorio, 263, 271, 275, 277, 283, 286, 288
Gwynne, John, vii, 43, 46

H.M.V. Records, 173
Haley, Sir William, 280–1, 283
Halifax, Earl of, 198
Harriet, servant at Tapeley, 17
Harrison, Julius, 178
Harvey, Mr, Glyndebourne gardener, 80–1, 176
Hastings, Sir Patrick, 133–7
Hay, Frances and Henrietta, 3, 56
Headlam, G. W. ("Tuppy"), 39, 40, 93*n*
Heinemann, Lili, 179
Helletsgruber, Luise, 167, 171
Henderson, Roy, 167, 179, 202
Herbert, Aubrey, 47
Herz, Das, 153–4
Hess, Dame Myra, 122, 227
Hill, Norman and Beard, 76, 103–10
Hirth, Walther and Johanna, 116–17, 123, 146
History of the War in Asia, 1780–2, 1–2
Hogg, Quintin (Lord Hailsham), 44, 268–9, 288
Hoggan, Dr, 8
Holloway, Lt G., 68–9
Holt, Harold, 235
Horder, Sir Thomas (afterwards Lord), 91

Hornby, Dr J. J., 20
Howard, Dr, 8
Howes, Frank, 281, 282–3
Hughes, Spike, vii, 56, 160*n*, 175, 176, 182–3, 240, 277, 283
Humby, Betty, *see* Beecham, Lady
Hunter, Ian, 260

Idomeneo, 146, 268, 271, 278
Impey, Lawrence, 98–9, 100–1
Incoronazione di Poppea, L', 286
Italiana in Algeri, L', 279

Jessop, Walter, 48–9
John Lewis Ltd, 200, 270
Jowitt, Lord, 229
Jurinac, Sena, 266, 268

Kallman, Chester, 285
Keynes, Lord, 226, 232, 233, 234, 237, 242–3, 260, 280–1
King's Royal Rifle Corps (60th), 60–9
Kipnis, Alexander, 205
Kleiber, Erich, 123
Kočová, Mìla, 176

Lampé, Dr, 146–7
Lampson, Mrs Alfred, 115, 121
Lancaster, Osbert, 275, 278
Langham, James, 56
Le Marchant, Edward, 59–60
Lewes Music Festival, the, 115
Lewis, John Spedan, 266
Lewis, Richard, 268, 280
Liebeslieder of Brahms, 122
Linklater, Eric, 284
Lloyd, Dr, master at Eton, 23, 33–4, 76
Lloyd-Baker, Col Arthur, viii, 41–3
London Symphony Orchestra, 166
Longman, R. H., 33–4
Loos, battle of, 68–9

Ludwig, Walther, 176
Lundy island, 51
Lymington, Viscount, 9–10
Lyttelton, Dr Edward, 36, 41, 45
Lyttelton, Hon George, 33–4
Lyttelton, Oliver (Lord Chandos), 257

Macbeth, 188–90, 194, 199, 209, 260, 265, 271
Macrae, Mrs John, 262
Magic Flute, The, see Zauberflöte, Die
Mallon, Dr J. J., 240, 241
Manén, Lucie, 167
Markan, Maria, 198
Marten, Sir Henry, 96
Meistersinger, Die, 120, 140, 159, 166, 276
Menotti, Tatiana, 179
Merrivale, Lord, 133, 134, 135, 137–8
Messel, Oliver, 267, 268, 277
Mildmay, Rev Sir Aubrey, 141, 181, 224, 265–6
Mildmay, Audrey, *see* Christie, Audrey
Mitchell, Frank, 119
Monthly Musical Record, 161–2
Moore, Grace, 170
Morgan, Miss, 211, 212, 213
Morley, Mary, 56
Morning Post, 166
Mounsey, Fanny, 113–20, 122, 123–4, 160, 225, 289
Mounsey, Johnnie, 113–18, 122, 123–4
Mounsey, Patrick, 113, 122
Musicians' Union, the, 165

Nash, Heddle, 167, 247
National Council of Music, 187, 212, 213, 219, 226–8, 231, 233, 234, 236, 242–3
Nemon, Oscar, 284
New Statesman, 171
New York World Fair, 197
Newman, Ernest, 171
Nicholson, Mary (Mrs George Christie), vii, 279, 287
Nicholson, Col, 128, 129
Nicholson, Otho, 132, 133, 138

Nightingale, Alfred, 165
Norman, E. S., 276
Norman, Herbert, 103
Nugent, Lord, 73

Observer, 181
Oerton, Col Gerald, 127–9, 130, 131, 132, 133–5, 138
Old Vic, the, 112
Oppenheim, Hans, 165, 180, 209
Orfeo (Monteverdi), 286
organs, 103–10
Orpheus or *Orphée et Euridice* (Gluck), 182, 258, 260
Orwell, George, 45*n*

Pacetti, Iva, 189, 190
Pagliacci, 141, 144
Parsifal, 34, 116, 164, 167, 275
Pelléas et Mélisande, 286
Petworth House, Sussex, 61
Philipps, Hon Wogan (Lord Milford), 47*n*
Probate Division of the High Court, 133–8
Pears, Peter, 254
Peter Grimes, 254
Piper, John, 256
Pomeroy, Jay, 235, 240
Pons, Lily, 170
Ponsonby, Sir Charles, 15
Ponsonby, Robert, 279
Porter, Rev Dr T. C., 22–3, 24
Portsmouth, Isaac Wallop, 5th Earl of (grandfather of J.C.), 4*n*, 8, 237
Portsmouth, Eveline, Countess of (grandmother of J.C.), 4, 7, 12
Portsmouth, 9th Earl of, *A Knot of Roots*, 5*n*
Potter, Mr, 93, 119, 120
Powell, Humphry, 80
Princeton University, U.S.A., 262, 263
Pritchard, John, 206–7, 208, 271
pugs, J.C.'s, 83, 153, 215, 263–4, 267
Puritani, I., 284

Queen Camel, Somerset, 145
Queen's Hall, London, 33

Rake's Progress, The, 275, 278
Rape of Lucretia, The, 179, 254, 255–8
Rautawaara, Aulikki, 167, 175, 176, 197
Redgrave, Sir Michael, 202
Reinhardt, Max, 163–4, 207
Rennert, Günther, 283
Residenztheater, Munich, 115 and *n*, 116
Rhys, Miss, 135, 147
Ring, The, 33, 34, 37, 116, 160, 161
Ringmer Building Works, 79, 107, 149*n*, 152, 165, 173, 225
Ringmer Motor Works, 79
Ringmer village, 29
Rising of the Moon, The, 179*n*
Robinson, Miss ("Dobbie"), 12, 16, 17, 39
Roe, W. N., 44
Roscoe, Sir Henry, 36, 70
Rosenkavalier, Der, 145, 167, 282
Rossini, Gioacchino, 271, 277
Rothenberger, Anneliese, 282

Sadler's Wells, 112, 178, 180, 186, 205, 252, 253, 254
St David's School, Reigate, 15–16
Samuel, Harold, 122
Sandow, Eugene, 5
Sargent, Sir Malcolm, 115, 201, 227
Saunton estate, N. Devon, 51–3, 129, 149
Saunton Sands Hotel, the, 149 and *n*, 214–15
Schauspieldirektor, Der, 119, 179, 279
Schuster, Sir George, 114, 234–5
Schwarz, Vera, 190
Segreto di Susanna, Il, 279
Sekers, Sir N. T., 270, 271
Selbstgeständnis, 13
Seraglio, Il, see Entführung aus dem Serail, Die
Serva Padrona, 120
Shaw, Bernard, 200–2
Shaxton, Mr, 127, 129, 130–1
Sheffield Theatre, 143–4
Simon, André, 50, 181*n*
Simon, Viscount, 133, 134, 137
Sitwell, Sir Osbert, 169
Smyth, Ethel, 178

Söderström, Elisabeth, 282
Somigli, Franca, 189
Souez, Ina, 167, 171, 175–6, 177, 181, 247
Stabile, Mario, 179, 180, 190, 247
Strasser, Janos (Jani), 155–6, 165, 203, 209, 253–4
Stratton, George, 166
Stutchbury, Rosamond, 162–3
Sunday Times, 193–6
Sutherland, Joan, 284

Tapeley Park, Devon, 51; 3, 6, 8, 12, 16, 17, 18, 19, 21, 56, 87, 88,
    125–6, 135–6, 214
  run by Lady Rosamond, 47–8, 54, 55, 67*n*, 77, 85–6, 132
  after Augustus's death, 148–51
  inheritance of, 127, 129, 131, 132, 138
Tatler, 47
Temple, William, Archbishop of Canterbury, 232
Théâtre des Nations, Paris, 279
Thomson, Sir J. J., 34
Times, The, 101, 171, 190, 191, 269, 274, 278, 279, 280–1, 282–3,
    283*n*, 285
Tom Brown's Schooldays, 4*n*, 216
Toscanini, Arturo, 189, 197, 199, 201
Tottenham, Admiral Sir Francis, 238
Toye, Dr Francis, 90, 125, 127, 128, 133, 134, 137, 166–7
Trinity College, Cambridge, 4, 28, 30–5
Tristan, 34, 276
Tunbridge Wells Opera House, 111–12, 116, 118–19
Tutté, Francis, 56

Valentino, Francesco, 189
Vansittart, Lord, 198–9
Vaughan, E. L., 49
Vaughan Williams, Dr Ralph, *see* William, Dr R. Vaughan
Veness, Tom, 80, 82
Vienna Mozart Society, the, 276
Voix Humaine, La, 284

Wagner, Wieland, 276
Walküre, Die, 159, 160, 161, 162

Wallop, Lady Rosamond, *see* Christie, Lady Rosamond
Walter, Bruno, 189
Warde, Philip, 122
Warre, Dr Edmond, 20, 22, 36, 76
Warre, Edmond ("Bear"), 76, 81, 152
Watney, Lady Margaret (née Wallop), 16–17, 21–2, 67, 94, 225
Watney, Rosalind, 67
Watney, Silvia, 48, 94, 114
Watney, Vernon James, 16–17, 31, 34–5, 48, 50, 67
Webber-Douglas opera school, the, 114, 140
Wells, C. M., 49–50, 96, 122–3, 181, 191, 274*n*
West Berlin Festival, 277
White-Thomson, R. W., master at Eton, 20–1, 22, 23–4, 25, 26, 36
    and *n*
Whitworth, Mrs A. W., 47
Williams, Dr R. Vaughan, 182, 227
Williamsburg, Virginia, U.S.A., 202
Willis, Constance, 167
Wilson, Hamish, 151, 152, 159, 163, 165, 170
Wilson, Sir Steuart, 120, 243–4
Witley Camp, Sussex, 62
Wolf, Bertie, 44, 60*n*
Wood, Anne, 257
Wood, Sir Henry, 228
Woodhouse, Violet Gordon, 40, 170*n*
Woolwich Royal Academy, 22, 25, 26, 27–8
Wykes, Nigel, 99, 101, 262

Ypres, France, 63–9

Zauberflöte, Die, 173, 175, 176, 180, 184, 251
Zeffirelli, Franco, 285